Practicing
Universal Design

Art Center College of Design
Library
1700 Lida Street
Pasadena, Calif. 91103

Art Center College of Design
Library
1700 Lida Street
Pasadena, Calif. 91103

ART CENTER COLLEGE OF DESIGN

3 3220 00140 1418

720.87 0973
W687
1994

Practicing
Universal Design

An Interpretation of the ADA

Wm. L. Wilkoff, FASID, IBD

Laura W. Abed

With a Foreword by James S. Brady

Art Center College of Design
Library
1700 Lida Street
Pasadena, Calif. 91103

VNR VAN NOSTRAND REINHOLD
_____ New York

Copyright © 1994 by Wm. L. Wilkoff and Laura W. Abed

Library of Congress Catalog Card Number 93-8488
ISBN 0-442-01376-0

All rights reserved. No part of this work covered by the copyright hereon may be reproduced or used in any form or by any means—graphic, electronic, or mechanical, including photocopying, recording, taping, or information storage and retrieval systems—without the written permission of the publisher.

I(T)P   Van Nostrand Reinhold is an International Thomson Publishing company. ITP logo is a trademark under license.

Printed in the United States of America

Van Nostrand Reinhold
115 Fifth Avenue
New York, NY 10003

International Thomson Publishing
Berkshire House
168–173 High Holborn
London WC1V7AA, England

International Thomson
   Publishing GmbH
Konigswinterer Str. 518
5300 Bonn 3
Germany

Thomas Nelson Australia
102 Dodds Street
South Melbourne 3205
Victoria, Australia

Nelson Canada
1120 Birchmount Road
Scarborough, Ontario
M1K 5G4, Canada

International Thomson Publishing Asia
38 Kim Tian Rd., #0105
Kim Tian Plaza
Singapore 0316

International Thomson Publishing
   Japan
Kyowa Building, 3F
2-2-1 Hirakawacho
Chiyada-Ku, Tokyo 102
Japan

16 15 14 13 12 11 10 9 8 7 6 5 4 3 2 1

Library of Congress Cataloging-in-Publication Data
Wilkoff, Wm. L. (William L.), 1925–
     Practicing universal design : an interpretation of the ADA / Wm. L.
Wilkoff, Laura W. Abed.
       p.   cm.
     Includes bibliographical references and index.
     ISBN 0-442-01376-0
     1. Architecture and the physically handicapped—United States.
2. United States. Americans with Disabilities Act of 1990.
I. Abed, Laura W.   II. Title
NA2545.P5W56   1994
720′.42′097309049—dc20   93-8488
                                                              CIP

To all the people with disabilities who have enriched our lives with their contributions to the development of the premise of universal design.

Contents

Art Center College of Design
Library
1700 Lida Street
Pasadena, Calif. 91103

Art Center College of Design
Library
1700 Lida Street
Pasadena, Calif. 91103

Foreword

With the passage of the ADA in 1990, the disability rights movement has witnessed a major victory which in time should break down many of the barriers that people with disabilities now face. Central to this goal is the removal of architectural barriers in the environment that will allow those of us in the disabled community to fully and independently mainstream ourselves into American society. Achieving such a difficult task will depend greatly on the training of design professionals. You will need to develop both a working knowledge of the fundamentals of universal design and, more importantly, a sensitivity to people with disabilities. This combination of technical knowledge and awareness of needs will help to break down the physical barriers in the environment. Eliminating these will be the essential first step toward the ultimate disintegration of pervasive attitudinal and social barriers—barriers which can never be abolished unless individuals with disabilities are able to pursue their civil rights.

As students in the design profession, you can begin to develop both the sensitivity and the technical expertise that you will need in your professional life. Cultivating these concepts now will better prepare you for the design challenges that lie ahead.

James S. Brady
Vice Chairman
National Organization on Disability

Preface

With the enactment of the Americans with Disabilities Act (ADA), the field of universal design (also known as barrier free design) has been transformed from a cause espoused by relatively few design professionals to a legislative mandate affecting all designers. Those who have fought long and hard for disability rights undoubtedly applaud the passage of the Act, not just for the advances it will bring in design, but for all its civil rights protections as well. However, laws alone will not bring about the needed changes. Designers now must be educated about strategies for implementing universal design in light of the ADA, and this book was developed for that purpose.

The goals of the book are twofold. First, we will attempt to heighten the designer's awareness of the needs of people with disabilities. Without sensitivity toward the disabled population, designers who try to implement universal design regulations will constantly fall short of the desired goal. Technical specifications do not always explain why they are a certain way, and without this understanding designers may inadvertently create inaccessible or only partially accessible designs. Second, we will provide practical applications for the technical guidelines found in the ADA so that designers may gain some experience in using these guidelines in a sensitive manner. Hopefully these practice scenarios will provide a "safe" environment for trial and error that will in turn become the foundation for a deeper comprehension of the needs of people with all degrees of ability.

The issues surrounding the community of people with disabilities are vast and varied. We have necessarily limited the scope of this book so that there are a great many topics that could be touched on only lightly or not at all. Although the Americans with Disabilities Act includes transportation and communications, we have chosen not to deal with these subjects and have instead concentrated on design of public spaces in the built environment. We have excluded housing altogether, since the legal aspects fall under different legislation. Similarly, we have not delved too deeply into industrial design, even though the products used in public spaces are every bit as important to consider as the physical design of those spaces. While it would be impossible to discuss such an emotional topic as disability without mentioning the social and psychological aspects, we have done this only to the extent needed in order to enhance awareness. Each of these topics has been treated extensively elsewhere.

Because of our efforts to narrow the scope of the book to a manageable size, we have not attempted to address every accessibility issue that might arise. Indeed it would be presumptuous to assume that we could conceive of every possible barrier situation. Instead we have tried to address a broad array of circumstances in order to provide the reader with as much information as possible. Our main objective is education: if we open the reader's eyes to the need for accessibility and the strategies for achieving it, then the reader will be well equipped to solve problems on his or her own. Also, it is important to note that the interpretations of the ADA presented here are our own, based on professional experience, and should in no way be considered as regulations in a legal sense.

In writing this book we have assumed our primary audience to be students, especially those in interior design and architecture. In addition, the book may appeal to individuals already involved in professional design work whose experiences in universal design have been limited. It may also appeal to individuals, either students or practitioners, in other design fields such as industrial design or landscape architecture. People working in fields closely related to design (such as contractors or facilities managers) may also benefit from this book. Finally, the book may be of general interest to anyone concerned with the interrelationship between the physical environment and disabilities.

We wish to acknowledge several people who contributed to this book, including all those who gave us permission to use their illustrations or excerpts from their text. John P. S. Salmen, AIA, and Bernard Posner offered valuable assistance in obtaining materials. David Carter, Eddie Espinosa, Marc Fiedler, Esq., Dr. Jack Gannon, and W. David Kerr all devoted time to interviews with us. Their insights greatly enhanced the quality of the book, as well as our own sensitivity toward living with a disability. Robert C. Wilkoff, AIA, spent considerable time and effort in producing the graphic illustrations for the book. We would also like to thank Cynthia Leibrock and Marsha Mazz for their generous support. Special thanks go to Paula C. Wilkoff, who worked tirelessly on everything from developing scenarios to editing to other tasks too numerous to mention; and to Farough Abed, whose instructional design strategies set the book into motion and whose layout design gave it the finishing touch. Without them this book would not have been possible.

Part One

Understanding Universal Design

Art Center College of Design
Library
1700 Lida Street
Pasadena, Calif. 91103

UNIVERSAL DESIGN:

The Mayflower Hotel

Guest room baths are designed with accessible elements such as grab bars, levered tap sets, and maneuvering clearance under the sink. (Designed by George A. Snode, AIA, ASID, for the Mayflower Hotel, Washington, D. C.)

Designing a hotel that is accessible to all guests is accomplished at the beginning of the project. Consider each area that will be used by the guest and ensure that it is accessible to everyone. Studies have shown that initial accessible design costs much less than renovations requiring accessibility modifications.

The individual guest room is definitely the area of greatest concern in the design of the hotel. In other areas there will be hotel staff on hand to assist guests with special accommodations. However, in the individuals' rooms, they are on their own. Consequently, extreme care must be taken in the design of these areas. Paths of travel within the room must be wide enough, and reach-zones should be within the ranges for front and side approaches.

Bathrooms need to allow for maneuverability, both in rooms with tubs and rooms with roll-in showers.

Additional design time needs to be given to the details of furnishings within the guest room. Elements such as drawer pulls, operating hardware, and lamp switches should be designed to accommodate guests with dexterity problems.

The design of the guest room needs to be rethought. The designer must ask, "How will persons with different disabilities be affected by my design? Can the guest function independently within this guest room?"

Talking with various disabled groups can be helpful; they can identify common problems encountered during hotel visits. It has been my experience that most groups are willing to discuss design problems. Hopefully, through a more sensitive design approach, many simple barriers may be eliminated.

George A. Snode, AIA, ASID
Stouffer Hotels and Resorts

Introduction

In recent years there has been a national trend toward awareness and celebration of cultural diversity. This term typically brings to mind different ethnic groups, and yet cultures do not necessarily have to reflect a common ancestry. The community of people with disabilities is an example of a cultural group that fits this category.

One of the ways in which a group is defined is through the language used to describe it, for language is one of the most powerful tools for shaping attitudes and emotions toward a cultural group. Descriptive terminology changes over time to keep pace with national trends and perceptions. The community of people with disabilities is no more immune to this than other cultural groups, and a plethora of terms has found its way into various media over the years. Though some of these may have been commonly used in the past, they are clearly unacceptable today. Others are still debated, and new terms crop up regularly. Even within the disability community there is disagreement about semantics. In our text we have tried to choose the most widely accepted terms possible. We know at the outset, though, that no matter how careful we are in phrasing, there are bound to be people who find our chosen terminology offensive. To these people we apologize in advance.

Currently one thing about which many people with disabilities agree is that *people* should be stressed first. It is a much more positive approach to speak of "a person who is deaf" than to speak of "a deaf person," as though deafness is the most important attribute of that person. Similarly, it is improper to use such terms as "the disabled" or "paraplegics." Instead one should speak about "people with disabilities" or "people who are paraplegic." Therefore we have endeavored to put the disability last, even though this often leads to awkward sentences. Likewise, we tried to use the term "people without disabilities" rather than "able-bodied" or "nondisabled."

Many familiar terms are now seen as inappropriate because of negative connotations, and these we have excluded. For instance, it is no longer acceptable to refer to someone as "confined to a wheelchair" or "wheelchair bound." Instead that person is a "wheelchair user." Similarly, it is not proper to speak of someone who is "afflicted with" or "suffering from" a disability (e.g., cerebral palsy), but simply "a person with cerebral palsy." The important thing to remember in choosing terminology is that a descriptor should put the person first, and it should present a positive tone rather than one that invites pity or charity. By remembering this simple rule we can encourage a more accurate perception of the disability community; one in which its members are accepted for their cultural diversity but are seen first and foremost as individuals.

Universal Design and the ADA

Chapter 1

Consider the questions below as a guide to understanding the fundamental points of this chapter. The answers are not necessarily found in one passage, but instead are meant to capture the essence of the material being presented here.

Why is sensitivity on the part of the designer as important as, or perhaps more important than, technical knowledge?

How does universal design compare to traditional design?

How have American disability laws progressed through the years?

What is the basic difference between the Americans with Disabilities Act and other disability laws?

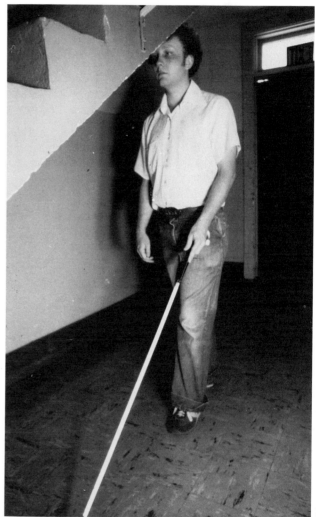

Photo: Barrier Free Environments, Inc. Raleigh, North Carolina

SENSITIVE DESIGN FOR PUBLIC USE

For whom are public buildings built? Obviously, they are built for the general public. But to whom do we refer when we speak of "the public?" By definition we should be speaking of *all* members of our community. In the past the standards used by the professional designer have reflected anthropometric data for "able-bodied" adult males in the prime of life.[1] What about the elderly? Children? People with disabilities? We, as designers, must be aware of the diversity among the users of the public spaces we design. Our responsibility lies not only in aesthetic and pragmatic design, but in universal design as well.

Let us further examine this idea of universal design. Suppose a new public library is to be built in town. Patrons of public libraries are a diverse group, and designers of both the interior and the exterior of the building should consider this fact and be aware of all possible needs. For instance, using large signage with a contrasting color scheme would be very useful to people who are elderly or visually impaired, not to mention parents with small children in tow and anyone else who might be in a hurry. People in wheelchairs, on crutches, or pushing strollers or book carts would require a ramp and/or an elevator. Perhaps there is a librarian or other staff member with a hearing loss. For such a person a visual alarm system would be essential to include along with the standard auditory system, and in an emergency having two systems increases the probability of escape for everyone. Adjusting the height of elevator call buttons, public telephones, and drinking fountains would make them available to people using wheelchairs (and easier for children to use as well). These are but a few of the specifications that allow for truly universal design. Not only do they make buildings accessible for those who would otherwise be unable to enter, they also make buildings safer, more functional, and more

"If doorways are too narrow to admit a wheelchair, if thresholds protrude unexpectedly, if drinking fountains are out of reach, if not even one toilet room is designed to accommodate wheelchair traffic, if elevators are too cramped or are inaccessible from the entrance level, if public telephone booths are not usable, if abrupt changes in floor level are not offset by gradually sloping ramps, then buildings constructed for the general public can be classified only as contradictions in concrete."

Edmund Leonard

---

1. Throughout this book we will use the word *designer* as a generic term to denote any person who is professionally involved in the design of a public site, including space planners, interior designers, architects, industrial designers, graphic designers, and landscape architects.

"Barrier removal and prevention have had the unintended benefit of revealing that the built environment is not perfectly accessible to anyone. All people face barriers that impede movement and restrict action, and these may change through time in relation to a person's physical size, age, health, and stamina. Indeed, the ordinary built environment is best suited to adults of average size and mobility in the prime of life. The more a person diverges from these conditions, the more barriers are likely to be encountered."

Kenneth E. Foote

convenient for everyone's use. The key to understanding universal design is awareness and sensitivity to the needs of *all* potential users; not just those who fit our definition of the "average" person. Likewise, accessibility in design is not strictly for the benefit of individuals with disabilities. It can improve the functionality of a space for people without physical limitations as well.

Buildings are not the only structures that must be designed in an accessible manner in order to achieve universal design. Exterior sites (e.g., sidewalks, parks, playgrounds, and streets) and transportation systems must be free of barriers as well. Many people will find an accessible building of little use if it is not served by accessible public transportation. Even if an individual with a disability is able to transport himself, there must be wide parking spaces in a nearby lot with an accessible path of travel to the building, including appropriate signage. In other words, the problem of accessibility must be considered throughout the entire exterior and interior circulation route. Just as a person without a disability would consider a broken bridge over a swiftly moving river to be a barrier, the person with a disability might consider stairs, curbs, and broken sidewalks to be barriers. A barrier is not an integral part of the disability; it is external to the person and therefore can be eliminated.

Neglecting any of these facets of interior or exterior site design amounts to nothing less than discrimination against a segment of our population. By constructing physical barriers we are infringing on the civil rights of people with disabilities (many of whom are taxpaying citizens), and preventing them from independently joining the mainstream of our society. A good deal of legislation has been enacted to remedy this situation, but until recently each act dealt with only a single aspect of the problems faced by people with disabilities (such as housing or education or voting rights). In July 1990 Congress passed the Americans with Disabilities Act, the first true civil rights law for American citizens with disabilities. Indeed, it is the only antidiscrimination legislation in the world specifically for this minority group. Briefly, it prohibits discrimination against Americans with disabilities in five sectors: employment, transportation, public accommodations, public services, and telecommunications. The breadth of the law allows for accessibility in a wide spectrum of situations encountered in daily life. We will discuss this Act in greater detail later in this chapter.

WHAT IS UNIVERSAL DESIGN?

For the designer who has no disability the concept of universal design can be elusive. Those of us without disabilities often happen upon barriers in everyday life without even thinking about them. While shopping we step over boxes in aisles and circuit around temporary display cases. We enter through revolving doors and turnstiles. We travel over broken sidewalks and driveways, streets and curbs. We read signs without raised lettering. Stairs and heavy doors may slow us down, but they do not completely impede our progress. But how does the person with a disability cope with such obstacles? Typically the term "disabled" brings to mind a person in a wheelchair. It is easy to understand that stairs, turnstiles, narrow doorways, and the like would totally bar this person's path, making it difficult if not impossible to cope. Individuals in wheelchairs, however, make up only a small percentage of the population of people with disabilities. Other barriers are less discernible because we are not as familiar with the needs of people with other types of disabilities. For instance, a person with leg braces might be able to negotiate stairs, but not those with a protruding tread nosing that could catch the toes. People with dexterity impairments such as severe arthritis might have difficulty with doorknobs, but would find lever-type hardware more manageable. As designers develop their sensitivity to the needs of people with varying disabilities, it becomes easier to focus on potential barriers and eradicate them. Technical knowledge about barriers is necessary but not sufficient for universal design. Sensitivity is the essential ingredient that allows a designer to create an accessible solution that truly works for the person with a disability.

From the examples given thus far we can now define the basic characteristics of universal design. First, new elements are generally not introduced into the environment. Instead, existing ones are redesigned to broaden their functionality. Such modifications require awareness on the part of the designer, since in many cases the traditional attributes of an element render it inaccessible. For instance, changing hardware or tap sets from knob types to lever types, lowering switches, controls, or drinking fountains, and widening doorways can all contribute to the elimination of barriers without adding elements. The apparent exception is the ramp. In cases where an existing site is being retrofitted, a ramp certainly can look like a new element, and often an out-of-place element as well. However, in new construction ramps can be used as a replacement for stairs or aesthetically incorporated into a design along with stairs to achieve a modification of the traditional element for vertical level change.

A second characteristic of universal design is that it creates a safe, more functional, and more convenient environment for everyone, not just those with disabilities. The person carrying a heavy load would appreciate an automatic door, and a parent pushing

FIGURE 1–1. People with mobility and/or auditory disabilities can take advantage of this TDD/telephone bank installed at an accessible height.

a stroller would be happy to see wide aisles in a store. Handrails, curb cuts,[2] adequate signage, and auditory/visual signals are but a few of the many other elements that make the built environment easier and safer for all users.

Traditionally, the term *barrier free design* has been applied to the definition as it now stands. The original concept was one of barrier removal specifically for the purpose of accommodating people with disabilities, which had the unintended but welcome benefit of improving the environment for everyone. Universal design embraces and extends this purpose with the idea that it should serve as a philosophy for all design disciplines connected with the environment; a philosophy advocating design that considers the changes taking place throughout the entire life span, from childhood to old age. To this end it encompasses graphic and product design as well as interior and exterior design. There is an attempt to extend accessibility into the environment to such a degree that it is accepted by both designers and the public as the norm rather than being viewed as an adaptation for special needs. Not only would architectural barriers be eliminated to achieve this, but signage would feature large, legible print and industrial designers would promote furniture, equipment, and utensils designed to meet the needs of as many users as possible. Products that are adjustable are ideal for this purpose. Telecommunications and transportation equipment would be similarly endowed with accessible traits (a notion that is mandated in the ADA, though discussion of these topics is beyond the scope of this book). When we think of universal design, then, we envision design that serves the maximum number of people in the safest and most convenient manner and endeavors to exclude no one.

THE ROLE OF THE DESIGNER

As designers, it is imperative that we remain sensitive to the needs of the whole of society when we design public buildings and sites. People may have disabilities, either permanent or temporary, but do not necessarily have to be handicapped by the environment. Disabilities vary widely in their severity, leaving some individuals with hardly any strength

"An emphasis on technical specifications alone simply transforms the disabled into impersonal objects, wheelchairs with a given turning radius. While specifications are important, they should serve as adjuncts to, not replacements for, an understanding of how disabled people can live independently in a world largely designed by and for the able-bodied."

Raymond Lifchez

---

2. The terms *curb cut* and *curb ramp* will be used interchangeably throughout this text.

"Consider a concept of design where the user is not known, but every possibility is accommodated. The architect may not be pregnant today, but she or a friend may become so. The planner may not have a broken leg today, but he or his father may soon fall down a flight of steps. The designer may not be in a wheelchair today, but tomorrow he or she could be in a car accident and confined to one for life. Why not plan for every possibility so the environment can continue to be as convenient, functional, efficient, and usable as it was originally conceived? This is the concept of barrier-free design. It is not 'special,' it is not 'traditional,' it is human."

Peter L. Lassen
Director, Compliance Division,
ATBCB 1975–79

or ability to function unaided and others with very little need for help. The built environment, though, makes a crucial difference. A person with a disability may be capable of living alone in a home that has been designed to meet his or her needs; yet that same person may be virtually helpless upon leaving home when the streets, buses, shops, and offices present barriers at every turn. At home the disability does not handicap the individual in any way, because the home environment is designed to ease the accomplishment of his or her daily routine. The handicapping obstacles have been eliminated since the interior and exterior design compensate for the individual's physical characteristics. In contrast, away from home he or she may find that the disability is definitely a handicap because of the design of the physical environment. This handicapping effect could easily be ameliorated by sensitive, universal design. One way that the designer can develop this essential sensitivity is to continually evaluate the needs of the disability community (through contact with its members) and compare their needs with the existing physical environment and the designer's own current design projects. Over time this process develops into an intuitive sense about universal design that further strengthens sensitivity. This concept is elaborated upon in the next chapter.

As important as physical change, or perhaps more important, is the need for attitudinal change in society. Individuals with disabilities, like all people, want respect from others instead of sympathy, pity, or charity. Moreover, they do not wish to be segregated from the rest of society either through institutionalization or through inaccessible building design. Harold Russell, a former chairman of the President's Committee on Employment of People with Disabilities (and an Academy Award winner for *The Best Years of Our Lives*), relates an incident that epitomizes the "ostrich mentality" that has been prevalent for centuries in the Western world. When the Governor's Committee in Iowa decided to retrofit public buildings to make them accessible, one postmaster in a small town scoffed at the idea. In all his years as postmaster, he asserted, he had never once seen a person with a disability come into the building. Small wonder that he had not, for the building had steps, a revolving door, and a high counter. Unfortunately, the ostrich's penchant for hiding from trouble in the hopes that it will disappear is echoed in our own Western traditions. For centuries we have chosen to erect inaccessible buildings that, along with the practice of institutionalization, would help us to hide from those we did not wish to acknowledge, or more accurately, hide them from us so that we would not have to deal with them on a daily basis. This exclusion of people with disabilities is a subtle form of segregation.

Designers can provide the stimulus for setting into motion an attitudinal change toward people with disabilities, and indeed, many designers have taken it upon themselves to create accessible designs. The more that individuals with disabilities can emerge from their homes to make their way in the environment, the more they are able to participate independently in the mainstream of everyday life, and this will lead to greater respect from and acceptance by others in society.

"Each new disabled person who shows up at the office or at the movies or on the bus nicks away at the wall of misconceptions and fears. And as that wall breaks down, so does discomfort at hiring and socializing with disabled people."

Editorial,
Christian Science Monitor

THE BARRIER FREE DESIGN MOVEMENT

Although Congress has been passing legislation to stimulate employment, rehabilitation, and care of people with disabilities since early in this century, it failed to make the fundamental association between accessibility of the built environment and procurement of services or employment until the mid-1960s. The importance of this connection is underscored by an event that took place in 1957, when Hugh Deffener, a barrier free design proponent using a wheelchair, submitted to being bodily carried up a flight of stairs in order to receive the Handicapped American of the Year Award. Surely this sort of humiliation takes place on a daily basis for many Americans with disabilities.

The government's primary concern in the past seems to have been employment, a concern that was demonstrated as early as 1920 with the Vocational Rehabilitation Act. This program was originally conceived as temporary aid to states for the purpose of finding employment for those with disabilities. During World War II Congress again expressed concern over job opportunities for individuals with disabilities, though this concern may have been motivated as much by the dwindling workforce as by any sense of civil injustice. The problem increased in magnitude as World War II ended, when veterans with disabilities returned home. Since then intensive lobbying by veterans, disability groups, and organizations advocating disability rights has encouraged Congress to chip away at discriminatory practices. In 1948 and again in 1954 new legislation attempted to provide services for people with disabilities, first with a law prohibiting discrimination in U.S. Civil Service employment based on disability, and later with an extension of the funding and services of the Vocational Rehabilitation Act. The problem with all these programs, of course, was that they did not consider physical accessibility as a prerequisite for accomplishing their goals.

Establishing ANSI Standards. In 1947 Congress established the President's Committee on Employment of the Handicapped (currently entitled the President's Committee on Employment of People with Disabilities) for the purpose of providing employment op-

FIGURE 1–2. Ramps can be aesthetically incorporated into the overall design. Carpeting the ramp prevents slipping. (Designed by George A. Snode, AIA, ASID, for the Mayflower Hotel, Washington, D.C.)

portunities. An offshoot of this was the Barrier Free Design subcommittee, which consisted of professionals from various design disciplines. This body represented the beginning of organized barrier free design. In 1958 this committee, together with the Veteran's Administration, published a guidebook for achieving accessibility in public buildings, though compliance was strictly voluntary. One year later the President's Committee and the Easter Seal Society hosted a conference for all interested parties on the problem of accessibility in public buildings. The conference resulted in accessibility standards for the physical environment, issued by the American National Standards Institute as ANSI 117.1 in 1961. These constituted the first minimum requirements to be released, and they included general criteria for various structures, including ramps, parking spaces, stairs, floor surfaces, public telephones, and so on. The document was only six pages long and did not detail any dimensional specifications. Again, no enforcement measures were included. These were simply standards for design and construction of public buildings.

In 1964, after almost half a century of legislation for the benefit of Americans with disabilities, Congress heard its first remarks regarding the need for accessibility in the built environment. These were made by Senator Frank E. Moss of Utah and Senator Hubert H. Humphrey of Minnesota. In explaining the need for accessibility Senator Moss said, "Because of America's thoughtlessness in erecting in many public buildings architectural barriers which the handicapped cannot hurdle, millions of our citizens cannot take care of their business personally in state, county, or federal office buildings" (*Congressional Record*, 1964, 110:3136). Senator Moss suggested that his state's programs for barrier removal might be viewed as models for other states and communities. Not only did he elaborate on physical barriers, but he also touched on social barriers when he stated:

It is a reflection on the level of our civilization, it seems to me, that in so many of our public buildings—including our Federal buildings—a person confined to a wheelchair, or in a heavy leg brace, or with a weak heart, must enter through a level freight entrance at the back of the building and reach public areas only after a trip through a boilerroom, or a storeroom, and in a freight elevator (*Congressional Record*, 1964, 110:3137).

"The greatest single obstacle to employment for the handicapped is the physical design of the buildings and facilities they must use."

National Commission on
Architectural Barriers to Rehabilitation
of the Handicapped

In 1965 the National Commission on Architectural Barriers to the Rehabilitation of the Handicapped was formed by Congress to investigate the progress toward accessibility thus far. Since the publication of the ANSI standards, a variety of interest groups and agencies had worked with state and local legislatures to encourage adoption of the standards at the state and local levels. At the time of the commission's survey, at least half the states had made some attempt to implement accessibility standards through local building codes. Nevertheless, the commission found that voluntary compliance was providing only minimal gains at all levels. Local building codes often were not comprehensive enough, and many designers were not even familiar with the ANSI standards (A117.1). Additionally, there were no monitoring systems in place to ensure compliance with the standards. Clearly what should have been the groundwork for change amounted to little more than a symbolic gesture. The commission concluded that nothing short of mandatory compliance would suffice in order to achieve the goal of accessibility for all Americans.

Architectural Barriers Act of 1968. The commission's report was not the only work advocating the removal of architectural barriers. In early 1967 bills were introduced in both the House and the Senate demanding that public buildings financed with federal dollars be barrier free. All of these efforts led to the passage of the Architectural Barriers Act of 1968 (PL90–480). This act mandated that all facilities funded partially or wholly by federal funds and intended for public use should be designed and constructed in an accessible manner. The law applied to new construction, renovations, and leased facilities. Although the ANSI standards were adopted under the act, new standards were to be drawn up by the Director of the General Services Administration, the Secretary of Housing and Urban Development, the Secretary of Defense, and the Postal Service.

PL90–480 was a step forward in that it was the first formal Congressional recognition of the integral role that physical barriers play in preventing some Americans from enjoying their natural rights as citizens. However, the act was not without its problems. First, it applied solely to federal buildings or programs, or other programs supported by federal funds. This of course excluded a good many buildings, including shops, theaters, restaurants, and private offices; in short, many of the places that citizens without disabilities can and do visit on a daily basis. Second, many federal programs lease space in public buildings. For instance, an IRS office might lease a portion of the second floor of a private office building. Although the law required the IRS office to be accessible, it did not cover the remainder of the building, which might not have an accessible path of travel to the office. Many people with disabilities, therefore, would be unable to obtain personal tax assistance or employment in the office even though the office itself would be accessible. Third, the Architectural Barriers Act did not impose any consequences for noncompliance with the law in spite of the commission's report suggesting the need for compliance measures. This omission was perhaps the most problematic element of the law, and was not resolved for another five years.

Rehabilitation Act of 1973. Whereas PL90–480 was concerned with accessibility in the (federal) built environment, the Rehabilitation Act of 1973 addressed the issue of discrimination. Section 504 of the act prohibited discrimination against those with disabilities in any federal agency or any program receiving federal financial assistance. It also mandated affirmative action in the federal government. By the spring of 1977, however, the regulations needed to implement Section 504 still had not been issued by the Department of Health, Education and Welfare (or HEW, the agency chosen to develop the regulations). After demonstrations by hundreds of individuals with disabilities at regional HEW offices and an encounter between some of these people and the Secretary of HEW in Washington, D.C., regulations were signed ensuring that programs funded by HEW would be conducted in barrier free facilities. This did not necessarily require retrofitting, since the regulations allowed for removal to accessible locations if a person with a disability so requested. The intent of the law was to provide equal access to *programs,* and alternative measures were acceptable to achieve this end.

The other major result of the Rehabilitation Act was the creation of the Architectural and Transportation Barriers Compliance Board (ATBCB), which was authorized to investigate complaints concerning noncompliance in federal agencies or federally funded programs, and to seek enforcement of compliance orders. The board consisted of the heads of eight federal agencies, including the Department of Health, Education and Welfare, the Department of Transportation, the Department of Housing and Urban Development, the Department of Labor, the Department of the Interior, the General Services Administration, the U.S. Postal Service, and the Veteran's Administration. This

FIGURE 1–3. Automatic doors allow wheelchair users easy access to building interiors regardless of the weight of the doors.

"These rights are diffused throughout the legal system; but the wisdom and power of a unified policy toward disabled citizens are still missing in America."

Robert A. Francis

was the first time that Congress provided for the enforcement of the accessibility laws that were in place. However, appropriations committees actually supplied less than one third of the funds needed to carry on the work of the board. The ATBCB did not issue its first citation until 1977, when it cited the Department of the Interior and the Department of Transportation for inaccessible renovations at Union Station in Washington, D.C.

Up to this point the ANSI A117.1 accessibility standard, originally issued in 1961 and reissued without changes in 1971, had been the accepted standard for the federal government and many state governments. However, it was very brief, contained ambiguous language, and limited itself almost exclusively to barriers affecting wheelchair usage. The Department of Housing and Urban Development, together with the President's Committee and the Easter Seal Society, sponsored the research and development of a revised and expanded ANSI standard, which was released in 1980 and updated in 1986. It is still considered the basic "how-to" standard. In 1982 the ATBCB issued its own Minimum Guidelines and Requirements for Accessible Design (MGRAD) for use by federal agencies in developing consistent federal standards. MGRAD was based on the 1980 ANSI technical provisions, with the addition of broad scoping requirements (scoping indicates how many accessible elements are needed and where they go). In 1984 the Uniform Federal Accessibility Standard (UFAS) was developed to be consistent with MGRAD, and it became the accepted government standard, as it still is today. Under the Americans with Disabilities Act, which provides its own guidelines, UFAS is considered the interim "safe harbor" standard for federal, state, or local government buildings. (How long this interim will last is not known, but as we go to press it is still valid.) Both UFAS and MGRAD frequently reference ANSI for technical provisions. In the future ANSI will periodically be reviewed and updated to be in accordance with the guidelines offered in the ADA. This abundance of standards and guidelines has been extremely confusing for designers concerned about compliance, and to make matters worse, local jurisdictions vary widely. Many states, cities, and counties have adopted the ANSI standard, or have developed their own codes, often based on ANSI, UFAS, or MGRAD. At this point there is an attempt to align the various federal standards and guidelines to reduce the level of confusion, but there will inevitably be some variance between state and federal standards. Fortunately the framers of these documents have wisely chosen to use the same numbering system in all of them so that designers and users do not have to learn a new language for each document.

By the early 1980s many other bills had passed in Congress upholding the rights of people with disabilities in other arenas, such as education and transportation. The spirit in Congress was certainly one of protecting the civil rights of citizens with disabilities. Clearly physical barriers must be removed to achieve this goal, and the 1968 and 1973 acts promoted the cause to some extent. Indeed, the Rehabilitation Act of 1973 has often been regarded as significant civil rights protection for citizens with disabilities. Nonetheless, it should be remembered that these two pieces of legislation pertained only to agencies or programs receiving federal funding. They did not apply at all to the private sector, thus thwarting Congress' efforts to truly protect against discrimination. The laws to this point in time guaranteed access only to places that received federal financial assistance, and compliance was moderate at best. Everything else was still essentially off limits to individuals with disabilities, except in cases where a designer involved in a project was aware of and sensitive to accessibility issues. It was not until 1990 that this state of affairs changed. A quarter of a century after Congress first discussed the crucial role that physical access plays in mainstreaming citizens with disabilities into American life, they passed a bill that would guarantee the basic civil rights that are due every American.

THE AMERICANS WITH DISABILITIES ACT:
A CIVIL RIGHTS LAW

"The passage of ADA is truly another emancipation, not only for the 43 million Americans with disabilities who will directly benefit but even more so for the rest of us, now free to benefit from the contributions that these Americans will make to our economy, our communities, and our individual well-being."

Dick Thornburgh

On July 26, 1990, President George Bush signed into law the Americans with Disabilities Act (ADA), which he likened to a Declaration of Independence for the 43 million citizens of America who have disabilities. This kind of civil rights protection was called for as early as 1969, when Professor Richard C. Allen stated:

> In some areas, at least transportation, places of public accommodation and perhaps even employment in business and institutions, under federal regulations, there should be a federal civil rights law with appropriate sanctions directed to discrimination against the physically handicapped, whose effects are every bit as demeaning and as incapacitating as they are when directed against other citizens because of the color of their skin (Allen, 1969).

Indeed, the ADA extends the protections of the Civil Rights Act of 1964 to include another minority, though by no means a small one. Over 30 million African Americans and over 8 million Americans of other ethnic minorities together make up 15.7 percent of the population, compared to 43 million Americans with disabilities, who comprise 17 percent of the population.

The law itself is modeled after the Civil Rights Act and Section 504 of the Rehabilitation Act of 1973. It consists of five titles, as follows: Title I–Employment, Title II–Public Services, Title III–Public Accommodations, Title IV–Telecommunications, and Title V–Miscellaneous Provisions. Of these, Titles I and III are of primary concern to designers. Title II, which covers state and local government facilities (including transportation), might also be relevant for some designers. Each of the titles has its own set of regulations and schedules for compliance, which are listed in Appendix 1.

Title I—Employment. According to this Title, employers may not discriminate against qualified individuals with disabilities. This begins with accurate job descriptions identifying specific tasks needed to qualify. For instance, a receptionist's position might require an individual who could type so many words per minute as a major duty of the job. If an applicant meets this criterion, he or she could not be rejected because of an inability to deliver a package across town or perform some other task outside the specified job description. Employers may require physical examinations only if they are given posthiring, and only if they are a condition for all new employees.

An employer must honor requests to reasonably accommodate qualified job applicants or employees with disabilities, including modifying work stations, equipment, and the work site, unless these modification requirements would result in undue hardship to the employer. As described in the ADA, "undue hardship" means that an accommodation would be unduly costly, extensive, substantial, or disruptive, or would fundamentally

FIGURE 1–4. Removing the ash urn from underneath these call buttons is a simple method of achieving barrier removal.

"The removal of physical barriers and access to reasonable accommodations are among the most essential elements of this measure. The lunch counter sit-ins of the early 1960s led to the great public accommodations title of the 1964 Act. But if the students demonstrating at those lunch counters had been in wheelchairs, they could not have made it through the door of the establishment. If Rosa Parks had been disabled, she could not have boarded the bus at all."

Senator Edward M. Kennedy

alter the nature or operation of the business. This is determined by the employer's size, financial resources, and the nature and structure of its operation. What would be a reasonable accommodation request for a large corporation might be too expensive for a small company.

What types of modifications should an employer consider? Systems furniture might be installed to provide adaptable work stations for people with mobility and dexterity disabilities. For individuals with sensory disabilities, audio and visual assists would be useful. Obviously, all the necessary modifications could not be made until an individual is hired and his or her needs are assessed. However, it is the designer's responsibility to determine from consultation with the client whether or not there are employees with needs that must be addressed. Also, the designer might recommend to a client that whenever remodeling is done, even before a person with a disability is hired, at least the bathrooms and the major accessible routes throughout the work environment should meet ADA regulations. Anticipating the need for these types of changes can save time and money later in the event that a person with a disability is hired.

If some of the necessary changes would present undue hardship, then the employer would be obliged to provide other reasonable accommodations to make the existing facility readily accessible to, and usable by, individuals with disabilities. For instance, since a law clerk who uses a wheelchair might not be able to reach the books on the top shelves of a law library, the librarian could assist when necessary.

Title II—Public Services. State and local governments may not discriminate against qualified individuals with disabilities. This means that all newly constructed state and local government buildings, including transit facilities, must be accessible. In addition, alterations to existing state and local government buildings must be done in an accessible manner. Particularly when alterations could affect accessibility to "primary function" areas of a transit facility, an accessible path of travel must be provided to the altered areas. The restrooms, drinking fountains, and telephones that serve the altered areas must meet the barrier free standards of the ADA, to the extent that the additional accessibility costs are not disproportionate to the overall alteration costs.

Title III—Public Accommodations. Public accommodation refers to privately operated establishments in which the public are served as customers, clients, or visitors, or to facilities that are potential places of employment and are commercial enterprises. This includes restaurants, hotels, theaters, shopping centers and malls, retail stores, museums, professional offices, libraries, parks, day-care centers, recreation facilities, and the like. Title III prohibits discrimination in these places on the basis of disability. It mandates that all new construction must be accessible, and that physical barriers in existing facilities must be removed if readily achievable; that is, if the removal is easily accomplished without much difficulty or expense (as in Title I, the size of the facility, its financial resources, and the nature and cost of the action are all considered in this determination). This does not mean that facilities must be totally accessible in every area. Instead a building must provide a high degree of accessibility in its public areas and reasonably accommodate people with disabilities. (Accessibility in private or employee areas comes under the jurisdiction of Title I.) However, as in state and local government facilities, alterations that affect accessibility to ''primary function'' areas must provide an accessible route to the altered areas. Restrooms, telephones, and drinking fountains serving these areas must be in compliance with ADA regulations insofar as the additional accessibility costs are not disproportionate to the overall alteration costs. Specific regulations are also given for elevators. They are not required in new or altered buildings under three stories or less than 3000 square feet per floor, unless the building is a shopping center, mall, or health-care provider's office.

What types of alterations might be appropriate in a public accommodation such as a retail clothing store? Widening aisles, lowering shelving, and adjusting the layout of racks are all readily achievable means of allowing wheelchair access. At least one dressing room in a cluster and at least one checkout counter should be accessible to wheelchairs, and at least one sales counter (or a portion of one) should be no taller than 36 inches. An accessible dressing room must allow space for more than one person in order to accommodate those who need help putting on clothing. This may necessitate a policy change if the store requires customers to enter dressing rooms one at a time. If the entrance to the store has a small stoop, then ramping would be a readily achievable alteration. Also installing grab bars in the restroom and removing fixtures or obstacles that block accessible paths would be easy methods of eliminating barriers.

Whatever accessibility changes are feasible must be carried out, even if all of the

"Accessibility permeates all other aspects of disabled persons' civil rights. Without access, rights to equal employment opportunity, rights to be "abroad in the land," and the full panoply of protections and duties can be rendered meaningless. To a disabled person, a six-inch curb may loom as large as the Berlin Wall."

Charles D. Goldman

necessary changes are not accomplished. However, the ADA has recommended certain priorities in retrofitting for accessibility. First, the exterior path of travel should be accessible to allow individuals with disabilities to enter the building. Second, access should be made available to areas providing goods and services. Third, restrooms should be accessible. Finally, any remaining barriers should be removed. It should be noted that these are only recommendations. In some instances it may serve the disability community better to invest a given amount of money in the removal of three less expensive barriers than in one costly barrier.

If certain alterations are not deemed readily achievable, then alternate methods of providing services must be initiated. For instance, goods and services can be provided at the door, sidewalk, or curb, or home delivery may be provided. Salespeople can retrieve merchandise from inaccessible shelves or racks. Activities can be relocated to accessible locations. All of these services help to make public accommodations more accessible without undue hardship to owners and operators. Such alternate methods, however, are not to be used if accessibility is readily achievable. The intent of the ADA is to integrate as much as possible, and segregation is not considered an appropriate way to achieve compliance.

When drafting the ADA, every attempt was made by Congress to protect the owners of businesses. For instance, only larger employers with 25 or more employees must adhere to the first scheduled compliance date for Title I. Two years later smaller employers with 15 or more employees must comply. This phasing in of schedules and timetables is one of the methods used to prevent overburdening of the public. Another method is the provision of tax credits that help to ease the burden of compliance with the law. In addition, the law is most stringent where it applies to new construction; the regulations are more lenient for existing facilities (except when major renovations are planned in an existing facility; then the more stringent standards apply to the alterations). In their attempt to promote civil rights for people with disabilities, Congress did not want to infringe on the rights of the public sector. It is this desire for balance that helped the Act to be passed by an overwhelming majority of 91–6 in the Senate and 377–28 in the House.

This attempt at fairness can also be seen in some of the language of the law, which is frequently worded in such a way as to indicate that the law should not be burdensome to the public. For instance, Title I asks for ''reasonable accommodation'' unless it would produce ''undue hardship.'' Such terms are nebulous and are defined only in the broadest sense. Narrowing down these terms to objective definitions will in all likelihood be the work of the courts as litigation occurs. Enforcement of the ADA regulations will take place there, as people who feel that they have been discriminated against in violation of the ADA institute civil action for preventive relief.

It is important to remember that this law is *not* a building code. Instead, it offers minimum guidelines for accessibility based on previous standards and, like UFAS and MGRAD, it provides scoping (i.e., how many, where) as well as the technical approach of ANSI (i.e., how to). State or local jurisdictions may submit their own accessibility codes to the Attorney General for certification. Certified codes must either meet or exceed the minimum requirements set forth in the ADA Accessibility Guidelines (ADAAG). Designers should adhere to the most stringent requirements, whether they are local or state codes or the regulations of the ADA. Five federal agencies are involved in developing these regulations and guidelines, and they will also be responsible for monitoring compliance.

Because of the technical provisions and, more importantly, the spirit of the Americans with Disabilities Act, designers in all disciplines are being encouraged to embrace the philosophy of universal design. Not only will universal design have a profound impact on the lives of people with disabilities, but the implementation of this type of design may have some educational impact as well. Each time a person without a disability becomes aware of a Braille sign, an automatic door, or a parking space with an access symbol, that person's eyes are opened a little wider to the diversity in our society and this will hopefully lead to a greater level of acceptance and mainstreaming of a population that has long been suppressed.

REFERENCES

Allen, R. C. 1969. *Legal Rights of Disabled and Disadvantaged.* Washington, D.C.: U.S. Department of HEW, National Citizen's Conference on Rehabilitation of Disabled and Disadvantaged.

Bednar, Michael J., ed. 1977. *Barrier-Free Environments.* Stroudsburg, Pa.: Dowden, Hutchinson and Ross.

Berkery, Peter M., Jr. 1990. "The Americans with Disabilities Act: Its Impact on Small Business." *National Public Accountant* 35 (September): 42–47.

Bowe, Frank. 1980. *Rehabilitating America: Toward Independence for Disabled and Elderly People.* New York: Harper and Row.

Christian Science Monitor, September 13, 1991.

Congressional Digest. 1989. "Americans with Disabilities Act of 1989." *Congressional Digest* 68(12):289–314.

Congressional Record. 88th Congress, 2d sess., 1964. Vol. 110, pt. 3.

DeJong, Gerben, and Raymond Lifchez. 1983. "Physical Disability and Public Policy." *Scientific American* 248 (June): 40–49.

Fisher, Thomas. 1985. "Enabling the Disabled." *Progressive Architecture* 7:119–24.

Foote, Kenneth E. 1986. "Mobility Impairment and Pharmacy Accessibility: Conflict in a Commercial Built Environment." *Environment and Behavior* 18 (September): 571–603.

Francis, Robert A. 1983. "The Development of Federal Accessibility Law." *Journal of Rehabilitation* 49 (January–March): 29–32.

Goldman, Charles D. 1983. "Architectural Barriers: A Perspective on Progress." *Western New England Law Review* 5:465–93.

Harkness, Sarah P., and James N. Groom, Jr. 1976. *Building Without Barriers for the Disabled.* New York: Whitney Library of Design.

Jones, Michael. 1980. "Access Today." *Progressive Architecture* 61 (September): 206–11.

Kennedy, Edward M. 1989. In Congressional Digest. *See* Congressional Digest, 1989.

Lassen, Peter L. 1976. In *Building without Barriers for the Disabled. See* Harkness, 1976.

Leonard, Edmund. 1978. "The Handicapped Building." *Rehabilitation Literature* 39 (September): 265–69. Published by National Easter Seal Society, 70 E. Lake St. Chicago, Illinois 60601.

Lewis, Sylvia. 1977. The Disabled Are Tired of Being Pushed Around. *Planning* 43 (July): 9–13.

Lifchez, Raymond. 1987. *Rethinking Architecture: Design Students and Physically Disabled People.* Berkeley: University of California Press.

Morton, David. 1978. "Bearing Down on Barriers." *Progressive Architecture* (April): 63–64.

National Commission on Architectural Barriers to Rehabilitation of the Handicapped. 1983. In *Journal of Rehabilitation. See* Francis, 1983.

Robinette, Gary O. 1985. *Barrier-Free Exterior Design.* New York: Van Nostrand Reinhold.

Rosentraub, Mark S., and John I. Gilderbloom. 1989. "The Invisible Jail." *Social Policy* 20 (Summer): 31–33.

Thornburgh, Dick. 1990. "The Americans with Disabilities Act: What It Means to All Americans." *Labor Law Journal* 41 (December): 803–7.

U.S. Dept. of Housing and Urban Development, Office of Policy

Development and Research. 1979. *Access to the Built Environment: A Review of Literature*. Washington, D.C.: Superintendent of Documents.

Vanderheiden, Gregg C. 1990. "Thirty-Something Million: Should They be Exceptions?" *Human Factors* 32:383–96.

Wagner, Michael. 1992. "Right of Access." *Interiors* 151 (August): 74–77.

Wilkoff, Wm. L. 1991. "The Americans with Disabilities Act: How It Affects Designers." *Interiors and Sources* 6 (July–August): 15–16.

———. 1991. "Are You Prepared for Disabled Americans?" *Visual Merchandising and Store Design* 122 (October): 16–18.

———. 1991. "Countdown to the ADA." *Contract Design* 33 (October): 82–83.

———. 1991. "The Americans with Disabilities Act: Are You Prepared?" *Journal of Property Management* 56 (November–December): 70–71.

———. 1992. "The ADA Law, Where It Came from and How It Impacts on What We Do." *Institute of Business Designers Perspective* (Winter): 12–16.

Types of Disabilities

Chapter 2

Consider the questions below as a guide to understanding the fundamental points of this chapter. The answers are not necessarily found in one passage, but instead are meant to capture the essence of the material being presented here.

How does knowledge about particular disabilities go beyond technical regulations to help achieve universal design?

Why is it important for designers to refrain from stereotyping people with disabilities and their needs?

What is the most appropriate way for designers to deal with the environment and its users in order to achieve universal design?

Photo: Farough Abed

MYTHS ABOUT DISABILITIES

In order to gain a full understanding of the contribution the designer can make to universal design, it is important to look at the population commonly referred to as "disabled." The use of such a term suggests the existence of a homogeneous group, but in fact this population is anything but homogeneous. The common denominator that loosely binds its members together is, of course, a physical or mental disability. But this very attribute can in turn be defined by so many characteristics that the diversity of this population quickly becomes evident. For instance, individuals may have a disability affecting only one function, such as vision, or more than one, such as mobility and hearing. Elderly people frequently fall into the latter category. Similarly, people vary in the severity of their disabilities, ranging from mild impairments to severe dysfunction. At the mild end of the continuum there is a fine line between ability and disability. A woman who requires the use of leg braces may be considered as having a disability for census-taking purposes due to the presence of a physical problem, but she may not consider the impairment a disability if she finds that it causes no significant lifestyle changes. Disabilities that are more severe may cause changes referred to as functional limitations, meaning that the disability limits a person's abilities to perform basic daily tasks.

When we refer to a person as "disabled," then the term is insufficient because it fails to describe the actual impairment. The term is also inaccurate since a totally disabled person would be unable to do anything independently, as Goldsmith (1977) has pointed out. The vast majority of people who are classed as "disabled" are not as dysfunctional as this label suggests. It covers individuals whose disability hinders them little or not at all in their daily activities, individuals who are able to be independent most of the time but may require some help, and individuals who require assistance on a daily basis. For some of these people the disability can result in a functional limitation; for some the environment is handicapping. The distinction between these two terms is an important one. A *functional limitation* pertains to the disability itself. A person has a functional limitation if his or her disability limits daily activities. For example, a man who requires assistance in dressing himself has a functional limitation, resulting in a less independent lifestyle. In contrast, *handicap* is a function of the environment. A person is handicapped if the environment (physical or social) puts him or her at a disadvantage, regardless of the type or severity of the disability. Thus a woman who is blind is handicapped if signage is not printed in raised characters or Braille. The two terms are independent and are not mutually exclusive; that is, either condition can occur without the other, or an individual can have a functional limitation *and* be handicapped by the environment.

In general, then, people with disabilities have little in common with each other. The mere fact that two people have a similar feature does not signify any relationship. People with muscular dystrophy are no more likely to have something in common with one another than are people with auburn hair. Like other human beings, individuals with disabilities are more inclined to seek out and develop friendships with those who share their interests and professions than with those who share their physical traits. This may seem like stating the obvious, but in fact people with disabilities traditionally have been institutionalized on the premise that they are more comfortable with "their own kind." Much of the federal legislation in recent years has functioned to dispel this myth.

FIGURE 2–1. Because the ramp is too steep it has been blocked off, leaving the loading dock as the only accessible entrance.

Another perpetual myth needing to be shattered is that the disability *is* the person. Certainly people with disabilities are multifaceted like everyone else. A man may be paraplegic, but he is also many other things. He may be an excellent chess player, a successful businessman, have average upper body strength, and above-average eyesight. Paraplegia is but one characteristic of the total person. In many cases the disability is a highly visible characteristic, making it difficult for others to focus on abilities. However, it should be remembered that all humans have a range of abilities; most of these abilities will be average, but a few will be exceptionally good or exceptionally poor. Knowing a person's ability level regarding one function (e.g., vision) gives no indication of that same person's ability in a fundamentally different function (e.g., cognition). Unfortunately, people without disabilities have a tendency to raise their voices when speaking to a person who is blind, or use simple language when speaking to an adult in a wheelchair, or worse still, speak to an able-bodied companion rather than the person with the disability. At an ADA seminar, one woman with blindness even said that on occasion she has asked strangers for directions and they have given the information to her guide dog. However subconscious these acts are, they indicate to people with disabilities that others make assumptions about their performance levels in all areas based solely on evidence of their disability. It is important, therefore, to judge people on their abilities, not on their *dis*abilities.

Similarly, it is important not to make assumptions about the *quality* of life for people with disabilities. Consider a woman without a disability. She may have average use of her limbs and her senses, but exceptional artistic skills that she uses to paint in her spare time. Now compare her with a woman who is deaf and is an excellent long-distance runner. Each of these women has developed her skills to their fullest potential in her chosen hobby. Does the second woman enjoy her hobby less because she cannot hear? Does the first woman get more out of painting because she has no physical problems? Surely the answer to both of these questions is no. Like everyone else, individuals with disabilities pursue a variety of interests in their lives, and it is erroneous to assume that a person who is blind will not have any use for a museum, or a person who is deaf could not possibly gain any enjoyment from a concert. All places of public accommodation should be as universally accessible as possible so anyone may utilize them.

"Many of the incapacities that we refer to as functional limitations, and which imprison the severely handicapped in a restricted milieu, can be diagnosed as the impact of architectural barriers."

Edmund Leonard

THE DESIGNER, THE USER, AND THE ENVIRONMENT: AN INTERACTIVE RELATIONSHIP

Comprehension of these concepts becomes important when one considers design of the built environment. There is a direct relationship between the designer, the environment, and the needs of the total population. Traditionally this relationship could be depicted in a linear model, as shown in Figure 2–2. The designer conceptualized his or her design based on preestablished anthropometric data about the average adult male. Assuming that these dimensions would be adequate for the general public, they served to shape the built environment in such a way that it excluded many potential users and inconvenienced still more. Further, the environment, once built, was not assessed by the designer to ensure that it was usable by the general public, nor was feedback about the design elicited from the general public. Hence, a linear model serves to depict this noninteractive relationship.

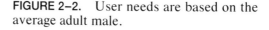

FIGURE 2–2.   User needs are based on the average adult male.

By contrast, Figure 2–3 demonstrates the possibility of an evolving relationship between the three variables. The designer makes use of broader anthropometric guidelines at the beginning of the design process, including information regarding the needs of people with various types of disabilities and people at different stages of life. In turn this information impacts the shape that the environment will take. Similarly, the designer continues to analyze environmental accessibility in order to better meet the needs of the general public, who also provide input about their experiences to the designer. In this model, then, the three variables in the relationship are constantly interacting with each other, creating the dynamics needed to achieve universal design.

The two models have omitted the client/owner as a variable in the process. Although the client's needs are undoubtedly paramount in any design project, they are extraneous to considerations of universal design. No matter how the client defines the parameters of the project, the design solution must still meet the accessibility requirements of the law and the universal design philosophy.

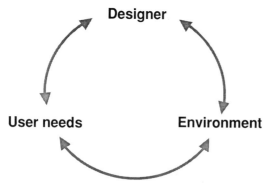

FIGURE 2–3.   User needs are based on users with all types of abilities.

What the designer must bring to this process is sensitivity, an understanding of disabilities that must be considered from the preliminary phase of design. It is critical that the needs of those with disabilities be addressed in the inital design phase; not only does this avoid costly design changes later, but more importantly, addressing these needs as an afterthought relegates individuals with disabilities to the status of second-class citizens, a position from which they have fought long and hard to emerge. Although it is the technical aspects of design elements that will be altered for accessibility, simply adhering to design regulations is not enough to serve the cause of accessibility. Sensitivity on the part of the designer is the main ingredient for a successful relationship among the designer, the environment, and the needs of those with disabilities (as well as other users). Without awareness, the designer can follow all the codes and still produce a design that falls short of being accessible. Below are two examples of "technically" accessible but otherwise insensitive designs.

Mr. David Carter, a member of the Indiana Civil Rights Commission who uses a wheelchair, often needs accessible lodging. In a hotel room advertised as accessible, he found two large armchairs and a table placed in front of the window, making it impossible for him to reach the cord to close the drapes. Mr. Carter left the drapes open and undressed in the dark, but consequently was awakened by daylight at 4:00 A.M. Although this room was in fact accessible and met all the code regulations, it was still an insensitive design. As such it did not comply with the *intent* of the ADA. A similar situation occurred when a woman using a wheelchair parked her car in a space labeled with the accessibility symbol. The space, to her relief, was in fact as wide as needed to comfortably remove her wheelchair from her car and transfer to it. Unfortunately the parking lot sloped and when she let go of the chair it rolled away to the middle of the lot, leaving her stranded in her car. Ironically she was on her way to speak at an ADA seminar and was 45 minutes late because she had to wait for someone to help her.

As barriers are removed the person with disabilities has greater access to the environment, including education, recreation, and employment. This independence can enhance self-esteem, allowing the person to become better equipped to contribute to society and enjoy his or her civil rights as an American citizen. Many designers have already begun to implement universal design, and others must join them. Only when individuals with

"[There must be] a partnership between the disabled and the designer. Each group must see the other not in an adversarial fashion but as a partner in achieving the ultimate goal of a barrier-free existence in the public and private spheres."

Itzhak Perlman

"The disabled are not a homogeneous group. Their impairments stem from different causes, manifest themselves in a different manner, and affect their functioning in drastically different ways. Their interaction with their surroundings, therefore, tends also to be different, according to the category of disability and degree of severity."

Edmund Leonard

disabilities attempt to patronize public and private buildings will they be able to voice their opinions on the accessibility and sensitivity in the design of those buildings; their input will aid designers in the process of learning how to create truly universal environments. It is imperative that we bring about these changes, for the estimated 43 million Americans who have disabilities as well as for the vast number who are likely to have them in the future.

RATES OF INCIDENCE

Although the figure of 43 million Americans has been accepted as the official government estimate, the actual figures pertaining to specific disabilities should be viewed with caution. Incidence rates vary tremendously from one source to another. Organizations that collect these data use different guidelines for determining the existence of a disability as well as different sources for data gathering. Moreover, persons with more than one disability may be counted under each disability category, increasing the probability of inaccurate figures.

More important than actual incidence figures is the realization that a great many people in America have some type of disability with the potential for restricting some aspect of their daily lives. With the current trend toward the "graying of America," that potential for loss of independence will continue to grow. Projected demographic figures indicate that by the middle of the twenty-first century about 35 percent of the population will be over 55 years of age, a critical point after which disabilities become more likely (Vanderheiden, 1990). Forty-five percent of 65-year-olds have functional limitations, while the figure jumps to 72.5 percent for 75-year-olds (Vanderheiden, 1990). Progress in medical technology also increases the chances that infants with birth defects, accident victims, or war veterans will live, often with physical or cognitive impairments. Some researchers even estimate that the population of people with disabilities in the United States could double before the middle of the next century (Congressional Digest, 1989). These statistics make it clear that each of us faces an ever-growing likelihood that at some point in our lives we will be faced with a disabling condition of our own or in someone we love.

On such a personal level it is easier to recognize the need for helping those with disabilities to lead independent and fulfilling lives as much as possible.

Disabilities may be loosely divided into four categories, namely mobility, dexterity, sensory, and cognitive disabilities. Each of the first three categories is greatly impacted by the built environment. To develop sensitivity the designer must know something about these broad categories and their effects on the individuals who must deal with them while maneuvering in the built environment. The remainder of this chapter offers information regarding the three categories. Many of the barrier solutions mentioned below reflect the ADA Accessibility Guidelines, or ADAAG. These can be found in Appendix 2.

People with cognitive disabilities, the fourth category, are much less impeded by architectural barriers. Nonetheless, there are a few related problems, most of which are addressed in relation to other disabilities. Signage is perhaps one of the biggest barriers since people with cognitive disabilities may be slow to assimilate information. Repetition of information is useful, as well as printing in large, easy-to-read letters. ADAAG does not call for repetition per se, but utilizing adequate signage as specified in the guidelines is helpful. Another beneficial requirement is the use of pictographs, such as the male/female symbols for restroom doors. These can clarify any uncertainty that may arise from the use of such nebulous terms as *Guys* and *Gals*, which are sometimes found in restaurants or places of recreation. Wider dimensions that are necessary for wheelchairs also serve the needs of people with cognitive disabilities who require assistance from a companion, as they might in dressing rooms or toilet stalls.

Keep in mind that there is a great deal of variability among people with disabilities. How many people will actually benefit from any given accessible feature is impossible to determine, since this depends on the severity of an individual's disability and the degree to which it limits activity (whether or not there is a functional limitation). For example, Braille in signage is useless to people with visual disabilities who do not read Braille or are able to read raised letters, but for those who use it as their only form of written communication it means the difference between independence and the need for aid. In designing for public accommodations we must always remember that the general public

"Now I know that no one is immune from disability. If we are not born with a disability, any of us can find ourselves in a wheelchair or without sight or hearing if we live long enough. Anyone can join the disability community in an instant, like I did."

James S. Brady

Art Center College of Design
Library
1700 Lida Street
Pasadena, Calif. 91103

FIGURE 2–4. Asymmetrical doors allow adequate width for a wheelchair in a space where two doors of equal width would have been inaccessible.

consists of all different types of people, and we must try to meet as many needs as possible to achieve maximal accessibility. This is the basis for universal design.

MOBILITY DISABILITIES

This category encompasses a vast array of conditions, often resulting in the need for a walking aid, and in the most severe disabling conditions, a wheelchair. The discussion below will be divided into two parts: the first dealing with wheelchair users and the second with people with other mobility impairments.

Problems of People Who Use Wheelchairs

Disorders such as cerebral palsy (loss of control over movement), muscular dystrophy (loss of muscular strength), and multiple sclerosis (motor incoordination) may necessitate the use of wheelchairs, though not everyone with these disorders is affected so severely in terms of mobility.

Often some type of paralysis results in wheelchair use. It may be in the lower half of the body (paraplegia), in all four limbs (quadriplegia), or in either the right half or left half of the body (hemiplegia). Paralysis may be accompanied by diminished body strength in other parts of the body. An individual with paraplegia might have weakened musculature in the back, chest, and/or arms, making tasks like opening doors more difficult. An associated loss of sensation is also not uncommon, leaving a person unable to feel temperature change, touch, or pain in the paralyzed limbs. People with this lack of sensitivity to external stimuli may not know when they have been injured and must constantly check their bodies for burns, abrasions, and the like. Noninsulated hot-water or drain pipes beneath sinks are an example of the type of hazard that must be avoided. Renal problems are also frequently associated with paralysis. These are potentially fatal, requiring that the individual have constant fluid intake and thus making accessible drinking fountains essential. It should be noted that not all people using wheelchairs have completely lost their mobility. Some may be able to move around a little without their wheelchairs, and may do so at home. Other people who are ambulatory may choose to use wheelchairs occasionally because of reduced body strength or other problems.

A moment's reflection will show that people in wheelchairs face a tremendous number of physical barriers. They may be shut out of a particular building by stairs or doorways that are not sufficiently wide. If they are able to enter (often through the back or service entrance), they still may face interior doorways or aisles that are too narrow. They may not be able to use a drinking fountain or bathroom facilities, reach merchandise or counters without assistance, or use office equipment. Section 4.2 of ADAAG details the minimum space requirements and reach ranges for wheelchair users. The problems commonly faced by individuals in wheelchairs may be loosely grouped together as vertical level change problems and dimensionality problems, though these categories cover only the most obvious barriers. Many more subtle problems exist, and talking with people who use wheelchairs can help the designer to comprehend them more fully.

One of the most important solutions to vertical level change problems is the elevator. While these are common in many places, they often have call buttons that are too high to reach, doors that are too narrow, small interiors that do not provide turning space, and interior control buttons that are too high. Also, they are frequently located away from the main path of travel, though they should be in a central location as escalators are.

For people in wheelchairs, vertical changes as small as 1 inch can impede movement. Often such level changes are present where they are not required, as in raised thresholds (though sometimes these are present as protection from the elements). It is essential that floors be even to allow those in wheelchairs to traverse an area easily. Floor surfaces should be of nonskid, firm materials. Carpets with a deep pile can make movement difficult for wheelchair users.

In the same vein, outdoor ground surfaces can create barriers. Ramps and curb cuts are becoming widespread solutions to level change barriers. However, small vertical changes at the bottom level of a ramp or curb cut are not uncommon, especially where

"Many places of public accommodation . . . have double-leaf doors, a pair of doors in front, each leaf of which is too narrow to accommodate a wheelchair. . . . Believe me when I say it's virtually impossible for a wheelchair user to sit in front of a pair of doors and pull both of them open at the same time."

Marc Fiedler, Esq.[1]

drainage is a problem. A raised surface of less than one half inch usually can be manipulated by those in wheelchairs, but anything exceeding this may pose a barrier. Slope is also an important consideration. A severe slope on a curb cut can send users of wheelchairs into traffic. Likewise, ramps can be difficult for some people in wheelchairs to maneuver. Although a gradient of 1:12 is commonly recommended and can be handled by many, a sensitive designer might choose a gentler slope in certain situations, such as for a nursing home or a convalescent center.

Dimensionality, of course, can be another major obstacle for people in wheelchairs. Doorways and corridors must be wide enough to accommodate a wheelchair, including turning radius. For doors that open toward the user, there also has to be sufficient space on the latch side of the door for it to swing open without hitting the chair. Another problem associated with doors is the force required to open one. Some, especially exterior doors, require a lot of strength to open, and can be heavy even for ambulatory people with good strength in their arms. (Often heavy doors are necessary to prevent them from being blown open by air pressure.) Wheelchair users vary a great deal in their upper body strength, and many find door pressure an obstacle. Automatic door openers are a good solution for such a situation; however, there is an associated risk with their use in that they are inoperable during power outages.

Bathrooms are yet another place where dimensions can present a problem. An individual in a wheelchair must not only be able to enter the room, but must often negotiate a privacy baffle followed by a stall door. Once inside, there must be room to shut the stall door, turn the wheelchair around, and effect a side or front transfer. Grab bars are necessary to complete a transfer. Having a spring-loaded stall door that shuts behind the user facilitates the process of locking the door. Because there is usually only one accessible stall required in a public restroom, it makes sense to have an accessible urinal as well.

Height can be an equally deterring factor for the individual in a wheelchair. It affects everything from controls (such as light switches and thermostats), to office equipment

1. From an interview with Marc Fiedler, Esq., Koonz, McKenney, Johnson, and Regan. Mr. Fiedler uses a wheelchair and has limited manual dexterity.

and furniture, to bathroom fixtures, drinking fountains, and public telephones. In stores merchandise is often inaccessible and checkout counters are frequently too high. Research and experience have determined the optimal height for reach by people who are either sitting or standing (see ADAAG 4.2), but often design elements do not conform to these recommendations.

Users of wheelchairs face many safety issues, particularly in terms of emergency egress from buildings and safe traversal of outdoor areas with cars. In parking lots, for instance, all accessible spaces should have direct access to the accessible route through the lot. A person in a wheelchair should not have to move behind parked cars in order to reach a curb cut because he or she may not be visible to other drivers and is therefore entering into a potentially hazardous situation.

FIGURE 2–5. A wheelchair lift may be installed when a ramp is architecturally infeasible.

"The test for most of the kind of hardware you should have is 'Can a fully able-bodied individual operate it with his fist closed?' If you can close your fist and operate it without using your fingers, then it will work."

Marc Fiedler, Esq.

Problems Related to People with Other Mobility Impairments

Certain conditions can result in less severe mobility impairments, including arthritis and rheumatism, diabetes, heart disease, an amputated lower limb, high blood pressure, or a temporary problem such as surgery, a broken leg, or pregnancy. Elderly people also frequently have mobility problems. Any of these conditions can create the need for a walking aid (for example, a walker, a cane, braces, or crutches), though many people do without them. Ambulatory individuals often experience insecurity or difficulty in walking, or problems with agility, balance, stamina, and/or speed. They may have trouble changing positions as well, as in kneeling, turning, or rising from a sitting position.

Dimensions are less of a problem with ambulatory people than with those in wheelchairs. In general, any width that is adequate for a wheelchair also will be sufficient for users of other mobility aids. The main problem for these individuals is vertical level change. Evenness in floors is imperative. Small level changes can be hazardous to ambulatory people who can trip easily or catch a walking aid. This same condition applies to stairs as well. Open risers and protruding tread nosings both have the capacity to catch the foot of someone who is wearing leg braces, who is not very agile, or who has trouble bending the knees. People with mobility impairments are also less likely to encounter problems on floors and stairs with nonskid, firm surfaces.

Handrails are an essential supportive device on stairs and ramps. When extended beyond the top and bottom risers, they provide users with a means for pulling themselves beyond the stairs. Also, installing handrails on both sides of a stairway is useful for people who have strength on only one side. Because people who rely on handrails usually rest their weight on them, a crucial consideration is the space between the rail itself and the wall. It must be small enough so that if a person slips and falls, the arm does not slide into the space, causing injury. Height, width, a surface material that is easy to grip, and the amount of pressure a handrail is able to sustain are all important variables to consider in making handrails supportive for people with a variety of needs.

DEXTERITY DISABILITIES

Certain motor difficulties may present dexterity problems. For example, arthritis, an artificial hand or arm, complete or partial paralysis, and reduced strength and agility can all contribute to dexterity difficulties. People who experience such problems may have trouble with reaching, grasping, pinching, twisting the wrist, or a combination of these or other manipulative tasks. Dexterity disabilities can be most incapacitating for two broad functions: grasping objects, such as handrails, and operating controls and hardware, such as that found on drawers or doors. Push buttons that do not require too much pressure, levers in place of knobs, and automatic controls can greatly enhance the abilities of individuals who have this type of disability.

VISUAL DISABILITIES

Like all disabilities, visual impairments cover a wide range from mild problems aided by corrective lenses to moderate visual impairments to the condition referred to as blindness, indicating a total lack of sight. Actually, some people who are blind can sense certain visual cues such as light/dark distinctions or changes in color. Typical visual problems other than blindness include difficulties with depth perception, reduced visual field, a sensitivity to glare, or difficulties in adjusting from dark to light conditions. Shadows can be particularly hazardous, especially where they obscure level changes. In the United States as much as 3.5 percent of the population has visual impairments, and 2 million people can be rated as either legally blind or severely visually impaired (Elkind, 1990).

Because of the extent to which humans rely on their visual sense, barriers are frequently encountered in the built environment by those with visual disabilities. Perhaps the least controllable barrier is the preponderance of temporary obstacles in the built environment. These include people moving across the path, objects such as boxes on a sidewalk or temporary exhibits placed in a path, and moveable objects such as furniture or display racks. Such nonpermanent objects may cause hazards to people with visual problems, whereas permanent fixtures can be memorized and thereby avoided.

"For a blind person, in some cases it makes no difference whether something is 20 feet away or 20 inches away if it's not where you expect it to be. You can feel around a little bit but once it gets beyond a foot or so, then you don't know whether it's worth continuing to feel around or whether you just have to start asking."

W. David Kerr[2]

2. From an interview with W. David Kerr, National Institutes of Health. Mr. Kerr is blind.

Protruding objects can cause another hazard for individuals with visual disabilities. Often objects such as signs hang at head level, or protrude from the wall at a level that cannot be detected by a cane, such as telephones and wall-hung drinking fountains. Guide dogs are trained to look for these obstacles and steer around them, but often they do not alert their owners to overhanging objects. It is not uncommon for people with severe visual problems to sustain facial injuries from colliding with such hazards. This problem can be solved by recessing fixtures or by continuing a projection to the floor so that it will be detectable by a cane.

A major barrier for people with visual disabilities is signage. Tactile and visual signs are essential contributions to the independence of individuals who are blind or visually impaired, but only if they can be perceived. Uniform locations for such signage aid people with visual disabilities by making locations predictable. Some people with visual impairments are able to read very large print, especially if they can get close to it. Also making information available both in Braille[3] and in raised letters (sans serif) maximizes the number of people who can utilize the information. (Only a small percentage of people with visual disabilities read Braille, so tactile lettering is imperative.) Tactile maps of a building or facility enhance the ability of those with visual impairments to maneuver through an unfamiliar space. Again, consistency in location is the key to providing useful signage since this allows people with visual impairments to obtain information independently.

A similar orientation problem exists with large, open spaces, such as expansive lobbies or transportation terminals. Consistently locating receptionists' stations or information booths just inside an entrance simplifies the task of orientation. In other large spaces such as shopping mall concourses or parking lots, textured or otherwise clearly demarcated pathways can help those with visual impairments to locate entrances, exits, and the like. Not providing these often means that a person with a severe visual disability will have to wander about until reaching the desired goal or locating someone to help, thereby limiting his or her independence.

3. There are two grades of Braille. Grade 1 consists of raised dot patterns representing letters and numbers, while Grade 2 is a group of contractions designed to make Braille messages shorter. The latter grade is required by the ADA Accessibility Guidelines to be used in signage.

Of great importance to individuals with visual disabilities are auditory signals. These include directional signals for elevators and auditory alarms, as well as recorded mes-

FIGURE 2–6.   Raised letters and symbols on this tactile map orient visitors with sight impairments at Independence National Historical Park. (Gift of The Guild of Prescription Opticians of Philadelphia as executed by the Philadelphia Architects Workshop.)

"The idea of having defined boundaries is very helpful to a blind person, whether the person is using a cane or a dog. With a dog it's not quite as critical because a dog can identify an exit or a sidewalk area and move to that area, whereas with a cane it is quite important because it gives you something to follow along."

W. David Kerr

sages to accompany signs and museum exhibits. In the event of an emergency, auditory alarms and signals can be as helpful in guiding those blinded by smoke as they can be in guiding those with poor visual acuity. This is a prime example of universal design that makes an environment safer for all users. Other auditory cues that may be helpful for orientation include the sounds of water fountains, escalators, traffic flow, turnstiles, and other environmental elements.

There are a variety of dangerous areas from which all pedestrians must be protected, as well as other areas that can be especially hazardous to those with little or no residual vision. For instance, loading docks, construction sites, and boiler rooms must be clearly demarcated with visual and tactile warnings. Stairs, ramps, and curb cuts must also have clear cues. A good many solutions can be used in eliminating these barriers, alone or in combination, depending on the situation. Contrasting texture or color on floor surfaces can highlight corridors or top and bottom stairs leading to dangerous zones (or to bathrooms). Handrails on stairs and ramps can be helpful as visual and tactile cues indicating level changes. Extending them above and below the flight of stairs and painting them a contrasting color can also serve as aids. Safety fences or rails, tactile ground surfaces, and roughened or knurled hardware can be effective warning devices at construction sites or other dangerous areas.

AUDITORY DISABILITIES

The number of Americans with hearing losses is estimated to be anywhere from 21 million to 28 million (American Speech-Language-Hearing Association, 1992). This includes people of all ages, and impairments ranging from mild losses (making soft sounds difficult to hear) to profound deafness (making even the loudest sounds difficult or impossible to hear). It should be reiterated that the numbers matter far less than the impact that the loss can have on daily life.

If deafness or severe auditory impairments are either congenital or incurred before language acquisition, they can make oral communication extremely difficult to master. As a primary means of communication, then, a child with deafness often is taught to communicate manually in sign language rather than orally. In part this is because it is difficult for such children to master speech without the auditory feedback that hearing children receive. Consequently, some people who are deaf or have severe hearing losses refrain from communicating in public because they have trouble articulating coherently and are accustomed to communicating in a different mode. Another reason is that people often perceive the speech of a person who is deaf to be strange and unintelligible, and they may not make an effort to understand it. When people who are deaf do communicate with hearing people, they frequently write messages or gesture rather than attempting to speak. There are many other people in the Deaf community who do not face these problems because their hearing losses occurred subsequent to language learning, making spoken conversation easier, or because they were taught oral communication as children despite the hearing loss.

People with hearing losses often have hearing aids. While these are generally thought of as corrective aids similar to eyeglasses, this is not always the case. A frequent problem with these aids is that they tend to amplify all sounds, not just communicative ones, making background noise competitive with speech. Also, some people have a hearing loss that distorts sounds besides making them less audible. Thus communication can once again be a problem.

An unfortunate effect of this communication problem surfaces when strangers attempt to speak to a person with a hearing loss, for instance, while shopping. A friendly comment may be completely ignored, not because the person who is deaf wishes to be rude, but because he or she simply did not hear the comment or see the other person initiating a conversation. This has nothing to do with intelligence; people with hearing losses are as capable of holding a conversation as people who hear, but may use an alternate, though equally sophisticated, form of communication (sign language).

In terms of barrier removal, one of the most beneficial tools for people with hearing losses (and everyone else) is signage that is noticeable and easy to read. Also, they benefit from closed captioning, sign language interpreting, and other such cues on video

"Noise and sound are strangers to me and other deaf people, which means that we are very, very visually oriented people. We use our eyes to hear."

Dr. Jack R. Gannon[4]

4. From an interview with Dr. Jack R. Gannon, Special Assistant to the President for Advocacy, Gallaudet University. Dr. Gannon is profoundly deaf.

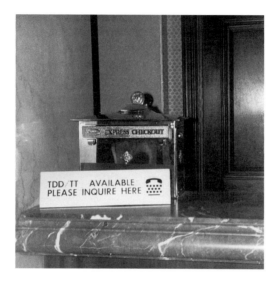

FIGURE 2–7. Well-displayed signage alerts the general public to the presence of accessible elements. Note the use of both text and symbol. (Designed by George A. Snode, AIA, ASID, for the Mayflower Hotel, Washington, D.C.)

monitors. Poor lighting or glares on signage or monitors can negate the helpful effects of these elements as quickly for individuals with hearing losses as for individuals with visual problems, so lighting should be considered carefully. Other visual information can also be extremely useful, such as elevators with visual directional signals and floor indicators. Visual alarms (strobes) are essential for the safety of people with hearing losses. Because they do not transmit signals in all directions like auditory alarms do, more of them may be necessary to cover a given space. Flashing lights can serve to signal a ringing telephone or doorbell.

Individuals with hearing losses are often unable to use public telephones because they lack special equipment. Volume control and text telephones, or TDDs, are essential aids for distance communication. Other auditory devices that increase accessibility include quality sound systems and assistive listening devices, which attenuate background noise while amplifying communicative sounds. Regarding sound systems, care should be taken to minimize the distance between the sound source and the listener.

Floor and wall surfaces must also be considered with respect to background noise, or they too can become barriers to communication. Sound-absorbing materials will reduce background noise, making the reception of speech and other communicative signals easier.

It is interesting to note that handrails serve a purpose for some people with hearing losses that may not at first be obvious. With a hearing loss originating in the inner ear there can occasionally be an associated problem with balance. Consequently, individuals with such a problem need to hold onto a rail when climbing or descending stairs.

Closely related to auditory impairments are speech and language impairments. These affect some 3 million Americans of all ages, and can be congenital disabilities or the result of stroke or head injury (American Speech-Language-Hearing Association, 1992). They frequently occur concomitantly with hearing loss. Communication barriers are the main factor that must be considered for this type of disability. As with auditory disabilities, adequate signage and lighting are useful in making the environment more accessible for people with speech and language impairments.

CONFLICTS BETWEEN DIFFERENT DISABILITIES

A good many of the barrier solutions mentioned thus far are advantageous for more than one type of disability. For instance, stairs with open risers can be hazardous for those with visual problems as well as ambulatory individuals who use aids or wear braces. They can also be dangerous for children and adults without disabilities. Prohibiting open risers thus promotes safety for all.

Unfortunately, not all solutions are that simple. Although the intent of the ADA is to make public spaces usable for the largest number of citizens, regardless of their physical or mental abilities, sometimes meeting these needs can create conflict. The ADA Accessibility Guidelines, provided by the federal government as minimum guidelines for accessibility, have dealt with some of these conflicts in an effective manner. A classic example is the curb-cut solution, which has evolved over time to meet various needs. Initially curb cuts were placed directly in the path of travel, allowing those with mobility disabilities to cross streets easily. This seemed appropriate until it was discovered that people who are blind and use canes could not distinguish between the curb cut and the natural surface undulations of concrete, thus losing the shoreline orientation and ending up in traffic as a result. This conflict was eventually resolved with a combination of two features: first, the curb cut was moved off to the side so as not to be in the direct line of pedestrian traffic and second, the curb cut was given a textured surface to alert people who are blind. Using both of these solutions in conjunction satisfies everyone's needs in a safe manner. This example underlines the importance of an interactive relationship in which the designer must receive feedback from users of the environment, and it also demonstrates the evolutionary process common to all types of design.

Another problem that has been effectively resolved concerns wall-hung drinking fountains and other such elements that project into the path of travel. Although these were originally designed to serve the needs of wheelchair users, it quickly became evident that they were a hazard to people with blindness who use canes because they could not detect projecting obstacles that high off the ground. The solution has been to recess the projecting object into the wall.

Still other issues have not been addressed by ADAAG. For instance, floor surfaces

"That is inevitable, that making an accommodation for one type of disability can cause some problems for others. . . . [By putting] elevator buttons low where a person in a wheelchair can reach them, if you have Braille it's more difficult to read . . . because you have to either read it sideways or upside down."

W. David Kerr

FIGURE 2–8. A recessed drinking fountain is lowered for wheelchair users.

have been discussed in terms of mobility, but not in terms of sound reverberation. While a certain amount of reverberation provides an orientation aid for individuals with visual disabilities, it can also confuse those with hearing losses, who prefer some sound absorbency from walls and floors. Certainly issues of potential conflict will continue to arise in the future, and new solutions will have to be devised to meet as many needs as possible.

UNIVERSAL DESIGN AND AESTHETICS

The designer reading through the ADA guidelines or other barrier free codes might easily feel aesthetically restricted by the extent of the regulations, on top of all the other types of codes that must be followed. However, they need not be restrictive, particularly if they are consistent in their content. The first set of ANSI standards was very broad in its scope, leaving many decisions to the designer. As experience and research have accumulated, each successive set of federal regulations has given the designer more specific details based on extensive data about accessibility. Indeed, regulations will in all likelihood continue to evolve in order to break down physical barriers, and this evolutionary process will occur in part as a direct result of the interaction among designers, the built environment, and its users. Designers must keep abreast of these changes but not let them constrain their creative efforts. As Thomas Fisher (1985, p. 124) so aptly stated, "There will, of course, always be architects [and designers] who see only the costs and not the benefits of accessibility, who see the handicapped codes only as an unwanted constraint upon their design freedom. For them, the inhibition of creativity lies not in the regulations, but in their own lack of imagination—the one disability no code can address."

REFERENCES

Allen, R. C. 1969. *Legal Rights of Disabled and Disadvantaged*. Washington, D.C.: U.S. Department of HEW, National Citizens Conference on Rehabilitation of Disabled and Disadvantaged.

American Speech-Language-Hearing Association. 1992. *Communication Fact Sheet*.

Brady, Jim. 1991. "New Federal Disabilities Law Goes into Effect: A Perspective on ADA." *DCCC Connections: Newsletter of the District of Columbia Chamber of Commerce* (Winter).

Congressional Digest. 1989. "Americans with Disabilities Act of 1989." *Congressional Digest* 68(12):289–314.

Elkind, Jerome. 1990. "Incidence of Disabilities in the United States." *Human Factors* 32:397–405.

Fisher, Thomas. 1985. "Enabling the Disabled." *Progressive Architecture* 7:119–24.

Foote, Kenneth E. 1986. "Mobility Impairment and Pharmacy Accessibility: Conflict in a Commercial Built Environment." *Environment and Behavior* 18 (September): 571–603.

Goldsmith, Selwyn. 1977. *Designing for the Disabled*. London: Royal Institute of British Architects.

Harkness, Sarah P., and James N. Groom, Jr. 1976. *Building Without Barriers for the Disabled*. New York: Whitney Library of Design.

Jones, Michael A., and John H. Catlin. 1978. "Design for Access." *Progressive Architecture* (April): 65–71.

Kaufman, Mervyn. 1992. "Universal Design in Focus." *Metropolis* 12 (November): 42–52.

Leonard, Edmund. 1978. "The Handicapped Building." *Rehabilitation Literature* 39 (September): 265–69.

New Internationalist. 1992. "Disabled Lives." *New Internationalist*, no. 233.

Nickerson, Raymond S. 1978. "Human Factors and the Handicapped." *Human Factors* 20:259–72.

Perlman, Itzhak. 1992. In *Metropolis. See* Kaufman, 1992.

Sorensen, R. J. 1979. *Design for Accessibility*. New York: McGraw-Hill Book Company.

Vanderheiden, Gregg C. 1990. "Thirty-Something Million: Should They Be Exceptions?" *Human Factors* 32:383–96.

The ADA: What Will It Cost?

Chapter 3

Consider the questions below as a guide to understanding the fundamental points of this chapter. The answers are not necessarily found in one passage, but instead are meant to capture the essence of the material being presented here.

How does the economic cost of accessibility compare with that of inaccessibility?

In what ways have social barriers kept people with disabilities from mainstreaming into American life?

What is the most important concept for designers to keep in mind in order to avoid litigation concerning public buildings?

Photo: Farough Abed

ECONOMIC EXPENDITURES: ACCESSIBILITY VS. INACCESSIBILITY

As a civil rights law, it would be difficult to argue with the intent of the ADA. The benefits to people with disabilities are unquestionably worth pursuing. However, all issues of moral and social responsibility must eventually be studied in terms of cost to society.

According to the National League of Cities and the U.S. General Accounting Office, studies have demonstrated that the inclusion of accessibility features in new site construction totals less than 1 percent, and usually less than one half of 1 percent, of the new construction costs. Authorities from around the world, reporting to the U.N., have concurred that accessibility features applied at the design stages of new construction add virtually nothing to the costs. On the other hand, alteration costs can be exceedingly variable, depending on the existing site and the type of alteration needed to bring about accessibility. Again, other countries agree with this estimate.

This variation can be understood readily when one considers that many accessible changes are achieved by adjusting the dimensions of existing elements rather than adding new ones. It costs nothing extra in new construction to install switches and controls lower than the traditional height, but moving these elements once they are installed would be somewhat more costly. Certainly features such as elevators and ramps, while expensive in new construction, would prove to be an even greater (and often unmanageable) expense if they were added to an existing building or site. Sometimes an increased cost due to accessibility will lower another cost, as in doors and walls. A 3'0'' door costs more than a 2'6'' door, but less drywall is needed and the costs are therefore nearly balanced out. Fortunately the costs of many accessibility features are decreasing gradually as manufacturers supply new products to meet ever-growing accessibility-market demands, and this of course will alleviate some of the expense involved in alterations. For instance, textured tiles, automatic door openers, handrails, levered handles, and any number of other products are being produced now in greater volume. Not only are these things more readily available and less expensive than they used to be, but they are offered in different styles and finishes to maintain aesthetic value and minimize the institutional look. Yet even with decreasing costs, it is certain that the designer who adopts barrier free features at little extra expense in the planning phase of a project will save a tremendous amount of expense and headache by not having to retrofit later or face litigation.

"Not since the abolition of slavery have Americans been denied equality for economic reasons. The principle of equality is not negotiable in the United States of America. ADA is not only affordable, we cannot afford not to have it."

*Justin Dart, Chairperson
Task Force on the Rights and
Empowerment of Americans
with Disabilities*

"There are choices and options available for any building designer at the concept stage of their planning that can almost entirely eliminate additional expense and the need for special accessibility features."

Ronald L. Mace, FAIA, President
Barrier Free Environments, Inc.

"The costs of disability are, all too often, simply that: the costs of maintaining inactivity rather than the costs of investing in peoples' productivity."

Prof. Edward D. Berkowitz,
The George Washington University
and Prof. David H. Dean,
University of Maryland

In drafting the Americans with Disabilities Act, Congress made provisions for keeping costs at a tolerable level. Tax credits will enable businesses to facilitate accessibility with minimal financial burden. Alterations in public accommodations are expected only when readily achievable, and the mandate requires up to 20 percent of renovation costs to be devoted to making the interior path of travel accessible. Alternative measures may be provided when costs of accessibility are too high. For employers who must provide reasonable accommodations to employees with disabilities, it has been estimated that 80 percent of such accommodations cost less than $1000 (Berkery, 1990).

In short, accessibility will cost little in terms of new construction, and the costs for retrofitting existing sites can be distributed over time. How does this assessment compare with the costs of inaccessibility? We have already seen that physical barriers can keep people with disabilities from gaining an education, goods and services, or employment. In 1990, Elkind estimated that almost half of the nation's 43 million citizens with disabilities live at or near the poverty level. One of the reasons for this staggering statistic is that, according to Berkery (1990), only 26 percent of people with disabilities are employed full-time, and for women with disabilities this rate drops to 13 percent. This leaves the disability community with the dubious distinction of having the highest unemployment rate of any minority group in America. Paradoxically, about 60–70 percent of working-age people with disabilities are seeking employment (Berkery, 1990).

Contrast these statistics with the national expenditure for supporting people with disabilities. In 1975 this figure was estimated to be $50 billion (Vanderheiden, 1990). It has steadily risen over the years so that the estimated figure now lies somewhere between $169 billion and $300 billion annually (Thornburgh, 1990). These figures cover both private- and public-sector funding, including governments at the local, state, and federal levels.

In weighing the costs of an accessible environment against the costs of remaining inaccessible, we find that in general society loses in the latter situation. Not only do we lose the potential contributions that people with disabilities can make to society, but we lose tax revenue as well. We also forfeit the potential expenditures in the consumer market that will undoubtedly be made by people with disabilities if they are able to earn money to spend *and* are able to shop in accessible stores. Many retail chains are beginning to use models with disabilities in their advertising in recognition of the fact that consumers come from *all* segments of the population.

An environment that is universally designed will allow those with disabilities to obtain an education and a job, something they often are unable to do. This is important not only from a moral standpoint, but it is also especially important in light of the fact that the post–World War II baby boomers are themselves having fewer children, suggesting the possibility of a labor shortage in the not-too-distant future. To compound this problem, as the general population ages and requires more disability benefits, there will be fewer workers to contribute to Social Security taxes. Integrating the population of people with disabilities into the mainstream of society could help to lessen the economic impact of a potential labor shortage. Of course the other benefit to society will be that once the built environment is made completely barrier free, it will remain that way for future citizens with disabilities.

Elderly people, too, will benefit from an accessible environment. Many senior citizens are forced to retire to nursing homes and other facilities where they incur exorbitant costs for their care. This is not always because they are unable to care for their personal needs at home, but because barriers in the environment make it difficult or impossible for them to remain independent (Bowe, 1980). In a barrier free environment, these people would no longer need to remove themselves to institutional settings.

Within institutional settings accessibility can be an asset as well. Researchers at the University of Michigan's Architecture and Planning Research Laboratory studied hospital patient rooms and found that anytime a patient was able to act independently rather than call a nurse, the hospital saved money (Fisher, 1985). In boarding schools for children with disabilities, in nursing homes, and in other settings, such measures are likely to give a psychological boost to residents, who will enjoy the feeling of independence that they might otherwise be denied.

"As a business person, think about first of all, this person wants to get in here and spend money. Why are you in business? Because you want people to come in and spend money. And the other thing is, it's good publicity. I can guarantee you I tell people word of mouth in the disability community that '[such and such] is a great place to go. They're real proactive on disability issues, they're great at accessibility, they're really working hard to do that.' And I tell one of my friends and that spreads the word."

Eddie Espinosa[1]

---

1. From an interview with Mr. Eddie Espinosa, ReeLife Solutions. Mr. Espinosa is a wheelchair user.

SOCIAL AND PSYCHOLOGICAL BARRIERS

Perhaps the most difficult barriers to change are the social and psychological barriers faced by people with disabilities. Finding a job has been a significant problem for many potential workers. Aside from the physical obstacles barring the way to employment, there have been attitudinal problems with employers who did not want to hire a person with a disability or hired that person for lower wages. In 1980 the average annual earnings were $6000 for people with disabilities compared to $11,300 for people without disabilities (Congressional Digest, 1989). Frequently people with disabilities have requested aid to supplement their incomes, but have found that they must be unemployed to receive funding. Unfortunately, many people have discovered that they can make a better living

FIGURE 3–1. This van-accessible space has a wide access aisle, proper signage, and a direct path to a curb ramp leading to an accessible entrance.

receiving government aid than with a job. In essence, then, our social programs focus on the disability rather than the abilities of a person, resulting in tax dollars that are used to keep people unemployed instead of helping them to gain employment and thereby become taxpaying citizens.

Hopefully the ADA will diminish this trend by providing opportunities for education and employment. While the ADA is not an affirmative-action program and does not require hiring quotas for people with disabilities, it does provide a level playing field for people who have not always had one in the past. The Act mandates that employment decisions be made on the basis of ability rather than disability; specifically, a qualified person may not be denied a job because of a disability.

Aside from these barriers, there is a less tangible barrier involving the nondisabled population and their perceptions of people with disabilities. While it is unrealistic to generalize to all citizens, it is certainly true that social interaction with people who do not have disabilities has caused many individuals with disabilities to feel stigmatized. This can arise from a simple misunderstanding of the nature of a disability and its accompanying physical limitations, but more frequently comes about through emphasis on a person's disability and denial of a person's abilities. Mr. Eddie Espinosa, who deals with disability rights in his professional work, is often called upon for advice by citizens whose rights have been violated. One example is that of a couple eating in a restaurant and using sign language to communicate with each other during their meal. They were asked by the maître d' to stop signing or leave because their manual communication offended the woman at the next table. They refused to leave, and after causing a scene the woman finally left. The true problem was not their mode of communication, but individual attitudes. First, the woman felt that she had the right to deny the couple their means of communication, and second, the maître d' looked upon the people with the disabilities as the problem rather than the woman with the unreasonable request. Prior to the passage of the ADA, many states did not have any means of legal recourse for people with disabilities who were denied their rights in such situations. (Although the couple obtained their rights in this particular situation, frequently it has been the other party that has prevailed in similar encounters.) Often it is not just the person with a disability who is

"As people with disabilities realize earnings commensurate with their productivity, the disincentives to work will be lessened. A higher earnings level, quite simply, will make working more attractive and will point our social welfare policy toward the participation of people with disabilities rather than their withdrawal from the mainstream of American life."

Prof. Edward D. Berkowitz,
The George Washington University
and Prof. David H. Dean,
University of Maryland

"The wonderful thing about the ADA is that it is not doing us favors. It's saying we're citizens with equal rights. The ADA is first and foremost civil rights legislation."

David Carter
Indiana Civil Rights Commission

denied his or her rights—often there are family members or friends accompanying the person, and these people too are denied their rights by association.

Education, employment, recreation, and shopping—activities that other people take for granted to be their rights—are systematically denied to many members of the disability community through social and physical barriers. Over time the denial of these rights, however inadvertent, chips away at the self-esteem of a person with a disability. Not being allowed to enter a building that others may enter, to sit with friends in a theater, to visit a cultural site—all these incidents multiplied over a lifetime add up to one conclusion: namely, that the person with a disability is not welcome to be a full participant in society.

WHO BEARS THE BURDEN OF NONCOMPLIANCE?

Although the ADA encourages conflict resolution through negotiation and arbitration rather than litigation, it is likely that liability questions will be determined through lawsuits. This is a civil rights law, and its fundamental purpose is to eliminate discrimination against people with disabilities. During a judicial review process, the court will view a dispute from this perspective. It is the most important point to bear in mind for anyone who might potentially become involved in litigation regarding the ADA, whether they are small business owners, prospective employers, or designers.

What does this mandate mean for the design profession? The law specifically states that the "failure to design and construct" in an accessible manner constitutes an act of discrimination, meaning that designers will share with building owners and tenants in the liability of an inaccessible design. Thus designers must make an effort to understand the law for their own protection.

Potential conflicts could arise over new construction, alterations, and even surveys of existing sites in terms of their compliance with Titles II and III. In fact, Title III provides private citizens with the right to challenge a project in its design stage on the issue of accessibility, a course that could lead to delays. Of equal importance is Title I (Employ-

"Probably the biggest barrier in this country or anywhere is just that of attitudes towards people with disabilities. That's the number one barrier in employment of people with disabilities and it's also the biggest barrier as far as just not getting into a facility or people not willing to really make a change."

Eddie Espinosa

ment). Although many discrimination cases will deal with employer/employee disputes, a designer could be drawn into a lawsuit over designs for reasonable accommodations.

The best defense for design professionals is knowledge and experience. The ADA is a civil rights law, not a building code. This statement has been made several times before, but its importance cannot be overstressed. The law mandates nondiscriminatory acts, but it does not mandate specific procedures for ensuring accessible design. Instead it offers minimum guidelines in the form of ADAAG, which may not always provide the best guidelines for compliance in a specific situation. Indeed, there are issues that ADAAG does not address at all, however comprehensive it may seem. A similar conflict can arise with state and local building codes. There may be situations in which these codes are not extensive enough to satisfy the intent of the law. In other words, even though the ADA seeks to ensure nondiscrimination, it does not provide a foolproof method of guaranteeing compliance, nor are there any officials to check for compliance. Unless the local building codes have been certified by the Attorney General to reflect their compliance with the ADA, there is no guarantee that buildings will be considered accessible in new construction. Likewise, there is no definite method for determining what is readily achievable in an alteration. Ultimately the designer must rely on personal experience and knowledge for guidance.

Becoming skilled at interpreting the ADA requires more than technical expertise. The designer must develop sensitivity by constantly assessing design plans; by keeping abreast of changes in product availability, research findings, and technological advances pertaining to accessibility; and by taking opportunities to speak with people with all types of disabilities. Increased awareness can result from simply maintaining an ongoing interaction among the designer, the environment, and the users of the space, as Figure 2–3 in Chapter 2 suggests. Keeping this interaction in mind can help the designer to develop sound judgment on compliance issues.

Information on liability is no doubt overwhelming. Based on the objective of the ADA and the fact that enforcement will probably occur through court proceedings, the safest route for designers to follow is the one that errs on the side of accessibility, the route that does the most to strengthen universal design. While ADAAG and building codes are invaluable resources for judging the best procedure, the designer would do well always

"Where we stayed, the swimming pool was up two flights of stairs. Although they have this color brochure with a cozy picture of everybody drinking cocktails around the swimming pool, I'm not one of those everybody, and it makes me feel like a second-class citizen and I don't like that."

David Carter
Indiana Civil Rights Commission

to keep in mind the spirit of the ADA and act accordingly. The judicial review process will take into account "good-faith efforts" in determining if a penalty is appropriate. Designers should discuss compliance issues with their clients and protect themselves through contractual agreements. The client contract should state that the design or recommended priorities (in the case of alterations) are based on the designer's professional

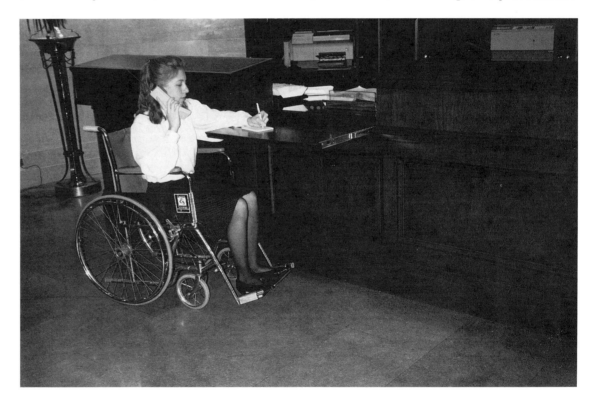

FIGURE 3–2. This concierge desk has a lowered portion with a touch-release extension shelf that retracts into a sleeve when not in use. (Designed by George A. Snode, AIA, ASID, for the Mayflower Hotel, Washington, D.C.)

interpretation of the ADA. Designers should never guarantee compliance with the ADA, since such a determination can only be made in the court. Further, the contract should recommend that the client refer to a lawyer for an opinion on compliance.[2]

When lawsuits are initiated, the ADA seeks to be fair to all parties by not allowing punitive damages to be paid to a private plaintiff, thereby making litigation financially unprofitable. This does not mean that the penalties for violations are light. They can include civil penalties, payment of attorney's fees, injunctive relief, or costly retrofitting to achieve accessibility. (Specific regulations and enforcement policies are shown in Appendix 1.)

"The architectural provisions of the ADA alone will vastly increase opportunities for disabled people by eliminating the subtle but pervasive discrimination that prohibits many disabled people from fully participating in society."

Ronald L. Mace, FAIA, President
Barrier Free Environments, Inc.

THE DESIGNER'S CHALLENGE

The Americans with Disabilities Act was conceived to address the issue of civil rights for the disability community. Efforts to adjust our attitudes as a society will have to come from numerous sectors, and no one body will be able to effect a positive change on its own. The key to change lies in the combined efforts of various entities that together will move our society toward an acceptance of people with disabilities.

What is the role of the designer in this process? We are an integral part of the change that must occur. Not only do we have to comply with the mandates of the ADA in creating an environment that is universally designed, but in so doing we are opening doors for millions who would otherwise be excluded. Accessibility is a means to an end.

---

2. As this book goes to press, we have been asked to comment on the Notice of Proposed Rulemaking to supplement the ADA as it relates to Title II. Although much preliminary debate took place prior to the passage of the ADA, in all likelihood there will continue to be amendments to the existing law in response to attempts to apply it in various situations. Designers should be sure to keep abreast of such changes. See Appendix 1, ADA Titles and Their Effective Dates.

It is a means by which people with disabilities will gain the enjoyment of their full rights as American citizens. As individuals with disabilities become more visible as productive members of our society, they will also become more accepted as humans with abilities like everyone else. We must accept this challenge, not only because we are legally mandated to do so, but because it is our moral and social responsibility to further this process of change.

REFERENCES

Berkery, Peter M., Jr. 1990. ''The Americans with Disabilities Act: Its Impact on Small Business.'' *National Public Accountant* 35 (September): 42-47.

Berkowitz, Edward D., and David H. Dean. 1989. In *Congressional Digest. See* Congressional Digest, 1989.

Bowe, Frank. 1980. *Rehabilitating America: Toward Independence for Disabled and Elderly People.* New York: Harper and Row.

Brady, Jim. 1991. ''New Federal Disabilities Law Goes into Effect: A Perspective on ADA.'' *DCCC Connections: Newsletter of the District of Columbia Chamber of Commerce* (Winter).

Congressional Digest. 1989. ''Americans with Disabilities Act of 1989.'' *Congressional Digest* 68(12):289–314.

Dart, Justin. 1989. In *Congressional Digest. See* Congressional Digest, 1989.

Elkind, Jerome. 1990. ''Incidence of Disabilities in the United States.'' *Human Factors* 32:397–405.

Fisher, Thomas. 1985. ''Enabling the Disabled.'' *Progressive Architecture* 7:119–24.

Francis, Robert A. 1983. ''The Development of Federal Accessibility Law.'' *Journal of Rehabilitation* 49 (January–March): 29–32.

Goldman, Charles D. 1983. ''Architectural Barriers: A Perspective on Progress.'' *Western New England Law Review* 5:465–93.

Jones, David K. 1992. ''The Ambiguities of the ADA.'' *Identity* 5 (Spring): 34–36, 38.

Kaufman, Mervyn. 1992. ''Universal Design in Focus.'' *Metropolis* 12 (November): 42–52.

Mace, Ronald L. 1989. In *Congressional Digest. See* Congressional Digest, 1989.

Stambul, Richard A. 1992. ''Americans with Disabilities Act.'' *Designers West* 39(3):117–18.

Thornburgh, Dick. 1990. ''The Americans with Disabilities Act: What It Means to All Americans.'' *Labor Law Journal* 41 (December): 803–7.

Vanderheiden, Gregg C. 1990. ''Thirty-Something Million: Should They Be Exceptions?'' *Human Factors* 32:383–96.

Wilkoff, Wm. L. 1991. ''The Americans with Disabilities Act: How It Affects Designers.'' *Interiors and Sources* 6 (July–August): 15–16.

———. 1991. ''The Americans with Disabilities Act: Are You Prepared?'' *Journal of Property Management* 56 (November–December): 70–71.

Part Two

Applying Universal Design

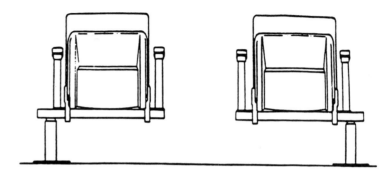

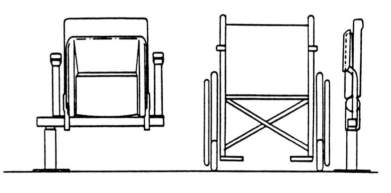

These seats can be occupied by fans with or without disabilities, or they can pivot into the pedestal sleeve, making clear space for wheelchair users. (Seating concept developed by the Stadium Accessibility Task Force for the Maryland Stadium Authority.)

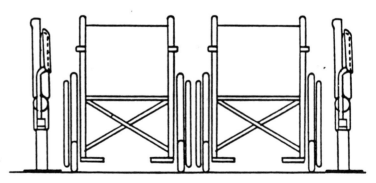

UNIVERSAL DESIGN:

Oriole Park at Camden Yards

When planning began for a new ballpark in Baltimore, the Baltimore Orioles, the Maryland Stadium Authority, and Governor William Donald Schaefer agreed that the new stadium must meet the needs of fans with disabilities. Initially the Governor's Office for Individuals with Disabilities set up a task force comprised of persons with disabilities, an architect for the Paralyzed Veterans of America, a building codes inspector, and an attorney. The task force traveled across the state to meet with members of the disabled community who provided recommendations to make the ballpark "user friendly" to people with disabilities.

One of the primary goals was to provide wheelchair seating in all areas and price ranges of the stadium. Consequently, a novel design for accessible seats was developed. These seats can be occupied by an able-bodied fan or they can easily be converted for use by someone in a wheelchair. Additionally, Oriole Park at Camden Yards has two elevators, many ramps, accessible restrooms and concession stands, an assistive listening system for the hard of hearing, handicapped parking, and other amenities for fans with disabilities.

Diane K. Ebberts, DIRECTOR
Office for Individuals with Disabilities
State of Maryland

Introduction

Being sensitive to the challenges associated with different disabilities is valuable only if one knows how to apply this knowledge in design situations. Presented in Part Two are a variety of scenarios that might be encountered by a professional designer. It is probably best to begin your task by familiarizing yourself with ADAAG (see Appendix 2). Note that ADAAG has an appendix where additional guidelines are described. This section can be very valuable for designers. Next, read through a design scenario and study the corresponding illustration(s). Refer to the relevant sections of ADAAG for information on the existing elements; for instance, if there are stairs in the scenario, read section 4.9 in ADAAG. Using the data collected thus far *and* your sensitivity to the general public, locate possible barriers in the scenario and design new solutions. Your solutions should include both drawing(s) and text, and should reference relevant sections from ADAAG.

Finally, check your solutions against the ones presented in Appendix 3. Remember that design is an art, not a science, and more than one right answer is possible. Your solution may look very different from the one presented in the book, but may address all the barriers and be equally feasible.

The scenarios are divided into three chapters representing the exterior path of travel (Chapter 4), the interior path of travel (Chapter 5), and general function areas (Chapter 6). This sequence follows the logical progression that would be used in surveying a building, and we suggest that you do the problems in the order given.

As a final note, try to keep in mind that the ultimate goal is universal design, and the more one practices this philosophy, the more innate it becomes. As Robert Anders expressed it: "The world of 'them' versus 'us' must give way to one of inclusion, where the needs of people with many different abilities and disabilities are routinely considered. Universal design is for everyone." Be creative with your solutions!

Chapter 4

The goal of universal design is sometimes misconstrued as one of creating *buildings* through which anyone can maneuver. However, accessibility inside a building matters precious little if it is unapproachable on the outside. Presented here are several problems representative of those the designer might encounter while considering the exterior of a building or the exterior environment in general. Keep in mind that potential users may have a variety of disabilities. Also, remember that sensitivity is as important as technical guidelines in devising a solution of high quality.

CURB RAMPS

The municipal department in your city is taking action to make the downtown area accessible. You have been invited to act as a consultant to address this issue. The proposed plan includes some curb ramps at intersections that will be running parallel to pedestrian traffic flow rather than being diagonal, due to fire alarm boxes mounted at the curved corners (see Figure 4–1). While this will provide accessibility for people in wheelchairs, it will also present a hazard for individuals with visual disabilities in that they could unknowingly step out into traffic. What advice will you give to avoid such an accident?

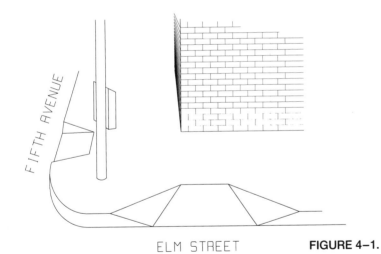

ELM STREET
FIGURE 4–1.

SIGNAGE FOR ACCESSIBLE PARKING

The management of a new shopping mall invites you to check its parking provision. There are a total of 332 available parking spaces. The owners of the mall have provided 8 accessible park-

ing slots for patrons with disabilities, and these slots are very clearly marked with the symbol of access stenciled on the pavement at each space (see Figure 4–2). The management was pleased that it had fulfilled the mandate of the ADA. Will you concur with their opinion regarding compliance?

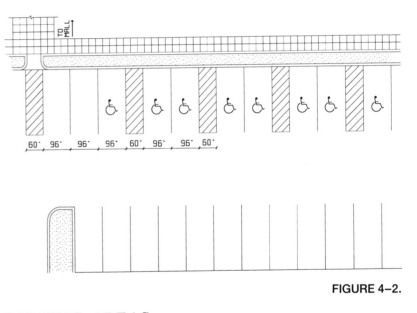

FIGURE 4–2.

PARKING AREAS

As a designer, one is occasionally asked by a client to survey an existing property to determine whether or not it is in compliance with various codes or laws. In this case you have been asked by a large corporation to assess the exterior of its local campus-type facility with respect to ADAAG compliance. The corporation has several employees with mobility disabilities who must

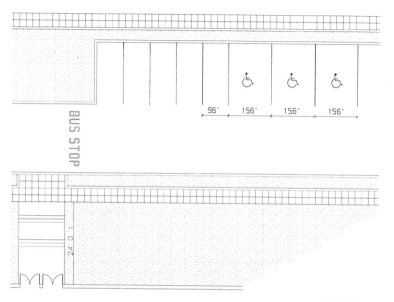

FIGURE 4–3.

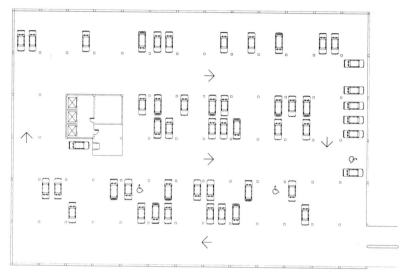

FIGURE 4–4.

use side or rear entrances to gain access to the building because they have found the approaches used by other employees to be inaccessible. Three major areas are to be included in the assessment: the outdoor parking area, the pedestrian route to the building's main entrance, and the indoor parking area. The outdoor parking area is served by a driveway with a public drop-off point for buses and cars, which is located directly in front of the pedestrian route to the main entrance (see Figure 4–3). The indoor parking area is shown in Figure 4–4. The corporation employs people with other disabilities; in your endeavor to alleviate barriers for people with mobility disabilities, be careful not to create barriers for another group.

EXTERIOR DOORS

Mr. Bernstein, a wheelchair user, wishes to enter a building situated on a corner (see Figure 4–5). There are two main entrances to the building. The one on Main Street has three sets of double-leaf bronze doors, each panel no more than 28 inches wide. Thus each clear opening is less than the minimum 32-inch requirement. This entrance is on grade both inside and outside, and accessible to the elevator lobby. Planters and lamp stanchions adorn the front of the building, with the lamp stanchions extending farther out into the sidewalk area than the planters. The management of the building will not change the configuration of the doors at this entrance because of the expense and the historical significance of the building.

Around the corner on Central Avenue is the second main entrance, which has two sets of double-leaf doors with 36-inch panels. These are on grade inside and out, and therefore are accessible. However, approximately 25 feet from the entrance is a set of three interior stairs with 6½-inch risers ascending to a hall leading to the same bank of elevators. At the bottom of this set of stairs on the right-hand side is a door leading to a retail store, and at the top of the stairs, against the left wall, is a pair of doors to the management office. Both doors open into the main hall. There is a great deal of traffic in and out of the management office. The door to the store is used less since the main entry to the store is on Central Avenue. As a designer, what could you do to help Mr. Bernstein and other wheelchair users gain access to the building? Consider the possibility of a solution for each of the main entrances, taking into account the fact that the management has already expressed some concern over cost and aesthetics.

Photo: Universal Designers and Consultants, Inc. Rockville, Maryland

FIGURE 4–6.

MANEUVERING CLEARANCE

Trying to gain entry to a medical facility, a person using a walker approaches a pair of double-leaf entry doors (see Figure 4–6). These doors open out and have glass sidelights on either side of the doors. The individual stops in front of the left door in order to open the right door for access. As this transpires, a person in a wheelchair exits the building through the left door, causing a collision of the two people. How can you alter the entry way in order to prevent this type of accident from occurring?

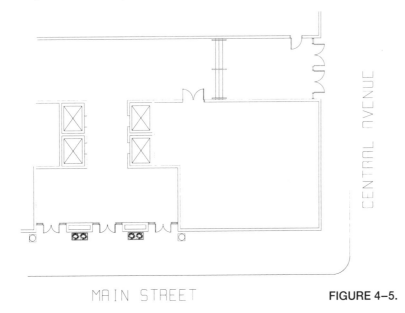

MAIN STREET

CENTRAL AVENUE

FIGURE 4–5.

Interior Path of Travel

Chapter 5

The interior path of travel provides a multitude of opportunities for accessibility improvements. The following scenarios present some of the issues one might encounter in design projects. As always, a good solution to a barrier problem depends as much on sensitivity to *all* disabilities as it does on technical requirements.

ELEVATORS AND SIGNAGE

A ten-story office building in a downtown area leases office space to various entities, some of whom require small suites, while others require one or more floors. Among the employees in these offices are several people with disabilities. Below are two scenarios regarding this building.

1. Ms. Carter, who is blind, is trying to reach a professional office on the seventh floor to interview for a job. Arriving at the elevator lobby (see Figure 5–1), she searches for the call buttons and is thwarted by a rather large ash urn on the floor. After much groping, she finds the call buttons, side by side, and has to determine which is the ''up'' button. There is a bank of six elevators and the far left cab door opens. She must traverse the corridor to the open cab, but does not arrive in time, and the door closes before she has a chance to enter. Several tries gain her entrance to one of the cabs. Once inside the elevator, she is unable to determine if the car is going up or down, and without assistance, she cannot tell which button to push for the seventh floor. Fortunately someone enters the elevator on another floor and assists her. Once outside the elevator cab, Ms. Carter does not know which direction to take because there are offices on either side of the elevator lobby and no indication of which way to turn. Eventually she does reach the office, is hired, and asks for reasonable accommodations to be made under Title I of the ADA. What would you, as a designer, do to relieve Ms. Carter of dependence on others in reaching her new office?

2. An employee in a large law firm is blind, but wishes to maintain his independence as much as possible. Within the office his needs might take him to the offices of colleagues, the library, conference rooms, the copy room, the kitchen, or the restroom. Because his firm occupies several floors of the office building and the layout on each floor is different, this employee often has trouble identifying the room he is trying to reach. As a design consultant to the law firm, what would you do to help him?

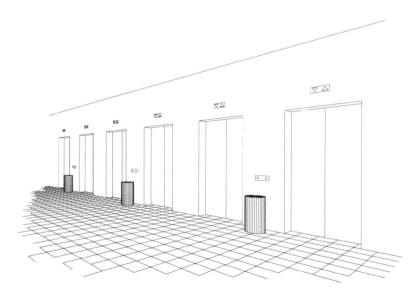

FIGURE 5–1.

STAIRWAYS

The local community center is housed in a nonelevator building. Mr. Lee, an elderly gentleman with arthritis in his hands and knees, must climb a staircase to the hall in the community center where he goes daily for social activity with other senior citizens.

Depicted in Figure 5–2 is the staircase and the door at the top leading into the hall. Are there any changes that could be made to help Mr. Lee and other elderly people who use this community service?

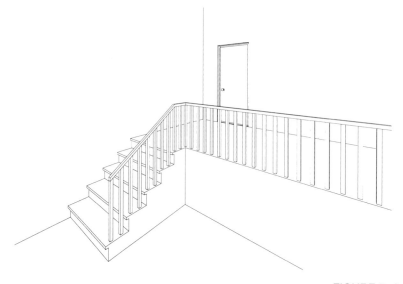

FIGURE 5–2.

(see Figure 5–3). One of the phones is equipped with volume control, but there is no signage to indicate this. You have been hired by the management to alter the telephones to be accessible. What steps will you take to comply with the ADA?

FIGURE 5–3.

TELEPHONES

The management of a shopping mall has received a number of complaints from patrons who are deaf or hearing impaired about the bank of public telephones in a hallway off of the concourse area. Currently the telephones are all at a height of 60 inches

GROUND AND FLOOR SURFACES

A large downtown hotel has advertised itself as accessible, and it has several accessible rooms in various locations, sizes, and price ranges to accommodate people with disabilities. Although the management has been pleased with the accolades it has received from its patrons with disabilities, there have been some suggestions for improvement. Specifically, the hotel has a large lobby area, which can be seen in Figure 5–4. It is carpeted throughout in low pile, and contains the registration desk, a bar area, an elevator, and an escalator with open floor space underneath (see Figure 5–5). Leading off of the lobby in different directions are the swimming pool and exercise room, the dining room beyond the bar, and a stairway/railed ramp (1:12) with a nonslip surface leading to a concourse with small shops. Visually impaired individuals have had trouble traversing the lobby and finding the areas they want. What steps could be taken to alleviate this problem?

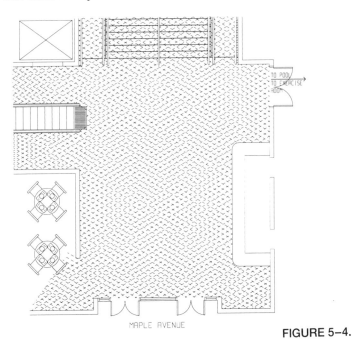

FIGURE 5–4.

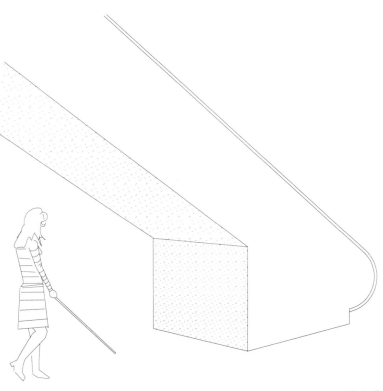

FIGURE 5–5.

DRINKING FOUNTAINS

Ms. Hernandez, a wheelchair user, tries to operate a floor-mounted hall drinking fountain (see Figure 5–6). She cannot get close enough to the spout to reach the water using either a

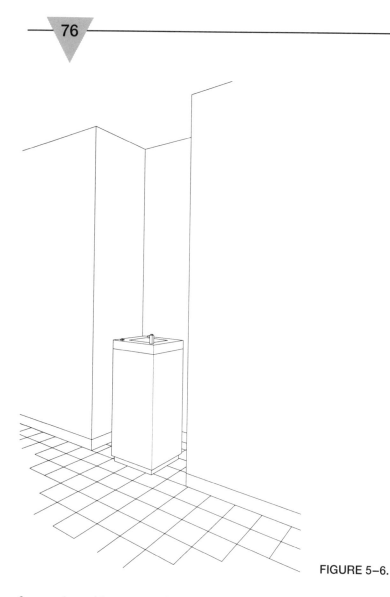

FIGURE 5–6.

forward or side approach, since the body of the fountain extends down towards the floor and it is too high. What accommodations can be made to enable her to use the drinking fountain?

ALARMS

Mr. Wylie, who is deaf, was working alone one evening in his systems office on the sixth floor of an office building when the audible fire alarm sounded. Unaware, he continued working. Fortunately it was a false alarm, but the building owners were concerned enough about the situation that they have asked you to advise them on what safety precautions they could take to alert Mr. Wylie in the event of an emergency. (See Figure 5–7 for a plan of the sixth floor.) Take into consideration the possibility that more people with disabilities may be hired in the future.

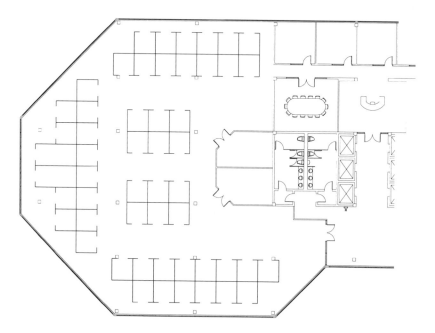

FIGURE 5–7.

BATHROOMS

A large department store has been endeavoring to meet the accessibility requirements for Title III (Public Accommodations) of the ADA. Thus far certain readily achievable alterations have been made, such as adjusting display racks to widen aisle space, providing large signage, and altering entrances to make them accessible as necessary. The retailer now wants to invest in retrofitting the bathrooms throughout the store. As a member of the major design firm that serves the store, you have been asked to submit plans for the alterations. There are three configurations used for public restroom facilities in various locations throughout the building.

1. The first, depicted in Figures 5–8 and 5–9, has three toilet stalls, which are all inaccessible, a vanity with three sinks, and various wall accessories. Consider what your solution would be if local codes happened to require three toilet stalls per public bathroom.

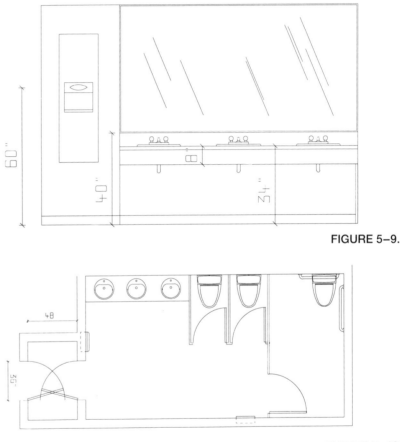

FIGURE 5–9.

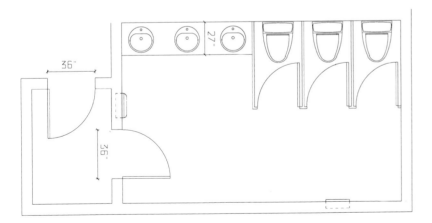

FIGURE 5–8.

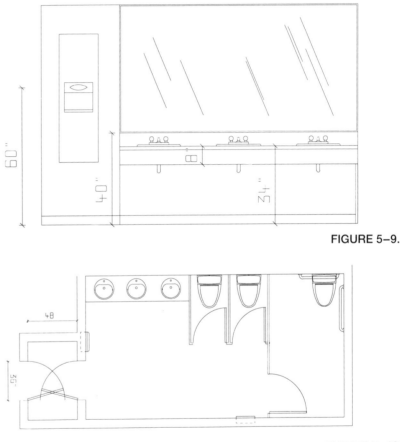

FIGURE 5–10.

2. The second bathroom, shown in Figure 5–10, is entered through two doors in series, the first taking 8 lbf. to open and the second taking 5 lbf. The inner door swings toward the outer door. Three toilet stalls and three lavatories are provided.

3. The third bathroom is entered through a vestibule, with toilet stalls and sinks at right angles to the vestibule (see Figure 5–11). Remember to be sensitive to all disabilities in trying to make the bathrooms accessible.

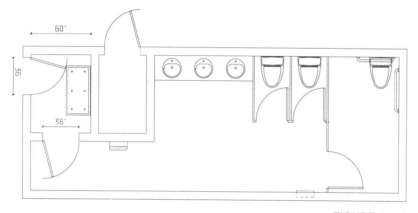

FIGURE 5–11.

INTERIOR STAIRS AND RAMPS

The management of an office building has engaged you to make some alterations, and you know that your plans must comply with the ADA regulations as well as other building codes. The local fire code demands two means of egress in case of fire for a building of this size. The lobby egress at the main entrance is on grade and is accessible. However, the rear fire egress is not on grade, and two possible scenarios are presented to describe it.

1. There are four interior steps down to the rear exit door at ground level, with a 48-inch landing before the door (see Figure 5–12).

2. A ramp exists to the exterior door, with a slope of 10 degrees (see Figure 5–13). How would you work with these two situations to accommodate people with disabilities?

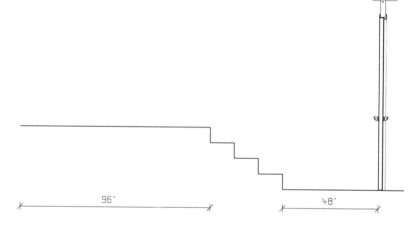

FIGURE 5–12.

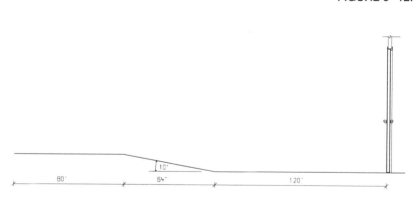

FIGURE 5–13.

ELEVATOR LOBBY LEADING TO A ROOF

A multiuse building has a roof garden that must be made accessible to all its tenants. The management knows that it has a problem with the elevator lobby, which gives access to the roof (see Figure 5–14). Upon exiting the elevator cab, one must ascend a set of stairs, traverse a hallway, and ascend one more step to a landing. The door rests on a curb raised 4 inches above the floor inside and outside to prevent water seepage. The door swings inward. There is also a hallway to one side of the stairs (see Figure 5–15). Not being familiar with the ADA, the management has hired you to determine a solution. How would you treat this problem?

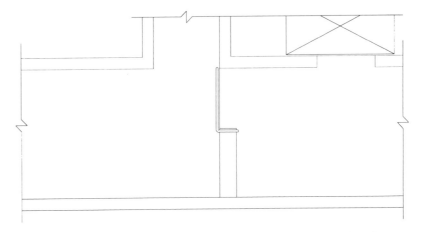

FIGURE 5–15.

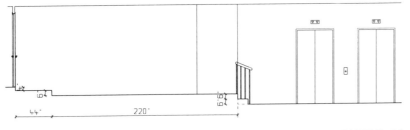

FIGURE 5–14.

General Function Areas

Chapters 4 and 5 dealt with the paths of travel serving the functional areas of a building or site. This chapter will present scenarios concerning accessibility within those functional areas, although barriers still may be present in the path of travel. The exterior and interior environment must be considered as a whole in real design situations even though we have treated them as separate entities for instructional purposes. As with previous scenarios, sensitivity combined with technical knowledge will lead to the best solutions.

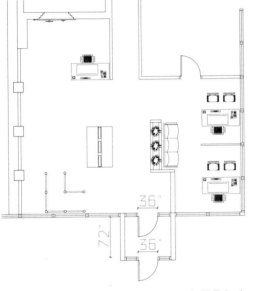

FIGURE 6–1.

INTERIOR OF A BANK

A neighborhood branch of a local bank is entered through two glass doors in series with a vestibule in between (see Figure 6–1). Both doors open out to meet the local building code, and each takes 10 lbf. to use. Inside the bank the customer desk provided for filling out deposit/withdrawal slips is 42 inches high. The teller windows are also 42 inches high with a flush facia and the usual clear security enclosure. The carpet is of dense level loop construction with a pile thickness of ½ inch, and was installed by the direct glue method. The bank manager has received several complaints from patrons who use wheelchairs, and has hired you as a consultant to survey the bank interior and make recommendations.

TRANSIENT LODGING

Mr. Connors, planning to attend a conference with a group of coworkers, requested an accessible hotel room due to the fact that he is a wheelchair user. He is also deaf and has limited manual dexterity. The hotel confirmation slip read "handicapped room," which the management interpreted as meaning that the room needed wider doors for wheelchair access into the sleeping room and the bathroom. After registering, Mr. Connors was shown to his room, which can be seen in Figure 6–2. Aside from certain problems with space design, he found that the thermostat control was at a height of 58 inches and the clothes rod in the closet was at 66 inches. The writing table had a knee clearance space of 26 inches AFF (above finish floor) and was 26 inches wide. The dresser drawer pulls were recessed. In the

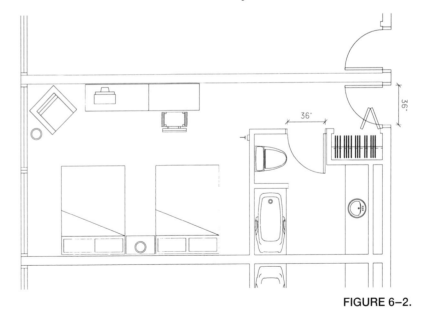

FIGURE 6–2.

bathroom the knee clearance beneath the lavatory apron was 27 inches AFF and the tap sets were of the knob type. In addition, because he is deaf Mr. Connors is concerned about his personal safety and about his ability to communicate with his office, though neither of these issues was addressed by the hotel. As Mr. Connors said, the room did indeed earn its name as a "handicapped room." What modifications should the hotel management make to change it from a handicapped room into an accessible room (1) for people using wheelchairs and (2) for people who are deaf?

(3) The hotel offers its guests shuttle-bus service to the tourist sites around town. Mr. Connors wished to participate in the sightseeing tour along with his group, but was unable to board the shuttle-bus as it did not have the lift necessary for a wheelchair user to gain access. Is this acceptable under the ADAAG regulations?

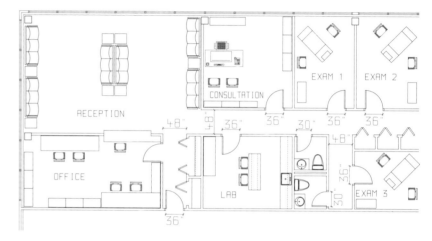

FIGURE 6–3.

MEDICAL OFFICE

Dr. Adams, a pediatrician, plans to move her office to a new medical facility. The suite in which she is interested was originally designed for a cardiologist, and needs modification in the reception area, the consultation offices, the examination rooms, and the restrooms (see Figure 6–3). Since Dr. Adams sees mostly young children, with and without disabilities, she is adamant that the design of her space be not only functional and aesthetically pleasing, but "patient-friendly" as well. How would you design her office to give the patients a feeling of being welcome?

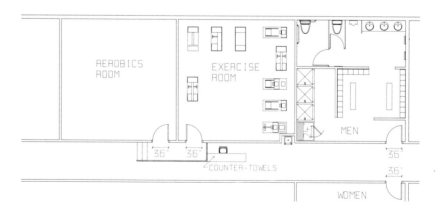
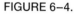

FIGURE 6–4.

HEALTH CLUB

A health club is provided in a multiuse complex. It contains a fully equipped exercise room, an aerobics room, a check-in desk where towels are distributed, identical men's and women's locker rooms with showers, a sauna, and a toilet room (see Figure 6–4). The drinking fountain indicated in the corridor is not fully illustrated in the drawing, but it is similar to the one shown in Figure 5–6. What accommodations, if any, would you deem appropriate to meet the mandate of the ADA? Consider this question both in terms of the information provided in the figures and in terms of other measures that might increase accessibility. Be sure to remain sensitive to the needs of *all* possible users.

MUSEUMS

An art museum will soon be having a special exhibit that will be viewed by the general public. Several groups have scheduled tours of the exhibit in advance, including groups of school children, senior citizens, and people with disabilities, and the museum staff wishes to be prepared for them. The building itself is highly accessible. Besides the exhibit areas, it has a coat room, a small gift shop, and accessible restrooms. What criteria must the designers of the special exhibit use to maintain the level of universal accessibility available throughout the rest of the museum? This scenario does not begin with an existing space design that needs alteration, and therefore no illustration has been provided. Instead designers must rely extensively on their sensitivity to, and knowledge of, people with varying capabilities to establish a set of criteria that could be used to create an exhibit that is truly universal.

RESTAURANT ALTERATIONS

Mr. Ortega, the proprietor of a restaurant on the ground floor of a building, has recently hired you to help him plan and carry out alterations to enlarge his restaurant. He is especially concerned

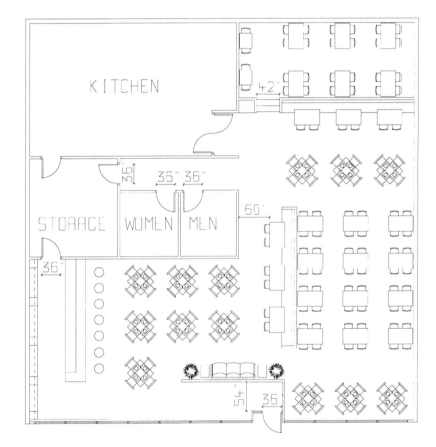

FIGURE 6–5.

about being in compliance with Title III of the ADA because he has two friends who frequent the restaurant together, one using a wheelchair and the other needing good lighting due to poor visual acuity. Preliminary drawings were made by another design firm, but Mr. Ortega was not sure the designers were sensitive enough to the needs of his friends and other people with disabilities. These drawings allocate space for a seated bar and a two-level dining room, as well as restrooms and an entry area. The plans are depicted in Figure 6–5. The main dining area was allotted 1300 square feet, while the raised dining area covers 340 square feet. What adjustments will you make to these plans to bring the project into compliance?

CLASSROOM ACCOMMODATIONS

At a community college one classroom has been designated to be wired for telebroadcasting so that the college will be able to receive courses from a nearby university, and this classroom will also be open to the local community as a teleconference room. Enrolled at this college are several people with disabilities, including two women who are deaf, some students with hearing aids, and three students using wheelchairs. The facilities manager is concerned about the classroom in question. In the past classes attended by people with disabilities have been relocated if they were scheduled in an inaccessible room, but in the present situation this is impossible since this will be the only classroom fitted with this communication equipment. Figure 6–6 shows the classroom, which is tiered, with fixed tables and loose chairs. A raised dais is accessed by two steps. On the dais

is another fixed table with a removable lectern and a telephone (to communicate with the host lecturer). Mounted on the wall

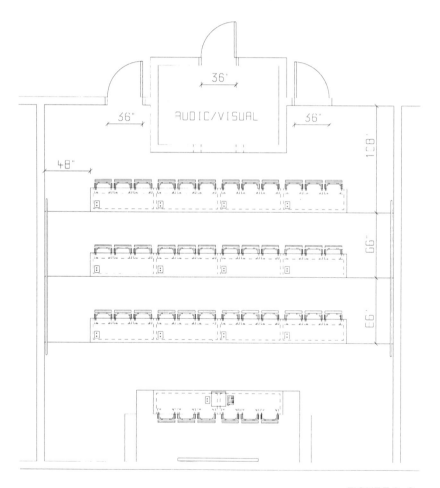

FIGURE 6–6.

behind the table is a large screen for TV projection (to view the broadcast). What needs to be done to make the classroom accessible? Keep in mind the broad spectrum of disabilities represented by students now on campus, as well as those that may attend in the future. Remember, when major alterations are done, they must be as accessible as new construction and therefore must take into account all possible physical abilities found in the general public.

OFFICE ENVIRONMENT

The Widget Corporation has just hired a person with a disability to fill a job opening in its Human Resources department. Ms. Allen, who has cerebral palsy, uses a wheelchair and has limited dexterity in her right hand. According to Title I of the ADA, she is entitled to reasonable accommodations to modify the systems work station she will occupy (see Figure 6–7). What steps should be taken to enable her to be as efficient as possible?

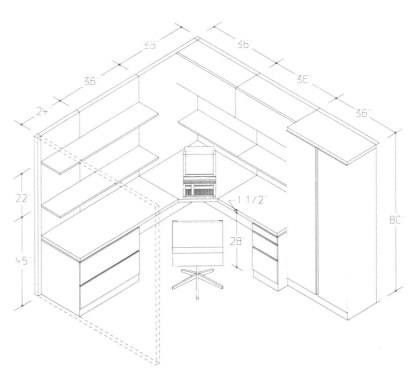

FIGURE 6–7.

Conclusion

Certain assumptions were made in the design scenarios that are not applicable in real design situations. First, we assumed that ADAAG was the prevailing technical guideline. In fact, the designer must be aware of state and local codes as well as ADAAG, and the more stringent code must always take precedence.

Second, we assumed that all steps necessary to achieve universal design would be financially feasible. Clearly this is not the case in the real world. Where new construction is concerned, we have seen that creating accessible designs is virtually no more expensive than creating inaccessible designs. In alterations, however, costs may very well be prohibitive. Ultimately it is the client who will decide whether or not all the goals for accessibility are carried out. If the client cannot afford to complete the necessary measures, then the designer can assist in prioritizing accessibility plans to achieve the greatest benefit allowable within the proposed budget.

Third, we have assumed that accessible elements will inevitably bring about independence for people who would otherwise need aid. While this is true much of the time, there still will be people for whom the environment is not maneuverable because their disabilities are too severe. Even when specific solutions may be found for them in their homes, these solutions may go beyond the general requirements in codes or in the ADA. As designers, we must realize the limitations of universal design for such individuals while remembering the countless others who will be helped.

In the design scenarios the reader explored possible solutions for altering existing spaces. While this reflects a vast amount of the work done by a professional designer, it also leaves out an enormous segment: namely, new construction. Aside from cost, the advantage to working with new construction is the ease with which accessible elements can be designed into a space from conception, rather than having to fit them in later. Although "fitting in" is generally not a problem, on occasion accessibility is architecturally infeasible in an existing site, as the scenarios indicated. Whatever the design project entails, though, the professional designer should always bear in mind that sensitivity, technical guidelines, and aesthetics go hand in hand in producing a satisfying solution to any design problem.

Will it be possible to achieve universal design? In one sense the idea is utopian. Truly achieving universal design would render the International Symbol of Accessibility obsolete, since accessibility would be the norm in the built environment. While such a level of acceptance is something to strive for, it is unlikely in a nation where most exisiting structures do not conform. Instead we will have to rely on the symbol to tell us where to find accessible design. Even so, designers can advance the environment in a positive direction as much as possible through universal design in buildings, landscaping, and products. This step will go a long way toward educating Americans about the existence of people with disabilities, and hopefully will help to bring about needed attitudinal changes. A feeling of acceptance in society together with a welcoming physical environment will create the right combination for the mainstreaming of people with disabilities into American life.

Appendix 1

ADA Titles and Their Effective Dates

TITLE I   EMPLOYMENT
- July 26, 1992 - for employers with 25 or more employees
- July 26, 1994 - for employers with 15 to 24 employees

TITLE II

A) STATE AND LOCAL GOVERNMENT SERVICES
- January 26, 1992 - unless otherwise noted below
- Structural changes to existing buildings to meet "the program accessibility" requirement must be made by January 26, 1995. Public entities with 50 or more employees must develop a "transition plan" for such changes by July 26, 1992
- Facilities must comply if construction bids are invited after January 26, 1992
- Alterations commenced after January 26, 1992

B) TRANSPORTATION
- Transit facilities must comply if "notice to proceed" is issued after January 25, 1992

Note: As this book goes to press, new rules are being proposed for four (4) sections of Title II:

- Section 11 - Access to and within judicial facilities, legislative facilities, regulatory facilities
- Section 12 - Detention and correctional facilities - jails, prisons and other holding areas
- Section 13 - Residential Housing - dwelling units owned or operated by a public entity
- Section 14 - Public rights-of-way, public streets and sidewalks - elements such as on-street parking, benches, telephones, emergency communication systems and public restrooms

TITLE III PUBLIC ACCOMMODATIONS

- January 26, 1992 for existing spaces - the obligation to engage in "readily achievable" barrier removal is a continuing one
- January 26, 1993 for facilities designed to be occupied after this date
- Alterations commenced after January 26, 1992
- New vehicles acquired by private entities to provide specific public transportation must comply if the closing date for submission of bids is after August 25, 1990
- Structural changes in over-the-road buses to provide access to wheelchair users are not required until July 26, 1996 (July 26, 1997 for small companies)

TITLE IV TELECOMMUNICATIONS

- By July 26, 1993, telephone companies must provide relay services for hearing impaired and speech impaired individuals 24 hours per day

Appendix 2

ADA Accessibility Guidelines for Buildings and Facilities

U.S. Architectural and Transportation
Barriers Compliance Board

Suite 1000
1331 F Street, N.W.
Washington, D.C. 20004-1111
202/272-5434 (Voice)
202/272-5449 (TDD)

August 1992

ADA ACCESSIBILITY GUIDELINES
FOR BUILDINGS AND FACILITIES
TABLE OF CONTENTS

1. PURPOSE.

This document sets guidelines for accessibility to buildings and facilities by individuals with disabilities under the Americans with Disabilities Act (ADA) of 1990. These guidelines are to be applied during the design, construction, and alteration of buildings and facilities covered by Titles II and III of the ADA to the extent required by regulations issued by Federal agencies, including the Department of Justice and the Department of Transportation, under the ADA.

The technical specifications 4.2 through 4.35, of these guidelines are the same as those of the American National Standard Institute's document A117.1-1980, except as noted in this text by italics. However, sections 4.1.1 through 4.1.7 and sections 5 through 10 are different from ANSI A117.1 in their entirety and are printed in standard type.

The illustrations and text of ANSI A117.1 are reproduced with permission from the American National Standards Institute. Copies of the standard may be purchased from the American National Standards Institute at 1430 Broadway, New York, New York 10018.

2. GENERAL.

2.1 Provisions for Adults. *The specifications in these guidelines are based upon adult dimensions and anthropometrics.*

2.2* Equivalent Facilitation. *Departures from particular technical and scoping requirements of this guideline by the use of other designs and technologies are permitted where the alternative designs and technologies used will provide substantially equivalent or greater access to and usability of the facility.*

3. MISCELLANEOUS INSTRUCTIONS AND DEFINITIONS.

3.1 Graphic Conventions. Graphic conventions are shown in Table 1. Dimensions that are not marked minimum or maximum are absolute, unless otherwise indicated in the text or captions.

Table 1
Graphic Conventions

Convention	Description
36 / 915	Typical dimension line showing U.S. customary units (in inches) above the line and SI units (in millimeters) below
9 / 230	Dimensions for short distances indicated on extended line
9 **36** / 230 915	Dimension line showing alternate dimensions required
(arrow)	Direction of approach
max	Maximum
min	Minimum
••••••••	Boundary of clear floor area
— ¢	Centerline

3.2 Dimensional Tolerances. All dimensions are subject to conventional building industry tolerances for field conditions.

3.3 Notes. The text of *these guidelines* does not contain notes or footnotes. Additional information, explanations, and advisory materials are located in the Appendix. Paragraphs marked with an asterisk have related, non-mandatory material in the Appendix. In the Appendix, the corresponding paragraph numbers are preceded by an A.

3.4 General Terminology.

comply with. Meet one or more specifications of *these guidelines.*

if...then. Denotes a specification that applies only when the conditions described are present.

may. Denotes an option or alternative.

shall. Denotes a mandatory specification or requirement.

should. Denotes an advisory specification or recommendation.

3.5 Definitions.

Access Aisle. An accessible pedestrian space between elements, such as parking spaces, seating, and desks, that provides clearances appropriate for use of the elements.

Accessible. Describes a site, building, facility, or portion thereof that complies with *these guidelines.*

Accessible Element. An *element* specified by *these guidelines* (for example, telephone, controls, and the like).

Accessible Route. A continuous unobstructed path connecting all accessible elements and spaces of a building or facility. Interior accessible routes may include corridors, floors, ramps, elevators, lifts, and clear floor space at fixtures. Exterior accessible routes may include parking access aisles, curb ramps, *crosswalks at vehicular ways,* walks, ramps, and lifts.

Accessible Space. Space that complies with *these guidelines.*

Adaptability. The ability of certain building spaces and elements, such as kitchen counters, sinks, and grab bars, to be added or altered so as to accommodate the needs of *individuals with or without disabilities* or to accommodate the needs of persons with different types or degrees of disability.

Addition. An expansion, extension, or increase in the gross floor area of a building or facility.

Administrative Authority. A governmental agency that adopts or enforces regulations and guidelines for the design, construction, or alteration of buildings and facilities.

Alteration. An alteration is a change to a building or facility made by, on behalf of, or for the use of a public accommodation or commercial facility, that affects or could affect the usability of the building or facility or part thereof. Alterations include, but are not limited to, remodeling, renovation, rehabilitation, reconstruction, historic restoration, changes or rearrangement of the structural parts or elements, and changes or rearrangement in the plan configuration of walls and full-height partitions. Normal maintenance, reroofing, painting or wallpapering, or changes to mechanical and electrical systems are not alterations unless they affect the usability of the building or facility.

Area of Rescue Assistance. An area, which has direct access to an exit, where people who are unable to use stairs may remain temporarily in safety to await further instructions or assistance during emergency evacuation.

Assembly Area. A room or space accommodating a group of individuals for recreational, educational, political, social, or amusement purposes, or for the consumption of food and drink.

Automatic Door. A door equipped with a power-operated mechanism and controls that open and close the door automatically upon receipt of a momentary actuating signal. The switch that begins the automatic cycle may be a photoelectric device, floor mat, or manual switch (see power-assisted door).

Building. Any structure used and intended for supporting or sheltering any use or occupancy.

Circulation Path. An exterior or interior way of passage from one place to another for pedestrians, including, but not limited to, walks, hallways, courtyards, stairways, and stair landings.

Clear. Unobstructed.

Clear Floor Space. The minimum unobstructed floor or ground space required to accommodate a single, stationary wheelchair and occupant.

Closed Circuit Telephone. A telephone with dedicated line(s) such as a house phone, courtesy phone or phone that must be used to gain entrance to a facility.

Common Use. Refers to those interior and exterior rooms, spaces, or elements that are made available for the use of a restricted group of people (for example, occupants of a homeless shelter, the occupants of an office building, or the guests of such occupants).

Cross Slope. The slope that is perpendicular to the direction of travel (see running slope).

Curb Ramp. A short ramp cutting through a curb or built up to it.

Detectable Warning. A standardized surface feature built in or applied to walking surfaces or other elements to warn visually impaired people of hazards on a circulation path.

Dwelling Unit. A single unit which provides a kitchen or food preparation area, in addition to rooms and spaces for living, bathing, sleeping, and the like. Dwelling units include a single family home or a townhouse used as a transient group home; an apartment building used as a shelter; guestrooms in a hotel that provide sleeping accommodations and food preparation areas; and other similar facilities used on a transient basis. For purposes of these guidelines, use of the term "Dwelling Unit" does not imply the unit is used as a residence.

Egress, Means of. A continuous and unobstructed way of exit travel from any point in a building or facility to a public way. A means of egress comprises vertical and horizontal travel and may include intervening room spaces, doorways, hallways, corridors, passageways, balconies, ramps, stairs, enclosures, lobbies, horizontal exits, courts and yards. An accessible means of egress is one that complies with these guidelines and does not include stairs, steps, or escalators. Areas of rescue assistance or evacuation elevators may be included as part of accessible means of egress.

Element. An architectural or mechanical component of a building, facility, space, or site, e.g., telephone, curb ramp, door, drinking fountain, seating, or water closet.

Entrance. Any access point to a building or portion of a building or facility used for the purpose of entering. An entrance includes the approach walk, the vertical access leading to the entrance platform, the entrance platform itself, vestibules if provided, the entry door(s) or gate(s), and the hardware of the entry door(s) or gate(s).

Facility. All or any portion of buildings, structures, site improvements, complexes, equipment, roads, walks, passageways, parking lots, or other real or personal property located on a site.

Ground Floor. Any occupiable floor less than one story above or below grade with direct access to grade. A building or facility always has at least one ground floor and may have more than one ground floor as where a split level entrance has been provided or where a building is built into a hillside.

Mezzanine or Mezzanine Floor. That portion of a story which is an intermediate floor level placed within the story and having occupiable space above and below its floor.

Marked Crossing. A crosswalk or other identified path intended for pedestrian use in crossing a vehicular way.

Multifamily Dwelling. Any building containing more than two dwelling units.

Occupiable. A room or enclosed space designed for human occupancy in which individuals congregate for amusement, educational or similar purposes, or in which occupants are engaged at labor, and which is equipped with means of egress, light, and ventilation.

Operable Part. A part of a piece of equipment or appliance used to insert or withdraw objects, or to activate, deactivate, or adjust the equipment or appliance (for example, coin slot, pushbutton, handle).

Path of Travel. (Reserved).

Power-assisted Door. A door used *for human passage* with a mechanism that helps to open the door, or relieves the opening resistance of a door, upon the activation of a switch or a continued force applied to the door itself.

Public Use. Describes interior or exterior rooms or spaces that are made available to the general public. Public use may be provided at a building or facility that is privately or publicly owned.

Ramp. A walking surface which has a running slope greater than 1:20.

Running Slope. The slope that is parallel to the direction of travel (see cross slope).

Service Entrance. An entrance intended primarily for delivery of goods or services.

Signage. Displayed verbal, symbolic, tactile, and pictorial information.

Site. A parcel of land bounded by a property line or a designated portion of a public right-of-way.

Site Improvement. Landscaping, paving for pedestrian and vehicular ways, outdoor lighting, recreational facilities, and the like, added to a site.

Sleeping Accommodations. Rooms in which people sleep; for example, dormitory and hotel or motel guest rooms or suites.

Space. A definable area, e.g., room, toilet room, hall, assembly area, entrance, storage room, alcove, courtyard, or lobby.

Story. That portion of a building included between the upper surface of a floor and upper surface of the floor or roof next above. If such

portion of a building does not include occupiable space, it is not considered a story for purposes of these guidelines. There may be more than one floor level within a story as in the case of a mezzanine or mezzanines.

Structural Frame. The structural frame shall be considered to be the columns and the girders, beams, trusses and spandrels having direct connections to the columns and all other members which are essential to the stability of the building as a whole.

Tactile. Describes an object that can be perceived using the sense of touch.

Text Telephone. Machinery or equipment that employs interactive graphic (i.e., typed) communications through the transmission of coded signals across the standard telephone network. Text telephones can include, for example, devices known as TDD's (telecommunication display devices or telecommunication devices for deaf persons) or computers.

Transient Lodging. A building, facility, or portion thereof, excluding inpatient medical care facilities, that contains one or more dwelling units or sleeping accommodations. Transient lodging may include, but is not limited to, resorts, group homes, hotels, motels, and dormitories.

Vehicular Way. A route intended for vehicular traffic, such as a street, driveway, or parking lot.

Walk. An exterior pathway with a prepared surface intended for pedestrian use, including general pedestrian areas such as plazas and courts.

NOTE: Sections 4.1.1 through 4.1.7 are different from ANSI A117.1 in their entirety and are printed in standard type (ANSI A117.1 does not include scoping provisions).

4. ACCESSIBLE ELEMENTS AND SPACES: SCOPE AND TECHNICAL REQUIREMENTS.

4.1 Minimum Requirements

4.1.1* Application.

(1) General. All areas of newly designed or newly constructed buildings and facilities required to be accessible by 4.1.2 and 4.1.3 and altered portions of existing buildings and facilities required to be accessible by 4.1.6 shall comply with these guidelines. 4.1 through 4.35, unless otherwise provided in this section or as modified in a special application section.

(2) Application Based on Building Use. Special application sections 5 through 10 provide additional requirements for restaurants and cafeterias, medical care facilities, business and mercantile, libraries, accessible transient lodging, and transportation facilities. When a building or facility contains more than one use covered by a special application section, each portion shall comply with the requirements for that use.

(3)* Areas Used Only by Employees as Work Areas. Areas that are used only as work areas shall be designed and constructed so that individuals with disabilities can approach, enter, and exit the areas. These guidelines do not require that any areas used only as work areas be constructed to permit maneuvering within the work area or be constructed or equipped (i.e., with racks or shelves) to be accessible.

(4) Temporary Structures. These guidelines cover temporary buildings or facilities as well as permanent facilities. Temporary buildings and facilities are not of permanent construction but are extensively used or are essential for public use for a period of time. Examples of temporary buildings or facilities covered by these guidelines include, but are not limited to: reviewing stands, temporary classrooms, bleacher areas, exhibit areas, temporary banking facilities, temporary health screening services, or temporary safe pedestrian passageways around a construction site. Structures, sites and equipment directly associated with the actual processes of construction, such as scaffolding, bridging, materials hoists, or construction trailers are not included.

(5) General Exceptions.

(a) In new construction, a person or entity is not required to meet fully the requirements of these guidelines where that person or entity can demonstrate that it is structurally impracticable to do so. Full compliance will be considered structurally impracticable only in those rare circumstances when the unique characteristics of terrain prevent the incorporation of accessibility features. If full compliance with the requirements of these guidelines is structurally impracticable, a person or entity shall comply with the requirements to the extent it is not structurally impracticable. Any portion of the building or facility which can be made accessible shall comply to the extent that it is not structurally impracticable.

(b) Accessibility is not required to (i) observation galleries used primarily for security purposes; or (ii) in non-occupiable spaces accessed only by ladders, catwalks, crawl spaces, very narrow passageways, or freight (non-passenger) elevators, and frequented only by service personnel for repair purposes; such spaces include, but are not limited to, elevator pits, elevator penthouses, piping or equipment catwalks.

4.1.2 Accessible Sites and Exterior Facilities: New Construction. An accessible site shall meet the following minimum requirements:

(1) At least one accessible route complying with 4.3 shall be provided within the boundary of the site from public transportation stops, accessible parking spaces, passenger loading zones if provided, and public streets or sidewalks, to an accessible building entrance.

(2) At least one accessible route complying with 4.3 shall connect accessible buildings, accessible facilities, accessible elements, and accessible spaces that are on the same site.

(3) All objects that protrude from surfaces or posts into circulation paths shall comply with 4.4.

(4) Ground surfaces along accessible routes and in accessible spaces shall comply with 4.5.

(5) (a) If parking spaces are provided for self-parking by employees or visitors, or both, then accessible spaces complying with 4.6 shall be provided in each such parking area in conformance with the table below. Spaces required by the table need not be provided in the particular lot. They may be provided in a different location if equivalent or greater accessibility, in terms of distance from an accessible entrance, cost and convenience is ensured.

Total Parking in Lot	Required Minimum Number of Accessible Spaces
1 to 25	1
26 to 50	2
51 to 75	3
76 to 100	4
101 to 150	5
151 to 200	6
201 to 300	7
301 to 400	8
401 to 500	9
501 to 1000	2 percent of total
1001 and over	20 plus 1 for each 100 over 1000

Except as provided in (b), access aisles adjacent to accessible spaces shall be 60 in (1525 mm) wide minimum.

(b) One in every eight accessible spaces, but not less than one, shall be served by an access aisle 96 in (2440 mm) wide minimum and shall be designated "van accessible" as required by 4.6.4. The vertical clearance at such spaces shall comply with 4.6.5. All such spaces may be grouped on one level of a parking structure.

EXCEPTION: Provision of all required parking spaces in conformance with "Universal Parking Design" (see appendix A4.6.3) is permitted.

(c) If passenger loading zones are provided, then at least one passenger loading zone shall comply with 4.6.6.

(d) At facilities providing medical care and other services for persons with mobility impairments, parking spaces complying with 4.6 shall be provided in accordance with 4.1.2(5)(a) except as follows:

(i) Outpatient units and facilities: 10 percent of the total number of parking spaces provided serving each such outpatient unit or facility;

(ii) Units and facilities that specialize in treatment or services for persons with mobility impairments: 20 percent of the total number of parking spaces provided serving each such unit or facility.

(e)*Valet parking: Valet parking facilities shall provide a passenger loading zone complying with 4.6.6 located on an accessible route to the entrance of the facility. Paragraphs 5(a), 5(b), and 5(d) of this section do not apply to valet parking facilities.

(6) If toilet facilities are provided on a site, then each such public or common use toilet facility shall comply with 4.22. If bathing facilities are provided on a site, then each such public or common use bathing facility shall comply with 4.23.

For single user portable toilet or bathing units clustered at a single location, at least 5% but no less than one toilet unit or bathing unit complying with 4.22 or 4.23 shall be installed at each cluster whenever typical inaccessible units are provided. Accessible units shall be identified by the International Symbol of Accessibility.

EXCEPTION: Portable toilet units at construction sites used exclusively by construction personnel are not required to comply with 4.1.2(6).

(7) Building Signage. Signs which designate permanent rooms and spaces shall comply with 4.30.1, 4.30.4, 4.30.5 and 4.30.6. Other signs which provide direction to, or information about, functional spaces of the building shall comply with 4.30.1, 4.30.2, 4.30.3, and 4.30.5. Elements and spaces of accessible facilities which shall be identified by the International Symbol of Accessibility and which shall comply with 4.30.7 are:

(a) Parking spaces designated as reserved for individuals with disabilities;

(b) Accessible passenger loading zones;

(c) Accessible entrances when not all are accessible (inaccessible entrances shall have directional signage to indicate the route to the nearest accessible entrance);

(d) Accessible toilet and bathing facilities when not all are accessible.

4.1.3 Accessible Buildings: New Construction. Accessible buildings and facilities shall meet the following minimum requirements:

(1) At least one accessible route complying with 4.3 shall connect accessible building or facility entrances with all accessible spaces and elements within the building or facility.

(2) All objects that overhang or protrude into circulation paths shall comply with 4.4.

(3) Ground and floor surfaces along accessible routes and in accessible rooms and spaces shall comply with 4.5.

(4) Interior and exterior stairs connecting levels that are not connected by an elevator, ramp, or other accessible means of vertical access shall comply with 4.9.

(5)* One passenger elevator complying with 4.10 shall serve each level, including mezzanines, in all multi-story buildings and facilities unless exempted below. If more than one elevator is provided, each full passenger elevator shall comply with 4.10.

EXCEPTION 1: Elevators are not required in facilities that are less than three stories or that have less than 3000 square feet per story unless the building is a shopping center, a shopping mall, or the professional office of a health care provider, or another type of facility as determined by the Attorney General. The elevator exemption set forth in this paragraph does not obviate or limit in any way the obligation to comply with the other accessibility requirements established in section 4.1.3. For example, floors above or below the accessible ground floor must meet the requirements of this section except for elevator service. If toilet or bathing facilities are provided on a level not served by an elevator, then toilet or bathing facilities must be provided on the accessible

ground floor. In new construction if a building or facility is eligible for this exemption but a full passenger elevator is nonetheless planned, that elevator shall meet the requirements of 4.10 and shall serve each level in the building. A full passenger elevator that provides service from a garage to only one level of a building or facility is not required to serve other levels.

EXCEPTION 2: Elevator pits, elevator penthouses, mechanical rooms, piping or equipment catwalks are exempted from this requirement.

EXCEPTION 3: Accessible ramps complying with 4.8 may be used in lieu of an elevator.

EXCEPTION 4: Platform lifts (wheelchair lifts) complying with 4.11 of this guideline and applicable state or local codes may be used in lieu of an elevator only under the following conditions:

(a) To provide an accessible route to a performing area in an assembly occupancy.

(b) To comply with the wheelchair viewing position line-of-sight and dispersion requirements of 4.33.3.

(c) To provide access to incidental occupiable spaces and rooms which are not open to the general public and which house no more than five persons, including but not limited to equipment control rooms and projection booths.

(d) To provide access where existing site constraints or other constraints make use of a ramp or an elevator infeasible.

(6) Windows: (Reserved).

(7) Doors:

(a) At each accessible entrance to a building or facility, at least one door shall comply with 4.13.

(b) Within a building or facility, at least one door at each accessible space shall comply with 4.13.

(c) Each door that is an element of an accessible route shall comply with 4.13.

(d) Each door required by 4.3.10, Egress, shall comply with 4.13.

(8) In new construction, at a minimum, the requirements in (a) and (b) below shall be satisfied independently:

(a)(i) At least 50% of all public entrances (excluding those in (b) below) must be accessible. At least one must be a ground floor entrance. Public entrances are any entrances that are not loading or service entrances.

(ii) Accessible entrances must be provided in a number at least equivalent to the number of exits required by the applicable building/fire codes. (This paragraph does not require an increase in the total number of entrances planned for a facility.)

(iii) An accessible entrance must be provided to each tenancy in a facility (for example, individual stores in a strip shopping center).

One entrance may be considered as meeting more than one of the requirements in (a). Where feasible, accessible entrances shall be the entrances used by the majority of people visiting or working in the building.

(b)(i) In addition, if direct access is provided for pedestrians from an enclosed parking garage to the building, at least one direct entrance from the garage to the building must be accessible.

(ii) If access is provided for pedestrians from a pedestrian tunnel or elevated walkway, one entrance to the building from each tunnel or walkway must be accessible.

One entrance may be considered as meeting more than one of the requirements in (b).

Because entrances also serve as emergency exits whose proximity to all parts of buildings and facilities is essential, it is preferable that all entrances be accessible.

(c) If the only entrance to a building, or tenancy in a facility, is a service entrance, that entrance shall be accessible.

(d) Entrances which are not accessible shall have directional signage complying with 4.30.1, 4.30.2, 4.30.3, and 4.30.5, which indicates the location of the nearest accessible entrance.

(9)* In buildings or facilities, or portions of buildings or facilities, required to be accessible, accessible means of egress shall be provided in the same number as required for exits by local building/life safety regulations. Where a required exit from an occupiable level above or below a level of accessible exit discharge is not accessible, an area of rescue assistance shall be provided on each such level (in a number equal to that of inaccessible required exits). Areas of rescue assistance shall comply with 4.3.11. A horizontal exit, meeting the requirements of local building/life safety regulations, shall satisfy the requirement for an area of rescue assistance.

EXCEPTION: Areas of rescue assistance are not required in buildings or facilities having a supervised automatic sprinkler system.

(10)* Drinking Fountains:

(a) Where only one drinking fountain is provided on a floor there shall be a drinking fountain which is accessible to individuals who use wheelchairs in accordance with 4.15 and one accessible to those who have difficulty bending or stooping. (This can be accommodated by the use of a "hi-lo" fountain; by providing one fountain accessible to those who use wheelchairs and one fountain at a standard height convenient for those who have difficulty bending; by providing a fountain accessible under 4.15 and a water cooler; or by such other means as would achieve the required accessibility for each group on each floor.)

(b) Where more than one drinking fountain or water cooler is provided on a floor, 50% of those provided shall comply with 4.15 and shall be on an accessible route.

(11) Toilet Facilities: If toilet rooms are provided, then each public and common use toilet room shall comply with 4.22. Other toilet rooms provided for the use of occupants of specific spaces (i.e., a private toilet room for the occupant of a private office) shall be adaptable. If bathing rooms are provided, then each public and common use bathroom shall comply with 4.23. Accessible toilet rooms and bathing facilities shall be on an accessible route.

Number of each type of telephone provided on each floor	Number of telephones required to comply with 4.31.2 through 4.31.8[1]
1 or more single unit	1 per floor
1 bank[2]	1 per floor
2 or more banks[2]	1 per bank. Accessible unit may be installed as a single unit in proximity (either visible or with signage) to the bank. At least one public telephone per floor shall meet the requirements for a forward reach telephone[3].

[1] Additional public telephones may be installed at any height. Unless otherwise specified, accessible telephones may be either forward or side reach telephones.

[2] A bank consists of two or more adjacent public telephones, often installed as a unit.

[3] EXCEPTION: For exterior installations only, if dial tone first service is available, then a side reach telephone may be installed instead of the required forward reach telephone (i.e., one telephone in proximity to each bank shall comply with 4.31).

(b)* All telephones required to be accessible and complying with 4.31.2 through 4.31.8 shall be equipped with a volume control. In addition, 25 percent, but never less than one, of all other public telephones provided shall be equipped with a volume control and shall be dispersed among all types of public telephones, including closed circuit telephones, throughout the build-ing or facility. Signage complying with appli-cable provisions of 4.30.7 shall be provided.

(c) The following shall be provided in accordance with 4.31.9:

(i) if a total number of four or more public pay telephones (including both interior and exterior phones) is provided at a site, and at least one is in an interior location, then at least one interior public text telephone shall be provided.

(ii) if an interior public pay telephone is provided in a stadium or arena, in a convention center, in a hotel with a convention center, or

(12) Storage, Shelving and Display Units:

(a) If fixed or built-in storage facilities such as cabinets, shelves, closets, and drawers are provided in accessible spaces, at least one of each type provided shall contain storage space complying with 4.25. Additional storage may be provided outside of the dimensions required by 4.25.

(b) Shelves or display units allowing self-service by customers in mercantile occupancies shall be located on an accessible route comply-ing with 4.3. Requirements for accessible reach range do not apply.

(13) Controls and operating mechanisms in accessible spaces, along accessible routes, or as parts of accessible elements (for example, light switches and dispenser controls) shall comply with 4.27.

(14) If emergency warning systems are provided, then they shall include both audible alarms and visual alarms complying with 4.28. Sleeping accommodations required to comply with 9.3 shall have an alarm system complying with 4.28. Emergency warning systems in medical care facilities may be modified to suit standard health care alarm design practice.

(15) Detectable warnings shall be provided at locations as specified in 4.29.

(16) Building Signage:

(a) Signs which designate permanent rooms and spaces shall comply with 4.30.1, 4.30.4, 4.30.5 and 4.30.6.

(b) Other signs which provide direction to or information about functional spaces of the building shall comply with 4.30.1, 4.30.2, 4.30.3, and 4.30.5.

EXCEPTION: Building directories, menus, and all other signs which are temporary are not required to comply.

(17) Public Telephones:

(a) If public pay telephones, public closed circuit telephones, or other public telephones are provided, then they shall comply with 4.31.2 through 4.31.8 to the extent required by the following table:

in a covered mall, at least one interior public text telephone shall be provided in the facility.

(iii) If a public pay telephone is located in or adjacent to a hospital emergency room, hospital recovery room, or hospital waiting room, one public text telephone shall be provided at each such location.

(d) Where a bank of telephones in the interior of a building consists of three or more public pay telephones, at least one public pay telephone in each such bank shall be equipped with a shelf and outlet in compliance with 4.31.9(2).

(18) If fixed or built-in seating or tables (including, but not limited to, study carrels and student laboratory stations), are provided in accessible public or common use areas, at least five percent (5%), but not less than one, of the fixed or built-in seating areas or tables shall comply with 4.32. An accessible route shall lead to and through such fixed or built-in seating areas, or tables.

(19)* Assembly areas:

(a) In places of assembly with fixed seating accessible wheelchair locations shall comply with 4.33.2, 4.33.3, and 4.33.4 and shall be provided consistent with the following table:

Capacity of Seating in Assembly Areas	Number of Required Wheelchair Locations
4 to 25	1
26 to 50	2
51 to 300	4
301 to 500	6
over 500	6, plus 1 additional space for each total seating capacity increase of 100

In addition, one percent, but not less than one, of all fixed seats shall be aisle seats with no armrests on the aisle side, or removable or folding armrests on the aisle side. Each such seat shall be identified by a sign or marker. Signage notifying patrons of the availability of such seats shall be posted at the ticket office. Aisle seats are not required to comply with 4.33.4.

(b) This paragraph applies to assembly areas where audible communications are integral to the use of the space (e.g., concert and lecture halls, playhouses and movie theaters, meeting rooms, etc.). Such assembly areas, if (1) they accommodate at least 50 persons, or if they have audio-amplification systems, and (2) they have fixed seating, shall have a permanently installed assistive listening system complying with 4.33. For other assembly areas, a permanently installed assistive listening system, or an adequate number of electrical outlets or other supplementary wiring necessary to support a portable assistive listening system shall be provided. The minimum number of receivers to be provided shall be equal to 4 percent of the total number of seats, but in no case less than two. Signage complying with applicable provisions of 4.30 shall be installed to notify patrons of the availability of a listening system.

(20) Where automated teller machines (ATMs) are provided, each ATM shall comply with the requirements of 4.34 except where two or more are provided at a location, then only one must comply.

EXCEPTION: Drive-up-only automated teller machines are not required to comply with 4.27.2, 4.27.3 and 4.34.3.

(21) Where dressing and fitting rooms are provided for use by the general public, patients, customers or employees, 5 percent, but never less than one, of dressing rooms for each type of use in each cluster of dressing rooms shall be accessible and shall comply with 4.35.

Examples of types of dressing rooms are those serving different genders or distinct and different functions as in different treatment or examination facilities.

4.1.4 (Reserved).

4.1.5 Accessible Buildings: Additions. Each addition to an existing building or facility shall be regarded as an alteration. Each space or element added to the existing building or facility shall comply with the applicable provisions of 4.1.1 to 4.1.3, Minimum Requirements (for New Construction) and the applicable technical specifications of 4.2 through 4.35 and sections 5 through 10. Each addition that affects or could affect the usability of an area containing a primary function shall comply with 4.1.6(2).

4.1.6 Accessible Buildings: Alterations.

(1) General. Alterations to existing buildings and facilities shall comply with the following:

(a) No alteration shall be undertaken which decreases or has the effect of decreasing accessibility or usability of a building or facility below the requirements for new construction at the time of alteration.

(b) If existing elements, spaces, or common areas are altered, then each such altered element, space, feature, or area shall comply with the applicable provisions of 4.1.1 to 4.1.3 Minimum Requirements (for New Construction). If the applicable provision for new construction requires that an element, space, or common area be on an accessible route, the altered element, space, or common area is not required to be on an accessible route except as provided in 4.1.6(2) (Alterations to an Area Containing a Primary Function.)

(c) If alterations of single elements, when considered together, amount to an alteration of a room or space in a building or facility, the entire space shall be made accessible.

(d) No alteration of an existing element, space, or area of a building or facility shall impose a requirement for greater accessibility than that which would be required for new construction. For example, if the elevators and stairs in a building are being altered and the elevators are, in turn, being made accessible, then no accessibility modifications are required to the stairs connecting levels connected by the elevator. If stair modifications to correct unsafe conditions are required by other codes, the modifications shall be done in compliance with these guidelines unless technically infeasible.

(e) At least one interior public text telephone complying with 4.31.9 shall be provided if:

(i) alterations to existing buildings or facilities with less than four exterior or interior public pay telephones would increase the total number to four or more telephones with at least one in an interior location; or

(ii) alterations to one or more exterior or interior public pay telephones occur in an existing building or facility with four or more public telephones with at least one in an interior location.

(f) If an escalator or stair is planned or installed where none existed previously and major structural modifications are necessary for such installation, then a means of accessible vertical access shall be provided that complies with the applicable provisions of 4.7, 4.8, 4.10, or 4.11.

(g) In alterations, the requirements of 4.1.3(9), 4.3.10 and 4.3.11 do not apply.

(h)*Entrances: If a planned alteration entails alterations to an entrance, and the building has an accessible entrance, the entrance being altered is not required to comply with 4.1.3(8), except to the extent required by 4.1.6(2). If a particular entrance is not made accessible, appropriate accessible signage indicating the location of the nearest accessible entrance(s) shall be installed at or near the inaccessible entrance, such that a person with disabilities will not be required to retrace the approach route from the inaccessible entrance.

(i) If the alteration work is limited solely to the electrical, mechanical, or plumbing system, or to hazardous material abatement, or automatic sprinkler retrofitting, and does not involve the alteration of any elements or spaces required to be accessible under these guidelines, then 4.1.6(2) does not apply.

(j) EXCEPTION: In alteration work, if compliance with 4.1.6 is technically infeasible, the alteration shall provide accessibility to the maximum extent feasible. Any elements or features of the building or facility that are being altered and can be made accessible shall be made accessible within the scope of the alteration.

Technically Infeasible. Means, with respect to an alteration of a building or a facility, that it has little likelihood of being accomplished because existing structural conditions would require removing or altering a load-bearing member which is an essential part of the structural frame; or because other existing physical or site constraints prohibit modification or addition of elements, spaces, or features which are in full and strict compliance with the minimum requirements for new construction and which are necessary to provide accessibility.

(k) EXCEPTION:

(i) These guidelines do not require the installation of an elevator in an altered facility that is less than three stories or has less than 3,000 square feet per story unless the building is a shopping center, a shopping mall, the professional office of a health care provider, or another type of facility as determined by the Attorney General.

(ii) The exemption provided in paragraph (i) does not obviate or limit in any way the obligation to comply with the other accessibility requirements established in these guidelines. For example, alterations to floors above or below the ground floor must be accessible regardless of whether the altered facility has an elevator. If a facility subject to the elevator exemption set forth in paragraph (i) nonetheless has a full passenger elevator, that elevator shall meet, to the maximum extent feasible, the accessibility requirements of these guidelines.

(2) Alterations to an Area Containing a Primary Function: In addition to the requirements of 4.1.6(1), an alteration that affects or could affect the usability of or access to an area containing a primary function shall be made so as to ensure that, to the maximum extent feasible, the path of travel to the altered area and the restrooms, telephones, and drinking fountains serving the altered area, are readily accessible to and usable by individuals with disabilities, unless such alterations are disproportionate to the overall alterations in terms of cost and scope (as determined under criteria established by the Attorney General).

(3) Special Technical Provisions for Alterations to Existing Buildings and Facilities:

(a) Ramps: Curb ramps and interior or exterior ramps to be constructed on sites or in existing buildings or facilities where space limitations prohibit the use of a 1:12 slope or less may have slopes and rises as follows:

(i) A slope between 1:10 and 1:12 is allowed for a maximum rise of 6 inches.

(ii) A slope between 1:8 and 1:10 is allowed for a maximum rise of 3 inches. A slope steeper than 1:8 is not allowed.

(b) Stairs: Full extension of handrails at stairs shall not be required in alterations where such extensions would be hazardous or impossible due to plan configuration.

(c) Elevators:

(i) If safety door edges are provided in existing automatic elevators, automatic door reopening devices may be omitted (see 4.10.6).

(ii) Where existing shaft configuration or technical infeasibility prohibits strict compliance with 4.10.9, the minimum car plan dimensions may be reduced by the minimum amount necessary, but in no case shall the inside car area be smaller than 48 in by 48 in.

(iii) Equivalent facilitation may be provided with an elevator car of different dimensions when usability can be demonstrated and when all other elements required to be accessible comply with the applicable provisions of 4.10. For example, an elevator of 47 in by 69 in (1195 mm by 1755 mm) with a door opening on the narrow dimension, could accommodate the standard wheelchair clearances shown in Figure 4.

(d) Doors:

(i) Where it is technically infeasible to comply with clear opening width requirements of 4.13.5, a projection of 5/8 in maximum will be permitted for the latch side stop.

(ii) If existing thresholds are 3/4 in high or less, and have (or are modified to have) a beveled edge on each side, they may remain.

(e) Toilet Rooms:

(i) Where it is technically infeasible to comply with 4.22 or 4.23, the installation of at least one unisex toilet/bathroom per floor, located in the same area as existing toilet facilities, will be permitted in lieu of modifying existing toilet facilities to be accessible. Each unisex toilet room shall contain one water closet complying with 4.16 and one lavatory complying with 4.19, and the door shall have a privacy latch.

(ii) Where it is technically infeasible to install a required standard stall (Fig. 30(a)), or where other codes prohibit reduction of the fixture count (i.e., removal of a water closet in order to create a double-wide stall), either alternate stall (Fig.30(b)) may be provided in lieu of the standard stall.

(iii) When existing toilet or bathing facilities are being altered and are not made accessible, signage complying with 4.30.1, 4.30.2, 4.30.3, 4.30.5, and 4.30.7 shall be provided indicating the location of the nearest accessible toilet or bathing facility within the facility.

(f) Assembly Areas:

(i) Where it is technically infeasible to disperse accessible seating throughout an altered assembly area, accessible seating areas may be clustered. Each accessible seating area shall have provisions for companion seating and shall be located on an accessible route that also serves as a means of emergency egress.

(ii) Where it is technically infeasible to alter all performing areas to be on an accessible route, at least one of each type of performing area shall be made accessible.

(g) Platform Lifts (Wheelchair Lifts): In alterations, platform lifts (wheelchair lifts) complying with 4.11 and applicable state or local codes may be used as part of an accessible route. The use of lifts is not limited to the four conditions in exception 4 of 4.1.3(5).

(h) Dressing Rooms: In alterations where technical infeasibility can be demonstrated, one dressing room for each sex on each level shall be made accessible. Where only unisex dressing rooms are provided, accessible unisex dressing rooms may be used to fulfill this requirement.

4.1.7 Accessible Buildings: Historic Preservation.

(1) Applicability:

(a) General Rule. Alterations to a qualified historic building or facility shall comply with 4.1.6 Accessible Buildings: Alterations, the applicable technical specifications of 4.2 through 4.35 and the applicable special application sections 5 through 10 unless it is determined in accordance with the procedures in 4.1.7(2) that compliance with the requirements for accessible routes (exterior and interior), ramps, entrances, or toilets would threaten or destroy the historic significance of the building or facility in which case the alternative requirements in 4.1.7(3) may be used for the feature.

EXCEPTION: (Reserved).

(b) Definition. A qualified historic building or facility is a building or facility that is:

(i) Listed in or eligible for listing in the National Register of Historic Places; or

(ii) Designated as historic under an appropriate State or local law.

(2) Procedures:

(a) Alterations to Qualified Historic Buildings and Facilities Subject to Section 106 of the National Historic Preservation Act:

(i) Section 106 Process. Section 106 of the National Historic Preservation Act (16 U.S.C. 470 f) requires that a Federal agency with jurisdiction over a Federal, federally assisted, or federally licensed undertaking consider the effects of the agency's undertaking on buildings and facilities listed in or eligible for listing in the National Register of Historic Places and give the Advisory Council on Historic Preservation a reasonable opportunity to comment on the undertaking prior to approval of the undertaking.

(ii) ADA Application. Where alterations are undertaken to a qualified historic building or facility that is subject to section 106 of the National Historic Preservation Act, the Federal agency with jurisdiction over the undertaking shall follow the section 106 process. If the State Historic Preservation Officer or Advisory Council on Historic Preservation agrees that compliance with the requirements for accessible routes (exterior and interior), ramps, entrances, or toilets would threaten or destroy the historic significance of the building or facility, the alternative requirements in 4.1.7(3) may be used for the feature.

(b) Alterations to Qualified Historic Buildings and Facilities Not Subject to Section 106 of the National Historic Preservation Act. Where alterations are undertaken to a qualified historic building or facility that is not subject to section 106 of the National Historic Preservation Act, if the entity undertaking the alterations believes that compliance with the requirements for accessible routes (exterior and interior), ramps, entrances, or toilets would threaten or destroy the historic significance of the building or facility and that the alternative requirements in 4.1.7(3) should be used for the feature, the entity should consult with the State Historic Preservation Officer. If the State Historic Preservation Officer agrees that compliance with the accessibility requirements for accessible routes (exterior and interior), ramps, entrances or toilets would threaten or destroy the historical significance of the building or facility, the alternative requirements in 4.1.7(3) may be used.

(c) Consultation With Interested Persons. Interested persons should be invited to participate in the consultation process, including State or local accessibility officials, individuals with disabilities, and organizations representing individuals with disabilities.

(d) Certified Local Government Historic Preservation Programs. Where the State Historic Preservation Officer has delegated the consultation responsibility for purposes of this section to a local government historic preservation program that has been certified in accordance with section 101(c) of the National Historic Preservation Act of 1966 (16 U.S.C. 470a (c)) and implementing regulations (36 CFR 61.5), the responsibility may be carried out by the appropriate local government body or official.

(3) Historic Preservation: Minimum Requirements:

(a) At least one accessible route complying with 4.3 from a site access point to an accessible entrance shall be provided.

EXCEPTION: A ramp with a slope no greater than 1:6 for a run not to exceed 2 ft (610 mm) may be used as part of an accessible route to an entrance.

(b) At least one accessible entrance complying with 4.14 which is used by the public shall be provided.

EXCEPTION: If it is determined that no entrance used by the public can comply with 4.14, then access at any entrance not used by the general public but open (unlocked) with directional signage at the primary entrance may be used. The accessible entrance shall also have a notification system. Where security is a problem, remote monitoring may be used.

(c) If toilets are provided, then at least one toilet facility complying with 4.22 and 4.1.6 shall be provided along an accessible route that complies with 4.3. Such toilet facility may be unisex in design.

(d) Accessible routes from an accessible entrance to all publicly used spaces on at least the level of the accessible entrance shall be provided. Access shall be provided to all levels of a building or facility in compliance with 4.1 whenever practical.

(e) Displays and written information, documents, etc., should be located where they can be seen by a seated person. Exhibits and signage displayed horizontally (e.g., open books), should be no higher than 44 in (1120 mm) above the floor surface.

NOTE: The technical provisions of sections 4.2 through 4.35 are the same as those of the American National Standard Institute's document A117.1-1980, except as noted in the text.

4.2 Space Allowance and Reach Ranges.

4.2.1* Wheelchair Passage Width. The minimum clear width for single wheelchair passage shall be 32 in (815 mm) at a point and 36 in (915 mm) continuously (see Fig. 1 and 24(e)).

4.2.2 Width for Wheelchair Passing. The minimum width for two wheelchairs to pass is 60 in (1525 mm) (see Fig. 2).

4.2.3* Wheelchair Turning Space. The space required for a wheelchair to make a 180-degree turn is a clear space of 60 in (1525 mm)

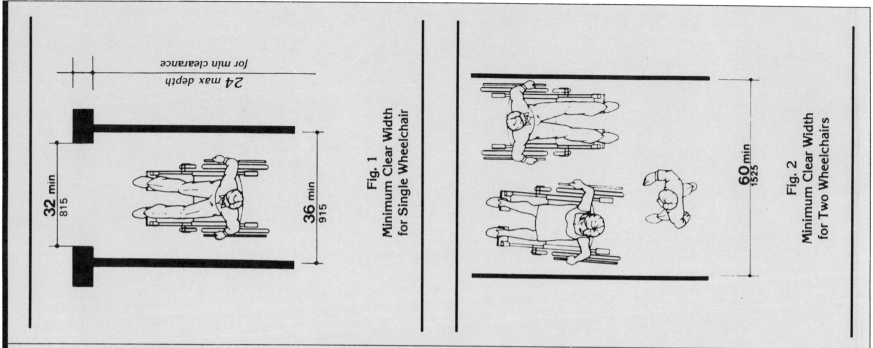

**Fig. 1
Minimum Clear Width
for Single Wheelchair**

**Fig. 2
Minimum Clear Width
for Two Wheelchairs**

diameter (see Fig. 3(a)) or a T-shaped space (see Fig. 3(b)).

4.2.4* Clear Floor or Ground Space for Wheelchairs.

4.2.4.1 Size and Approach. The minimum clear floor or ground space required to accommodate a single, stationary wheelchair and occupant is 30 in by 48 in (760 mm by 1220 mm) (see Fig. 4(a)). The minimum clear floor or ground space for wheelchairs may be positioned for forward or parallel approach to an object (see Fig. 4(b) and (c)). Clear floor or ground space for wheelchairs may be part of the knee space required under some objects.

4.2.4.2 Relationship of Maneuvering Clearance to Wheelchair Spaces. One full unobstructed side of the clear floor or ground space for a wheelchair shall adjoin or overlap an accessible route or adjoin another wheelchair clear floor space. If a clear floor space is located in an alcove or otherwise confined on all or part of three sides, additional maneuvering clearances shall be provided as shown in Fig. 4(d) and (e).

4.2.4.3 Surfaces for Wheelchair Spaces. Clear floor or ground spaces for wheelchairs shall comply with 4.5.

4.2.5* Forward Reach. If the clear floor space only allows forward approach to an object, the maximum high forward reach allowed shall be 48 in (1220 mm) (see Fig. 5(a)). *The minimum low forward reach is 15 in (380 mm).* If the high forward reach is over an obstruction, reach and clearances shall be as shown in Fig. 5(b).

4.2.6* Side Reach. If the clear floor space allows parallel approach by a person in a wheelchair, the maximum high side reach allowed shall be 54 in (1370 mm) and the low side reach shall be no less than 9 in (230 mm) above the floor (Fig. 6(a) and (b)). If the side reach is over an obstruction, the reach and clearances shall be as shown in Fig 6(c).

4.3 Accessible Route.

4.3.1* General. All walks, halls, corridors, aisles, *skywalks, tunnels,* and other spaces that are part of an accessible route shall comply with 4.3.

4.3.2 Location.

(1) At least one accessible route *within the boundary of the site* shall be provided from public transportation stops, accessible parking, and accessible passenger loading zones, and public streets or sidewalks to the accessible building entrance they serve. *The accessible route shall, to the maximum extent feasible, coincide with the route for the general public.*

(2) At least one accessible route shall connect accessible buildings, facilities, elements, and spaces that are on the same site.

(3) At least one accessible route shall connect accessible building or facility entrances with all accessible spaces and elements and with all accessible dwelling units within the building or facility.

(4) An accessible route shall connect at least one accessible entrance of each accessible

dwelling unit with those exterior and interior spaces and facilities that serve the accessible dwelling unit.

4.3.3 Width.
The minimum clear width of an accessible route shall be 36 in (915 mm) except at doors (see 4.13.5 and 4.13.6). If a person in a wheelchair must make a turn around an obstruction, the minimum clear width of the accessible route shall be as shown in Fig. 7(a) and (b).

4.3.4 Passing Space.
If an accessible route has less than 60 in (1525 mm) clear width, then passing spaces at least 60 in by 60 in (1525 mm by 1525 mm) shall be located at reasonable intervals not to exceed 200 ft (61 m). A T-intersection of two corridors or walks is an acceptable passing place.

4.3.5 Head Room.
Accessible routes shall comply with 4.4.2.

4.3.6 Surface Textures.
The surface of an accessible route shall comply with 4.5.

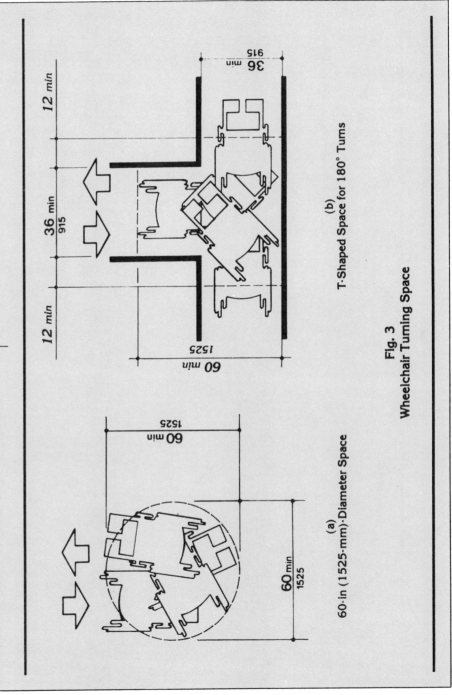

(a)
60-in (1525-mm)-Diameter Space

(b)
T-Shaped Space for 180° Turns

Fig. 3
Wheelchair Turning Space

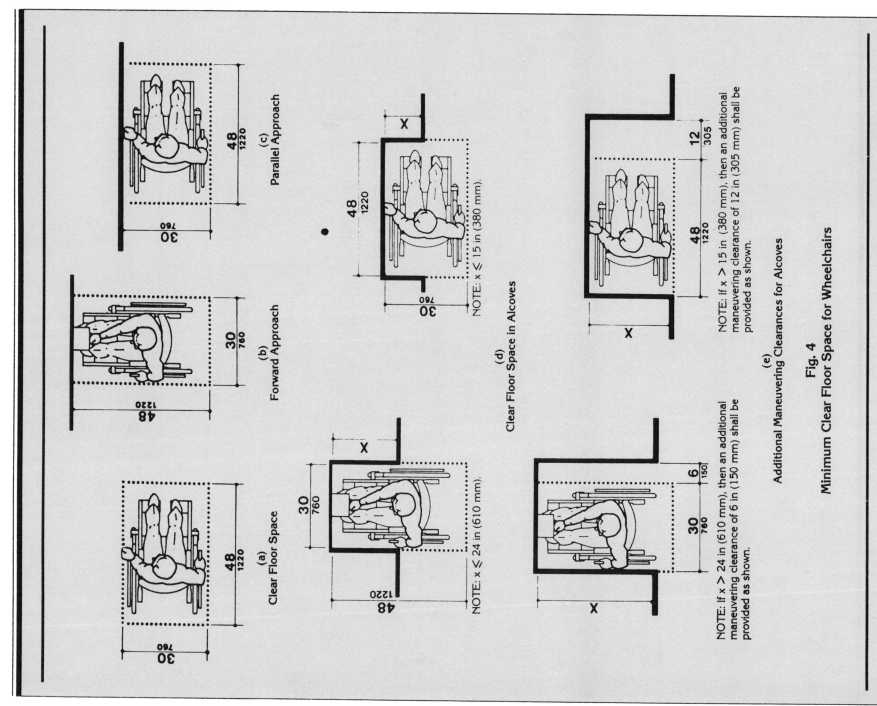

(a)
Clear Floor Space

(b)
Forward Approach

(c)
Parallel Approach

(d)
Clear Floor Space in Alcoves

NOTE: x ≤ 24 in (610 mm).

NOTE: x ≤ 15 in (380 mm).

NOTE: If x > 24 in (610 mm), then an additional maneuvering clearance of 6 in (150 mm) shall be provided as shown.

NOTE: If x > 15 in (380 mm), then an additional maneuvering clearance of 12 in (305 mm) shall be provided as shown.

(e)
Additional Maneuvering Clearances for Alcoves

Fig. 4
Minimum Clear Floor Space for Wheelchairs

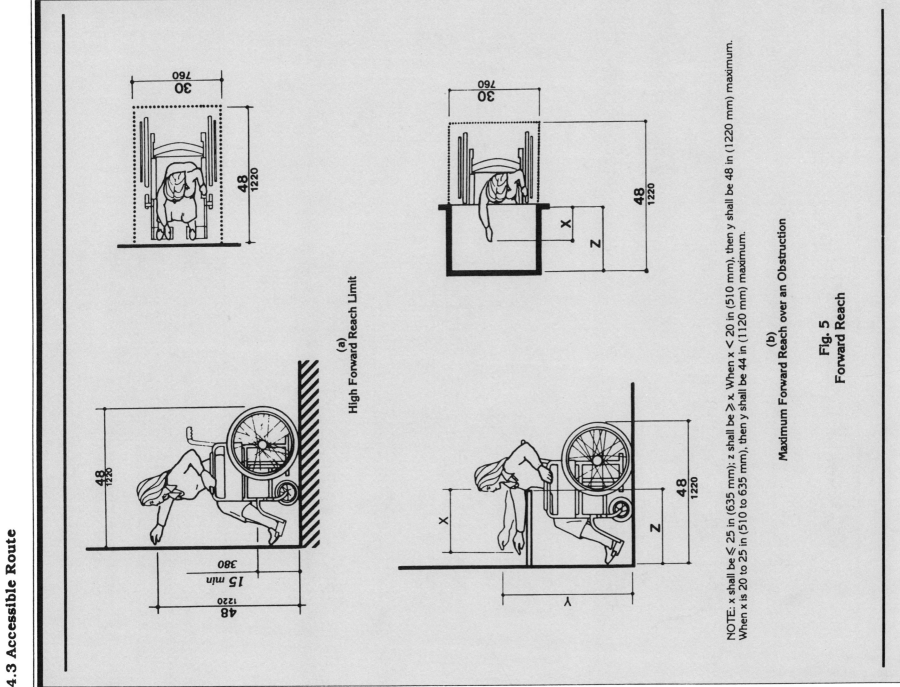

(a)
High Forward Reach Limit

(b)
Maximum Forward Reach over an Obstruction

Fig. 5
Forward Reach

NOTE: x shall be ≤ 25 in (635 mm); z shall be ≥ x. When x < 20 in (510 mm), then y shall be 48 in (1220 mm) maximum. When x is 20 to 25 in (510 to 635 mm), then y shall be 44 in (1120 mm) maximum.

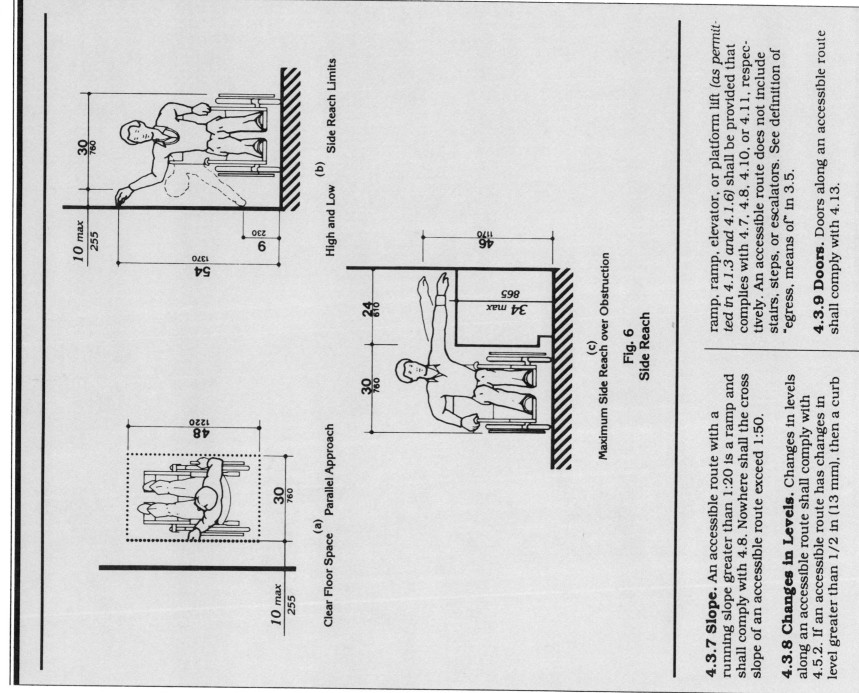

Clear Floor Space   Parallel Approach
(a)

High and Low   Side Reach Limits
(b)

Maximum Side Reach over Obstruction
(c)

**Fig. 6
Side Reach**

4.3.7 Slope. An accessible route with a running slope greater than 1:20 is a ramp and shall comply with 4.8. Nowhere shall the cross slope of an accessible route exceed 1:50.

4.3.8 Changes in Levels. Changes in levels along an accessible route shall comply with 4.5.2. If an accessible route has changes in level greater than 1/2 in (13 mm), then a curb

ramp, ramp, elevator, or platform lift (*as permitted in 4.1.3 and 4.1.6*) shall be provided that complies with 4.7, 4.8, 4.10, or 4.11, respectively. An accessible route does not include stairs, steps, or escalators. See definition of "egress, means of" in 3.5.

4.3.9 Doors. Doors along an accessible route shall comply with 4.13.

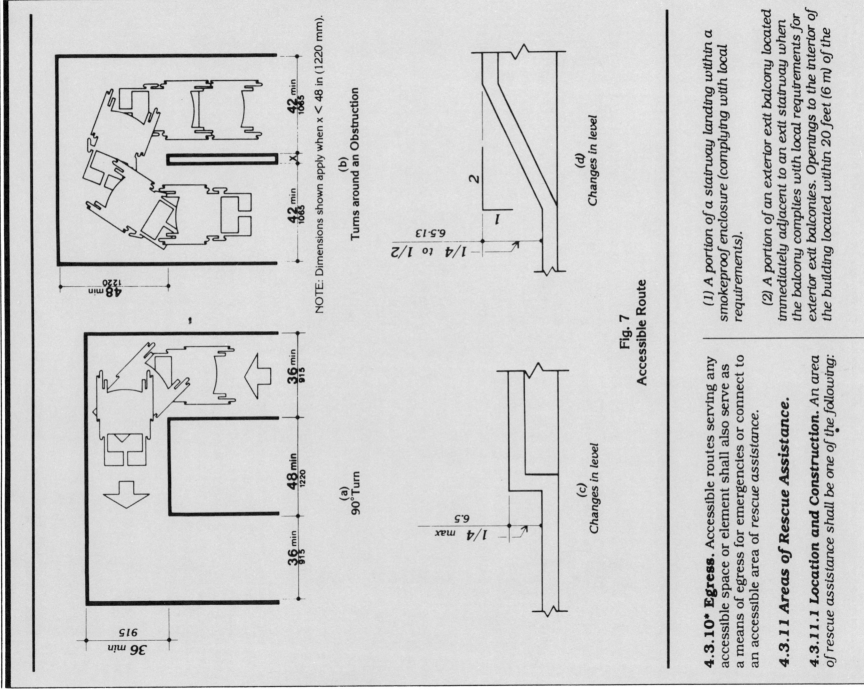

(a) 90° Turn

36 min 915

48 min 1220

36 min 915

36 min 915

(b) Turns around an Obstruction

48 min 1220

42 min 1065

X

42 min 1065

NOTE: Dimensions shown apply when x < 48 in (1220 mm).

(c) Changes in level

1/4 max 6.5

(d) Changes in level

1/4 to 1/2 6.5-13

1
2

Fig. 7
Accessible Route

4.3.10* Egress. Accessible routes serving any accessible space or element shall also serve as a means of egress for emergencies or connect to an accessible area of rescue assistance.

4.3.11 Areas of Rescue Assistance.

4.3.11.1 Location and Construction. An area of rescue assistance shall be one of the following:

(1) A portion of a stairway landing within a smokeproof enclosure (complying with local requirements).

(2) A portion of an exterior exit balcony located immediately adjacent to an exit stairway when the balcony complies with local requirements for exterior exit balconies. Openings to the interior of the building located within 20 feet (6 m) of the

area of rescue assistance shall be protected with fire assemblies having a three-fourths hour fire protection rating.

(3) A portion of a one-hour fire-resistive corridor (complying with local requirements for fire-resistive construction and for openings) located immediately adjacent to an exit enclosure.

(4) A vestibule located immediately adjacent to an exit enclosure and constructed to the same fire-resistive standards as required for corridors and openings.

(5) A portion of a stairway landing within an exit enclosure which is vented to the exterior and is separated from the interior of the building with not less than one-hour fire-resistive doors.

(6) When approved by the appropriate local authority, an area or a room which is separated from other portions of the building by a smoke barrier. Smoke barriers shall have a fire-resistive rating of not less than one hour and shall completely enclose the area or room. Doors in the smoke barrier shall be tight-fitting smoke- and draft-control assemblies having a fire-protection rating of not less than 20 minutes and shall be self-closing or automatic closing. The area or room shall be provided with an exit directly to an exit enclosure. Where the room or area exits into an exit enclosure which is required to be of more than one-hour fire-resistive construction, the room or area shall have the same fire-resistive construction, including the same opening protection, as required for the adjacent exit enclosure.

(7) An elevator lobby when elevator shafts and adjacent lobbies are pressurized as required for smokeproof enclosures by local regulations and when complying with requirements herein for size, communication, and signage. Such pressurization system shall be activated by smoke detectors on each floor located in a manner approved by the appropriate local authority. Pressurization equipment and its duct work within the building shall be separated from other portions of the building by a minimum two-hour fire-resistive construction.

4.3.11.2 Size. *Each area of rescue assistance shall provide at least two accessible areas each being not less than 30 inches by 48 inches (760 mm by 1220 mm). The area of rescue*

assistance shall not encroach on any required exit width. The total number of such 30-inch by 48-inch (760 mm by 1220 mm) areas per story shall be not less than one for every 200 persons of calculated occupant load served by the area of rescue assistance.

EXCEPTION: The appropriate local authority may reduce the minimum number of 30-inch by 48-inch (760 mm by 1220 mm) areas to one for each area of rescue assistance on floors where the occupant load is less than 200.

4.3.11.3* Stairway Width. *Each stairway adjacent to an area of rescue assistance shall have a minimum clear width of 48 inches between handrails.*

4.3.11.4* Two-way Communication. *A method of two-way communication, with both visible and audible signals, shall be provided between each area of rescue assistance and the primary entry. The fire department or appropriate local authority may approve a location other than the primary entry.*

4.3.11.5 Identification. *Each area of rescue assistance shall be identified by a sign which states "AREA OF RESCUE ASSISTANCE" and displays the international symbol of accessibility. The sign shall be illuminated when exit sign illumination is required. Signage shall also be installed at all inaccessible exits and where otherwise necessary to clearly indicate the direction to areas of rescue assistance. In each area of rescue assistance, instructions on the use of the area under emergency conditions shall be posted adjoining the two-way communication system.*

4.4 Protruding Objects.

4.4.1* General. Objects projecting from walls (for example, telephones) with their leading edges between 27 in and 80 in (685 mm and 2030 mm) above the finished floor shall protrude no more than 4 in (100 mm) into walks, halls, corridors, passageways, or aisles (see Fig. 8(a)). Objects mounted with their leading edges at or below 27 in (685 mm) above the finished floor may protrude any amount (see Fig. 8(a) and (b)). Free-standing objects mounted on posts or pylons may overhang 12 in (305 mm) maximum from 27 in to 80 in (685 mm to 2030 mm) above the ground or

4.4 Protruding Objects

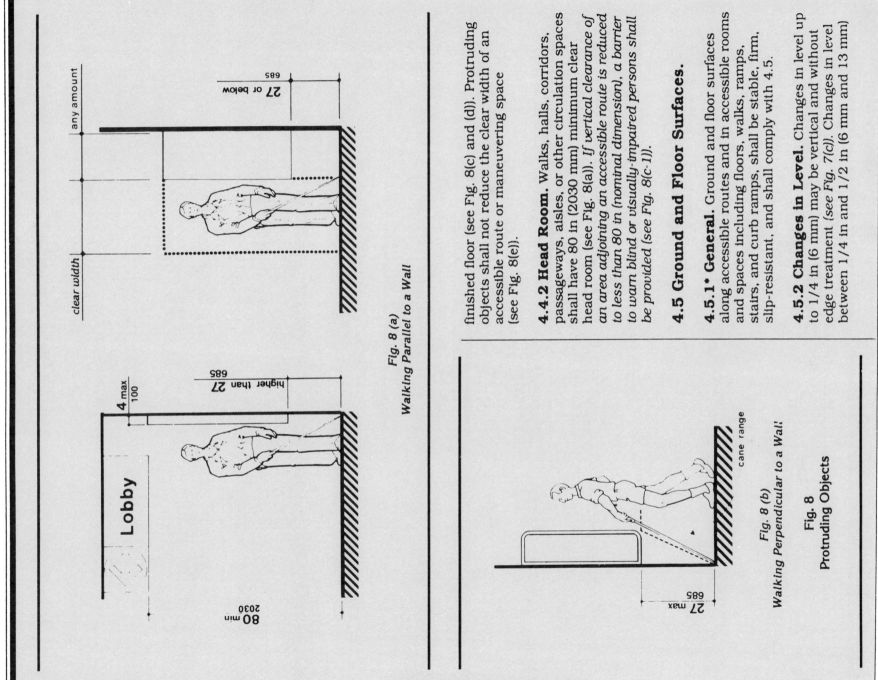

Fig. 8 (a)
Walking Parallel to a Wall

Fig. 8 (b)
Walking Perpendicular to a Wall

Fig. 8
Protruding Objects

finished floor (see Fig. 8(c) and (d)). Protruding objects shall not reduce the clear width of an accessible route or maneuvering space (see Fig. 8(e)).

4.4.2 Head Room. Walks, halls, corridors, passageways, aisles, or other circulation spaces shall have 80 in (2030 mm) minimum clear head room (see Fig. 8(a)). *If vertical clearance of an area adjoining an accessible route is reduced to less than 80 in (nominal dimension), a barrier to warn blind or visually-impaired persons shall be provided (see Fig. 8(c-1)).*

4.5 Ground and Floor Surfaces.

4.5.1* General. Ground and floor surfaces along accessible routes and in accessible rooms and spaces including floors, walks, ramps, stairs, and curb ramps, shall be stable, firm, slip-resistant, and shall comply with 4.5.

4.5.2 Changes in Level. Changes in level up to 1/4 in (6 mm) may be vertical and without edge treatment *(see Fig. 7(c)). Changes in level between 1/4 in and 1/2 in (6 mm and 13 mm)*

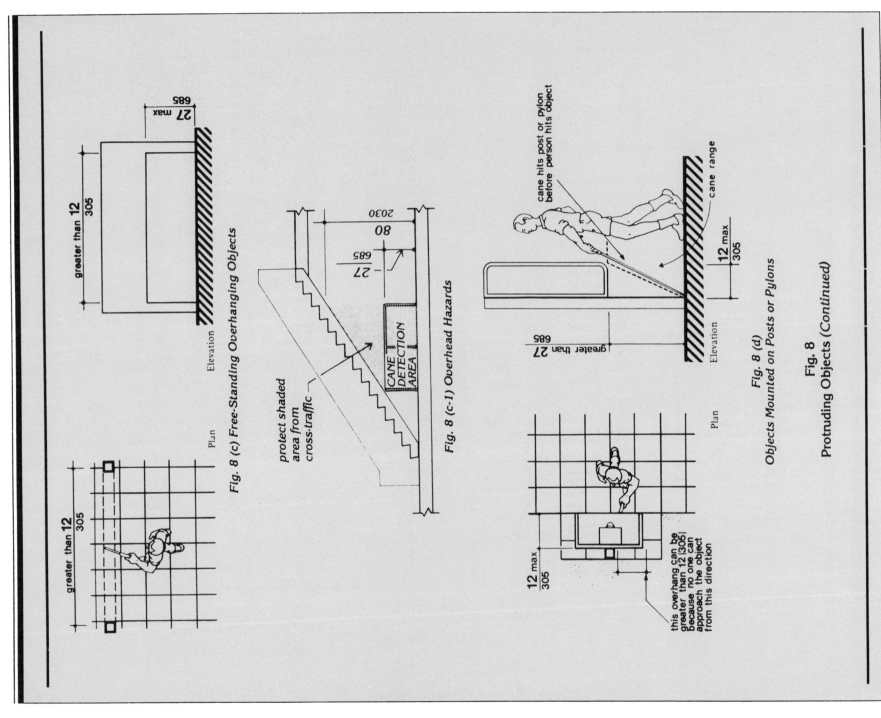

greater than **12**
305

Plan

greater than **12**
305

Elevation

27 max
685

Fig. 8 (c) Free-Standing Overhanging Objects

protect shaded
area from
cross-traffic

CANE
DETECTION
AREA

27
685

80

2030

Fig. 8 (c-1) Overhead Hazards

cane hits post or pylon
before person hits object

cane range

12 max
305

greater than **27**
685

Elevation

Fig. 8 (d)
Objects Mounted on Posts or Pylons

12 max
305

this overhang can be
greater than 12 [305]
because no one can
approach the object
from this direction

Plan

Fig. 8
Protruding Objects (Continued)

4.5 Ground and Floor Surfaces

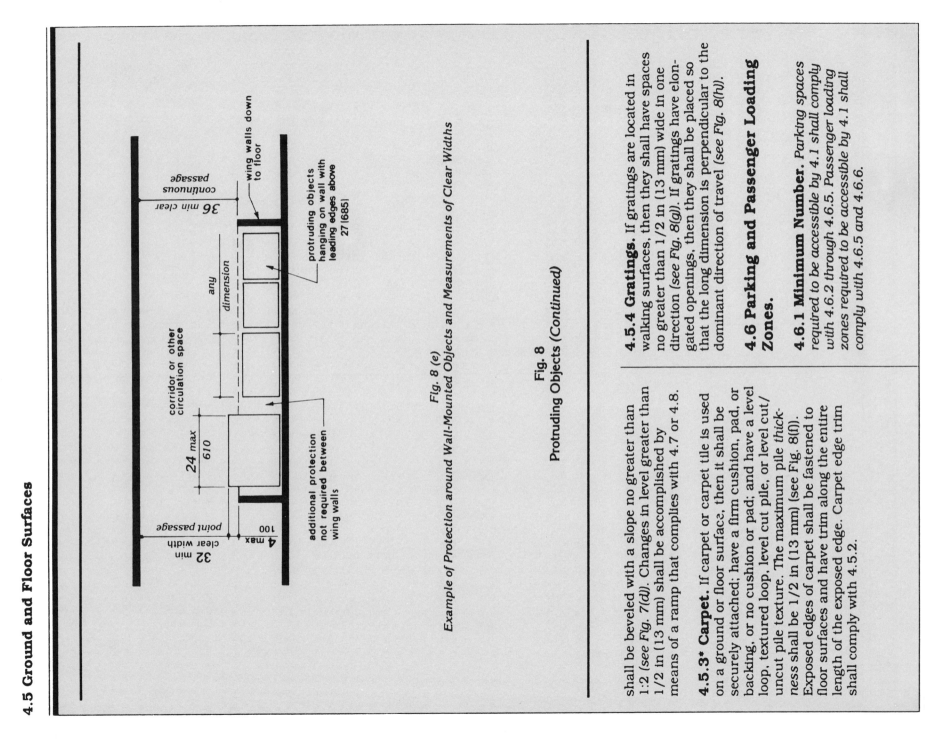

Fig. 8 (e)
Example of Protection around Wall-Mounted Objects and Measurements of Clear Widths

Fig. 8
Protruding Objects (Continued)

shall be beveled with a slope no greater than 1:2 *(see Fig. 7(d))*. Changes in level greater than 1/2 in (13 mm) shall be accomplished by means of a ramp that complies with 4.7 or 4.8.

4.5.3* Carpet. If carpet or carpet tile is used on a ground or floor surface, then it shall be securely attached; have a firm cushion, pad, or backing, or no cushion or pad; and have a level loop, textured loop, level cut pile, or level cut/uncut pile texture. The maximum pile *thickness* shall be 1/2 in (13 mm) (see Fig. 8(f)). Exposed edges of carpet shall be fastened to floor surfaces and have trim along the entire length of the exposed edge. Carpet edge trim shall comply with 4.5.2.

4.5.4 Gratings. If gratings are located in walking surfaces, then they shall have spaces no greater than 1/2 in (13 mm) wide in one direction *(see Fig. 8(g))*. If gratings have elongated openings, then they shall be placed so that the long dimension is perpendicular to the dominant direction of travel *(see Fig. 8(h))*.

4.6 Parking and Passenger Loading Zones.

4.6.1 Minimum Number. *Parking spaces required to be accessible by 4.1 shall comply with 4.6.2 through 4.6.5. Passenger loading zones required to be accessible by 4.1 shall comply with 4.6.5 and 4.6.6.*

4.6.2 Location. *Accessible parking spaces serving* a particular building shall be located on the shortest accessible route of travel from *adjacent parking* to an accessible entrance. In *parking facilities that do not serve a particular building, accessible parking shall be located on the shortest accessible route of travel to an accessible pedestrian entrance of the parking facility. In buildings with multiple accessible entrances with adjacent parking, accessible parking spaces shall be dispersed and located closest to the accessible entrances.*

4.6.3* Parking Spaces. *Accessible parking spaces* shall be at least 96 in (2440 mm) wide. Parking access aisles shall be part of an accessible route to the building or facility entrance and shall comply with 4.3. Two accessible parking spaces may share a common access aisle (see Fig. 9). *Parked vehicle overhangs shall not reduce the clear width of an accessible route. Parking spaces and access aisles shall be level with surface slopes not exceeding 1:50 (2%) in all directions.*

4.6.4* Signage. Accessible parking spaces shall be designated as reserved by a sign showing the symbol of accessibility (see 4.30.7). *Spaces complying with 4.1.2(5)(b) shall have an additional sign "Van-Accessible" mounted below the symbol of accessibility. Such signs shall be located so they cannot be obscured by a vehicle parked in the space.*

4.6.5* Vertical Clearance. *Provide minimum vertical clearance of 114 in (2895 mm) at accessible passenger loading zones and along at least one vehicle access route to such areas from site entrance(s) and exit(s). At parking spaces complying with 4.1.2(5)(b), provide minimum vertical clearance of 98 in (2490 mm) at the parking space and along at least one vehicle access route to such spaces from site entrance(s) and exit(s).*

4.6.6 Passenger Loading Zones. Passenger loading zones shall provide an access aisle at least 60 in (1525 mm) wide and 20 ft (240 in) (6100 mm) long adjacent and parallel to the vehicle pull-up space (see Fig. 10). If there are curbs between the access aisle and the vehicle pull-up space, then a curb ramp complying with 4.7 shall be provided. *Vehicle standing spaces and access aisles shall be level with*

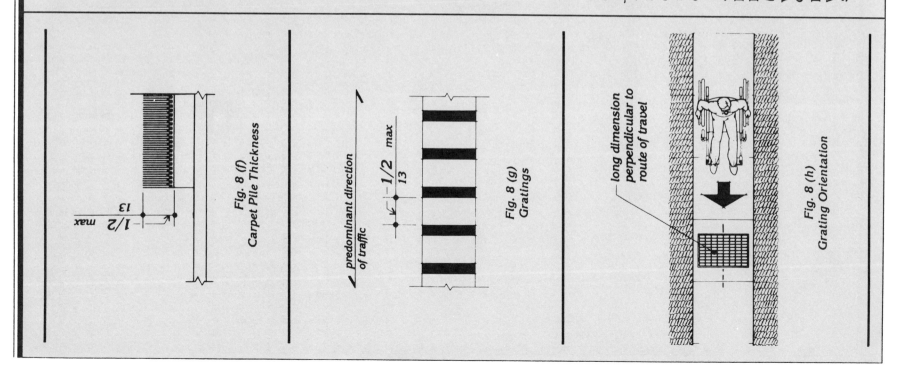

1/2 max
13

Fig. 8 (f)
Carpet Pile Thickness

predominant direction
of traffic

1/2 max
13

Fig. 8 (g)
Gratings

long dimension
perpendicular to
route of travel

Fig. 8 (h)
Grating Orientation

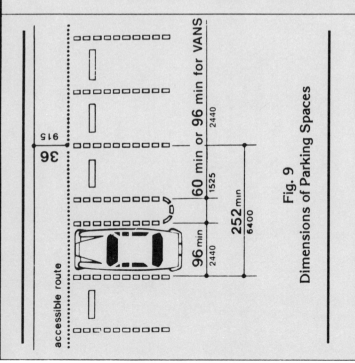

accessible route

36
915

96 min
2440

60 min or 96 min for VANS
1525   2440

252 min
6400

**Fig. 9
Dimensions of Parking Spaces**

surface slopes not exceeding 1:50 (2%) in all directions.

4.7 Curb Ramps.

4.7.1 Location. Curb ramps complying with 4.7 shall be provided wherever an accessible route crosses a curb.

4.7.2 Slope. Slopes of curb ramps shall comply with 4.8.2. The slope shall be measured as shown in Fig. 11. *Transitions from ramps to walks, gutters, or streets shall be flush and free of abrupt changes. Maximum slopes of adjoining gutters, road surface immediately adjacent to the curb ramp, or accessible route shall not exceed 1:20.*

4.7.3 Width. The minimum width of a curb ramp shall be 36 in (915 mm), exclusive of flared sides.

4.7.4 Surface. Surfaces of curb ramps shall comply with 4.5.

4.7.5 Sides of Curb Ramps. If a curb ramp is located where pedestrians must walk across the ramp, *or where it is not protected by hand-rails or guardrails*, it shall have flared sides; the maximum slope of the flare shall be 1:10 (see Fig. 12(a)). Curb ramps with returned curbs

may be used where pedestrians would not normally walk across the ramp (see Fig. 12(b)).

4.7.6 Built-up Curb Ramps. Built-up curb ramps shall be located so that they do not project into vehicular traffic lanes (see Fig. 13).

4.7.7 Detectable Warnings. A curb ramp shall have a *detectable* warning complying with 4.29.2. *The detectable warning shall extend the full width and depth of the curb ramp.*

4.7.8 Obstructions. Curb ramps shall be located or protected to prevent their obstruction by parked vehicles.

4.7.9 Location at Marked Crossings. Curb ramps at marked crossings shall be wholly contained within the markings, excluding any flared sides (see Fig. 15).

4.7.10 Diagonal Curb Ramps. If diagonal (or corner type) curb ramps have returned curbs or other well-defined edges, such edges shall be parallel to the direction of pedestrian flow. The bottom of diagonal curb ramps shall have 48 in (1220 mm) minimum clear space as shown in Fig. 15(c) and (d). If diagonal curb ramps are provided at marked crossings, the 48 in (1220 mm) clear space shall be within the markings (see Fig. 15(c) and (d)). If diagonal curb ramps have flared sides, they shall also have at least a 24 in (610 mm) long segment of straight curb located on each side of the curb ramp and within the marked crossing (see Fig. 15(c)).

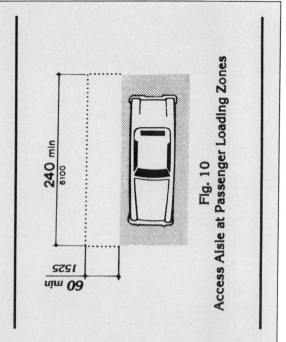

240 min
6100

60 min
1525

**Fig. 10
Access Aisle at Passenger Loading Zones**

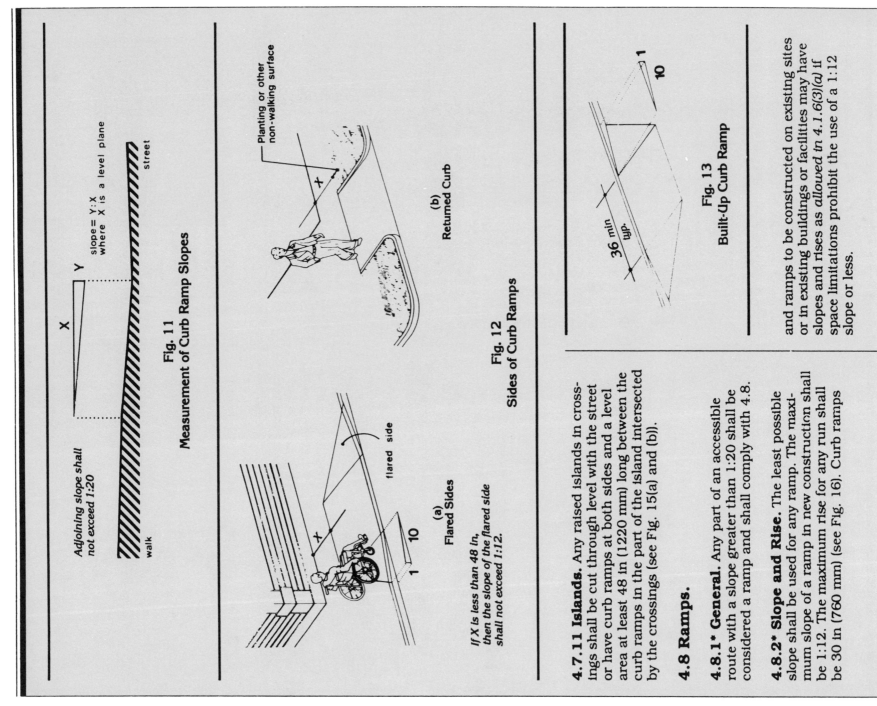

X

Y

slope = Y:X
where X is a level plane

*Adjoining slope shall
not exceed 1:20*

walk

street

**Fig. 11
Measurement of Curb Ramp Slopes**

flared side

X

1

10

**(a)
Flared Sides**

*If X is less than 48 in,
then the slope of the flared side
shall not exceed 1:12.*

Planting or other
non-walking surface

X

**(b)
Returned Curb**

**Fig. 12
Sides of Curb Ramps**

36 min
typ.

1

10

**Fig. 13
Built-Up Curb Ramp**

4.7.11 Islands. Any raised islands in crossings shall be cut through level with the street or have curb ramps at both sides and a level area at least 48 in (1220 mm) long between the curb ramps in the part of the island intersected by the crossings (see Fig. 15(a) and (b)).

4.8 Ramps.

4.8.1* General. Any part of an accessible route with a slope greater than 1:20 shall be considered a ramp and shall comply with 4.8.

4.8.2* Slope and Rise. The least possible slope shall be used for any ramp. The maximum slope of a ramp in new construction shall be 1:12. The maximum rise for any run shall be 30 in (760 mm) (see Fig. 16). Curb ramps

and ramps to be constructed on existing sites or in existing buildings or facilities may have slopes and rises as *allowed in 4.1.6(3)(a)* if space limitations prohibit the use of a 1:12 slope or less.

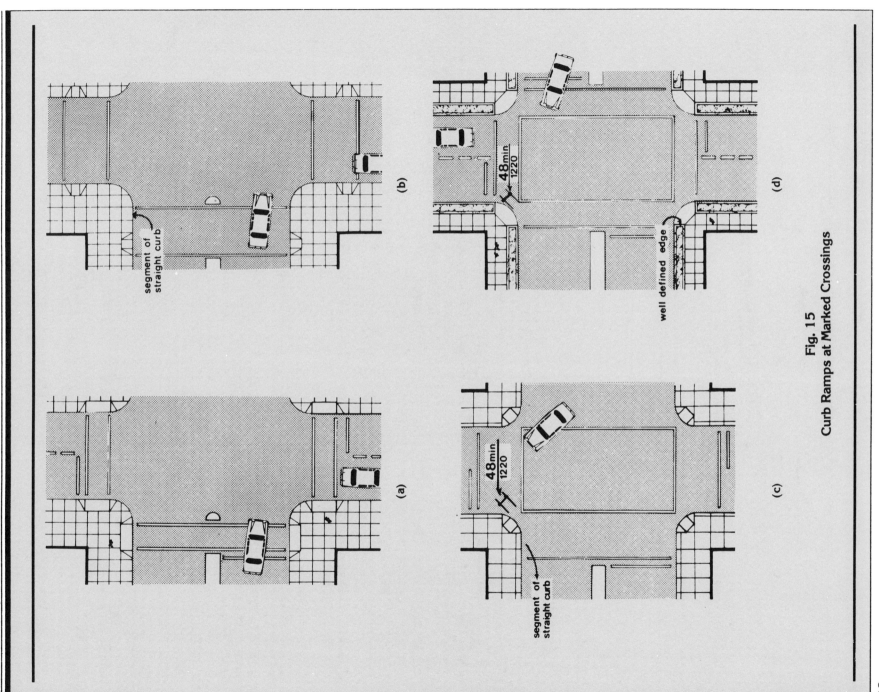

Fig. 15
Curb Ramps at Marked Crossings

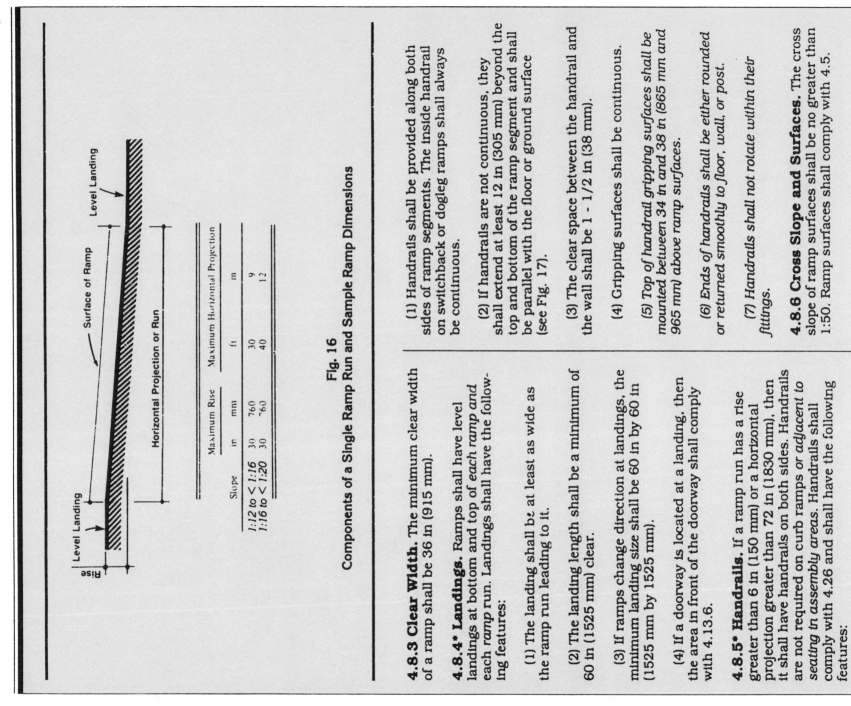

	Maximum Rise		Maximum Horizontal Projection		
Slope	in	mm	ft	m	
1:12 to < 1:16	30	760	30	9	
1:16 to < 1:20	30	760	40	12	

Fig. 16

Components of a Single Ramp Run and Sample Ramp Dimensions

4.8.3 Clear Width. The minimum clear width of a ramp shall be 36 in (915 mm).

4.8.4* Landings. Ramps shall have level landings at bottom and top of *each ramp and each ramp run*. Landings shall have the following features:

(1) The landing shall be at least as wide as the ramp run leading to it.

(2) The landing length shall be a minimum of 60 in (1525 mm) clear.

(3) If ramps change direction at landings, the minimum landing size shall be 60 in by 60 in (1525 mm by 1525 mm).

(4) If a doorway is located at a landing, then the area in front of the doorway shall comply with 4.13.6.

4.8.5* Handrails. If a ramp run has a rise greater than 6 in (150 mm) or a horizontal projection greater than 72 in (1830 mm), then it shall have handrails on both sides. Handrails are not required on curb ramps or *adjacent to seating in assembly areas*. Handrails shall comply with 4.26 and shall have the following features:

(1) Handrails shall be provided along both sides of ramp segments. The inside handrail on switchback or dogleg ramps shall always be continuous.

(2) If handrails are not continuous, they shall extend at least 12 in (305 mm) beyond the top and bottom of the ramp segment and shall be parallel with the floor or ground surface (see Fig. 17).

(3) The clear space between the handrail and the wall shall be 1 - 1/2 in (38 mm).

(4) Gripping surfaces shall be continuous.

(5) *Top of handrail gripping surfaces shall be mounted between 34 in and 38 in (865 mm and 965 mm) above ramp surfaces.*

(6) *Ends of handrails shall be either rounded or returned smoothly to floor, wall, or post.*

(7) *Handrails shall not rotate within their fittings.*

4.8.6 Cross Slope and Surfaces. The cross slope of ramp surfaces shall be no greater than 1:50. Ramp surfaces shall comply with 4.5.

4.8.7 Edge Protection. Ramps and landings with drop-offs shall have curbs, walls, railings, or projecting surfaces that prevent people from slipping off the ramp. Curbs shall be a minimum of 2 in (50 mm) high (see Fig. 17).

4.8.8 Outdoor Conditions. Outdoor ramps and their approaches shall be designed so that water will not accumulate on walking surfaces.

4.9 Stairs.

4.9.1* Minimum Number. *Stairs required to be accessible by 4.1 shall comply with 4.9.*

4.9.2 Treads and Risers. On any given flight of stairs, all steps shall have uniform riser heights and uniform tread widths. Stair treads shall be no less than 11 in (280 mm) wide, measured from riser to riser (see Fig. 18(a)). *Open risers are not permitted.*

4.9.3 Nosings. The undersides of nosings shall not be abrupt. The radius of curvature at the leading edge of the tread shall be no greater than 1/2 in (13 mm). Risers shall be sloped or the underside of the nosing shall have an angle not less than 60 degrees from the horizontal. Nosings shall project no more than 1-1/2 in (38 mm) (see Fig. 18).

4.9.4 Handrails. Stairways shall have handrails at both sides of all stairs. Handrails shall comply with 4.26 and shall have the following features:

(1) Handrails shall be continuous along both sides of stairs. The inside handrail on switchback or dogleg stairs shall always be continuous (see Fig. 19(a) and (b)).

(2) If handrails are not continuous, they shall extend at least 12 in (305 mm) beyond the top riser and at least 12 in (305 mm) plus the width of one tread beyond the bottom riser. At the top, the extension shall be parallel with the floor or ground surface. At the bottom, the handrail shall continue to slope for a distance of the width of one tread from the bottom riser; the remainder of the extension shall be horizontal (see Fig. 19(c) and (d)). Handrail extensions shall comply with 4.4.

(3) The clear space between handrails and wall shall be 1-1/2 in (38 mm).

(4) Gripping surfaces shall be uninterrupted by newel posts, other construction elements, or obstructions.

(5) *Top of handrail gripping surface shall be mounted between 34 in and 38 in (865 mm and 965 mm) above stair nosings.*

(6) *Ends of handrails shall be either rounded or returned smoothly to floor, wall or post.*

(7) *Handrails shall not rotate within their fittings.*

4.9.5 Detectable Warnings at Stairs. *(Reserved).*

4.9.6 Outdoor Conditions. Outdoor stairs and their approaches shall be designed so that water will not accumulate on walking surfaces.

4.10 Elevators.

4.10.1 General. *Accessible* elevators shall be on an accessible route and shall comply with 4.10 and with the ASME A17.1-1990. Safety Code for Elevators and Escalators. *Freight elevators shall not be considered as meeting the requirements of this section unless the only elevators provided are used as combination passenger and freight elevators for the public and employees.*

4.10.2 Automatic Operation. Elevator operation shall be automatic. Each car shall be equipped with a self-leveling feature that will automatically bring the car to floor landings within a tolerance of 1/2 in (13 mm) under rated loading to zero loading conditions. This self-leveling feature shall be automatic and independent of the operating device and shall correct the overtravel or undertravel.

4.10.3 Hall Call Buttons. Call buttons in elevator lobbies and halls shall be centered at 42 in (1065 mm) above the floor. Such call buttons shall have visual signals to indicate when each call is registered and when each call is answered. Call buttons shall be a minimum of 3/4 in (19 mm) in the smallest dimension. The button designating the up direction shall be on top. (See Fig. 20.) *Buttons shall be raised or flush. Objects mounted beneath hall call buttons shall not project into the elevator lobby more than 4 in (100 mm).*

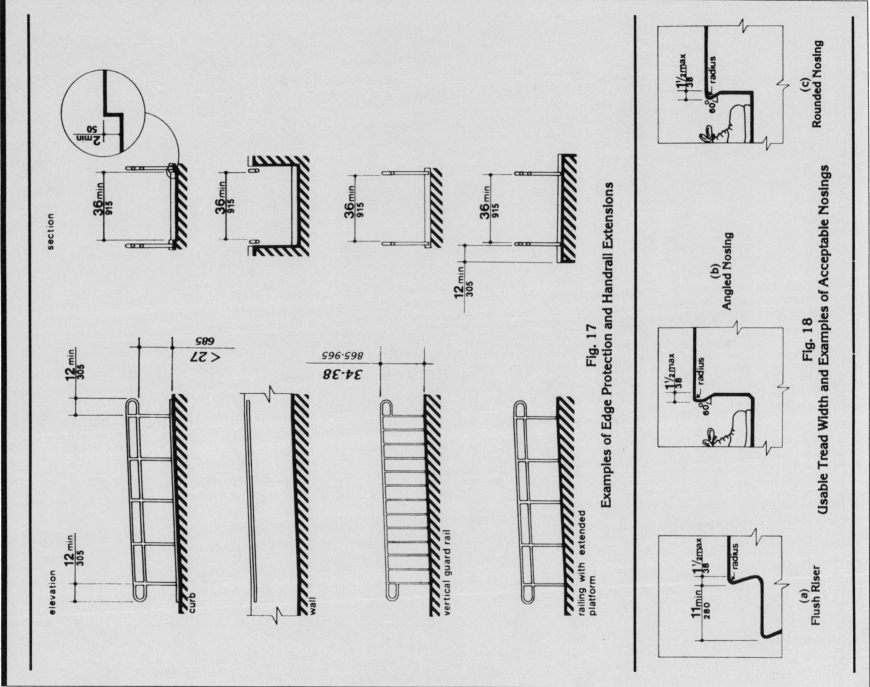

Fig. 17
Examples of Edge Protection and Handrail Extensions

Fig. 18
Usable Tread Width and Examples of Acceptable Nosings

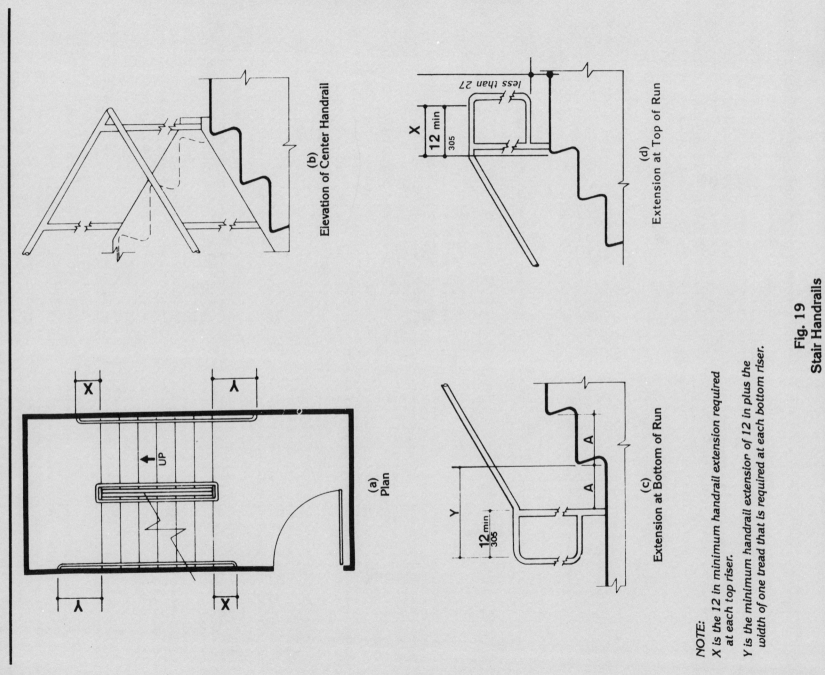

(b)
Elevation of Center Handrail

(a)
Plan

(c)
Extension at Bottom of Run

(d)
Extension at Top of Run

X
12 min
305

less than 27

Y
12 min
305

A A

NOTE:
X is the 12 in minimum handrail extension required at each top riser.

Y is the minimum handrail extension of 12 in plus the width of one tread that is required at each bottom riser.

Fig. 19
Stair Handrails

4.10.5 *Raised and Braille Characters on Hoistway Entrances.*

All elevator hoistway entrances shall have *raised and Braille floor* designations provided on both jambs. The centerline of the characters shall be 60 in (1525 mm) *above finish floor.* Such characters shall be 2 in (50 mm) high and shall comply with 4.30.4. Permanently applied plates are acceptable if they are permanently fixed to the jambs. (See Fig. 20).

4.10.6* Door Protective and Reopening Device.

Elevator doors shall open and close automatically. They shall be provided with a reopening device that will stop and reopen a car door and hoistway door automatically if the door becomes obstructed by an object or person. The device shall be capable of completing these operations without requiring contact for an obstruction passing through the opening at heights of 5 in and 29 in (125 mm and 735 mm) above finish floor (see Fig. 20). Door reopening devices shall remain effective for at least 20 seconds. After such an interval, doors may close in accordance with the requirements of *ASME A17.1-1990.*

4.10.7* Door and Signal Timing for Hall Calls.

The minimum acceptable time from notification that a car is answering a call until the doors of that car start to close shall be calculated from the following equation:

$$T = D/(1.5 \text{ ft/s}) \text{ or } T = D/(445 \text{ mm/s})$$

where T total time in seconds and D distance (in feet or millimeters) from a point in the lobby or corridor 60 in (1525 mm) directly in front of the farthest call button controlling that car to the centerline of its hoistway door (see Fig. 21). For cars with in-car lanterns, T begins when the lantern is visible from the vicinity of hall call buttons and an audible signal is sounded. *The minimum acceptable notification time shall be 5 seconds.*

4.10.8 Door Delay for Car Calls.

The minimum time for elevator doors to remain fully open in response to a car call shall be 3 seconds.

4.10.9 Floor Plan of Elevator Cars.

The floor area of elevator cars shall provide space for wheelchair users to enter the car, maneuver

---

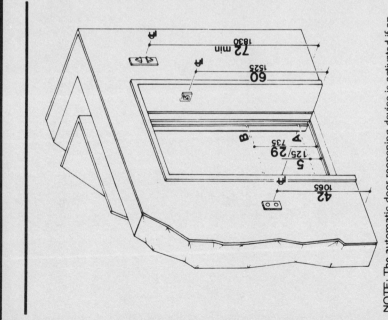

NOTE: The automatic door reopening device is activated if an object passes through either line A or line B. Line A and line B represent the vertical locations of the door reopening device not requiring contact.

Fig. 20

Hoistway and Elevator Entrances

4.10.4 Hall Lanterns.

A visible and audible signal shall be provided at each hoistway entrance to indicate which car is answering a call. Audible signals shall sound once for the up direction and twice for the down direction or shall have verbal annunciators that say "up" or "down." Visible signals shall have the following features:

(1) Hall lantern fixtures shall be mounted so that their centerline is at least 72 in (1830 mm) above the lobby floor. (See Fig. 20.)

(2) Visual elements shall be at least 2-1/2 in (64 mm) in the smallest dimension.

(3) Signals shall be visible from the vicinity of the hall call button (see Fig. 20). In-car lanterns located in cars, visible from the vicinity of hall call buttons, and conforming to the above requirements, shall be acceptable.

4.10.12 Car Controls

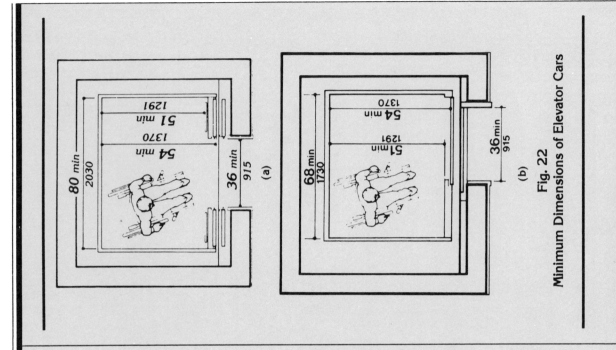

Fig. 22
Minimum Dimensions of Elevator Cars

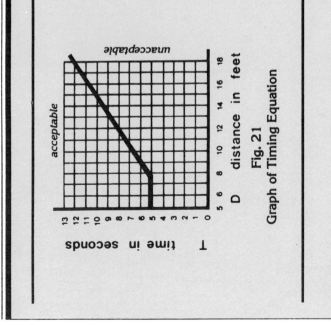

Fig. 21
Graph of Timing Equation

within reach of controls, and exit from the car. Acceptable door opening and inside dimensions shall be as shown in Fig. 22. The clearance between the car platform sill and the edge of any hoistway landing shall be no greater than 1-1/4 in (32 mm).

4.10.10 Floor Surfaces. Floor surfaces shall comply with 4.5.

4.10.11 Illumination Levels. The level of illumination at the car controls, platform, and car threshold and landing sill shall be at least 5 footcandles (53.8 lux).

4.10.12* Car Controls. Elevator control panels shall have the following features:

(1) Buttons. All control buttons shall be at least 3/4 in (19 mm) in their smallest dimension. They *shall be raised or flush.*

(2) Tactile, *Braille,* and Visual Control Indicators. All control buttons shall be designated by *Braille and by raised* standard alphabet characters for letters, arabic characters for numerals, or standard symbols as shown in Fig. 23(a), and as required in *ASME A17.1-1990. Raised and Braille characters and symbols* shall comply with 4.30. The call button for the main entry floor shall be designated by a *raised* star at the left of the floor designation (see Fig. 23(a)). All raised designations for control buttons shall be placed immediately to the left of the button to which they apply. Applied plates,

permanently attached, are an acceptable means to provide raised control designations. Floor buttons shall be provided with visual indicators to show when each call is registered. The visual indicators shall be extinguished when each call is answered.

(3) Height. All floor buttons shall be no higher than 54 in (1370 mm) above the *finish floor for side approach* and 48 in (1220 mm) *for front approach.* Emergency controls, including the emergency alarm and emergency stop, shall be grouped at the bottom of the panel and shall have their centerlines no less than 35 in (890 mm) above the finish floor (see Fig. 23(a) and (b)).

34

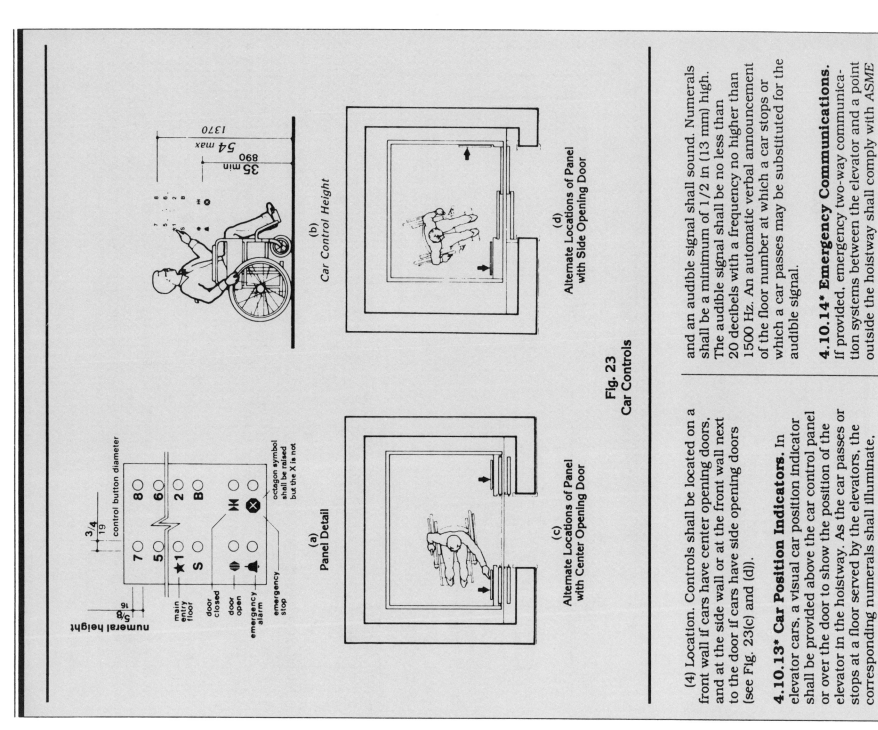

(a) Panel Detail

numeral height

3/4
19
control button diameter

5/8
16

7 ◯ 8 ◯
5 ◯ 6 ◯
★1 ◯ 2 ◯
S ◯ B ◯
⬗ ◯ ⊗ ◯

main entry floor
door closed
door open
emergency alarm
emergency stop

octagon symbol shall be raised but the X is not

(b) Car Control Height

35 min 890
54 max 1370

7 8
5 6
★1 2
S B
⬗ ⊗

(c) Alternate Locations of Panel with Center Opening Door

(d) Alternate Locations of Panel with Side Opening Door

Fig. 23
Car Controls

(4) Location. Controls shall be located on a front wall if cars have center opening doors, and at the side wall or at the front wall next to the door if cars have side opening doors (see Fig. 23(c) and (d)).

4.10.13* Car Position Indicators. In elevator cars, a visual car position indicator shall be provided above the car control panel or over the door to show the position of the elevator in the hoistway. As the car passes or stops at a floor served by the elevators, the corresponding numerals shall illuminate,

and an audible signal shall sound. Numerals shall be a minimum of 1/2 in (13 mm) high. The audible signal shall be no less than 20 decibels with a frequency no higher than 1500 Hz. An automatic verbal announcement of the floor number at which a car stops or which a car passes may be substituted for the audible signal.

4.10.14* Emergency Communications. If provided, emergency two-way communication systems between the elevator and a point outside the hoistway shall comply with *ASME*

35

A17.1-1990. The highest operable part of a two-way communication system shall be a maximum of 48 in (1220 mm) from the floor of the car. It shall be identified by a raised symbol and lettering complying with 4.30 and located adjacent to the device. If the system uses a handset then the length of the cord from the panel to the handset shall be at least 29 in (735 mm). If the system is located in a closed compartment the compartment door hardware shall conform to 4.27. Controls and Operating Mechanisms. The emergency intercommunication system shall not require voice communication.

4.11 Platform Lifts (*Wheelchair Lifts*).

4.11.1 Location. *Platform lifts (wheelchair lifts) permitted by 4.1 shall comply with the requirements of 4.11.*

4.11.2* Other Requirements. *If platform lifts (wheelchair lifts) are used, they shall comply with 4.2.4, 4.5, 4.27, and ASME A17.1 Safety Code for Elevators and Escalators, Section XX, 1990.*

4.11.3 Entrance. *If platform lifts are used then they shall facilitate unassisted entry, operation, and exit from the lift in compliance with 4.11.2.*

4.12 Windows.

4.12.1* General. *(Reserved).*

4.12.2* Window Hardware. *(Reserved).*

4.13 Doors.

4.13.1 General. *Doors required to be accessible by 4.1 shall comply with the requirements of 4.13.*

4.13.2 Revolving Doors and Turnstiles. Revolving doors or turnstiles shall not be the only means of passage at an accessible entrance or along an accessible route. An accessible gate or door shall be provided adjacent to the turnstile or revolving door and shall be so designed as to facilitate the same use pattern.

4.13.3 Gates. Gates, including ticket gates, shall meet all applicable specifications of 4.13.

4.13.4 Double-Leaf Doorways. If doorways have two *independently operated* door leaves, then at least one leaf shall meet the specifications in 4.13.5 and 4.13.6. That leaf shall be an active leaf.

4.13.5 Clear Width. Doorways shall have a minimum clear opening of 32 in (815 mm) with the door open 90 degrees, measured between the face of the door and the *opposite stop* (see Fig. 24(a), (b), (c), and (d)). Openings more than 24 in (610 mm) in depth shall comply with 4.2.1 and 4.3.3 (see Fig. 24(e)).

EXCEPTION: Doors not requiring full user passage, such as shallow closets, may have the clear opening reduced to 20 in (510 mm) minimum.

4.13.6 Maneuvering Clearances at Doors. Minimum maneuvering clearances at doors that are not automatic or power-assisted shall be as shown in Fig. 25. The floor or ground area within the required clearances shall be level and clear.

EXCEPTION: Entry doors to acute care hospital bedrooms for in-patients shall be exempted from the requirement for space at the latch side of the door (see dimension "x" in Fig. 25) if the door is at least 44 in (1120 mm) wide.

4.13.7 Two Doors in Series. The minimum space between two hinged or pivoted doors in series shall be 48 in (1220 mm) plus the width of any door swinging into the space. Doors in series shall swing either in the same direction or away from the space between the doors (see Fig. 26).

4.13.8* Thresholds at Doorways. Thresholds at doorways shall not exceed 3/4 in (19 mm) in height for exterior sliding doors or 1/2 in (13 mm) for other types of doors. Raised thresholds and floor level changes at accessible doorways shall be beveled with a slope no greater than 1:2 (see 4.5.2).

4.13.9* Door Hardware. Handles, pulls, latches, locks, and other operating devices on accessible doors shall have a shape that is easy

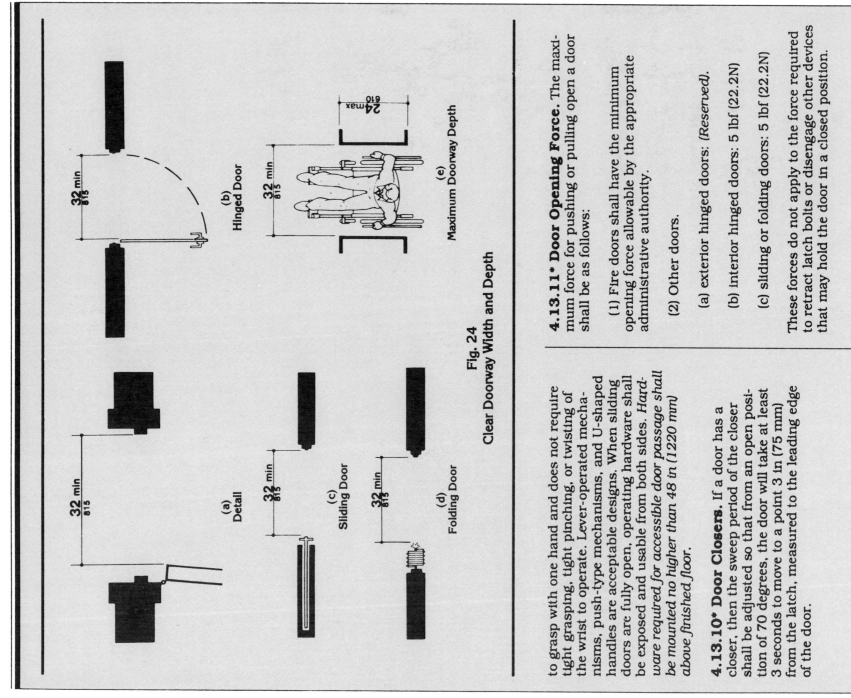

(a)
Detail

32 min
815

(b)
Hinged Door

32 min
815

(c)
Sliding Door

32 min
815

(d)
Folding Door

32 min
815

24 max
610

32 min
815

(e)
Maximum Doorway Depth

Fig. 24
Clear Doorway Width and Depth

to grasp with one hand and does not require tight grasping, tight pinching, or twisting of the wrist to operate. Lever-operated mechanisms, push-type mechanisms, and U-shaped handles are acceptable designs. When sliding doors are fully open, operating hardware shall be exposed and usable from both sides. *Hardware required for accessible door passage shall be mounted no higher than 48 in (1220 mm) above finished floor.*

4.13.10* Door Closers. If a door has a closer, then the sweep period of the closer shall be adjusted so that from an open position of 70 degrees, the door will take at least 3 seconds to move to a point 3 in (75 mm) from the latch, measured to the leading edge of the door.

4.13.11* Door Opening Force. The maximum force for pushing or pulling open a door shall be as follows:

(1) Fire doors shall have the minimum opening force allowable by the appropriate administrative authority.

(2) Other doors.

(a) exterior hinged doors: *(Reserved)*.

(b) interior hinged doors: 5 lbf (22.2N)

(c) sliding or folding doors: 5 lbf (22.2N)

These forces do not apply to the force required to retract latch bolts or disengage other devices that may hold the door in a closed position.

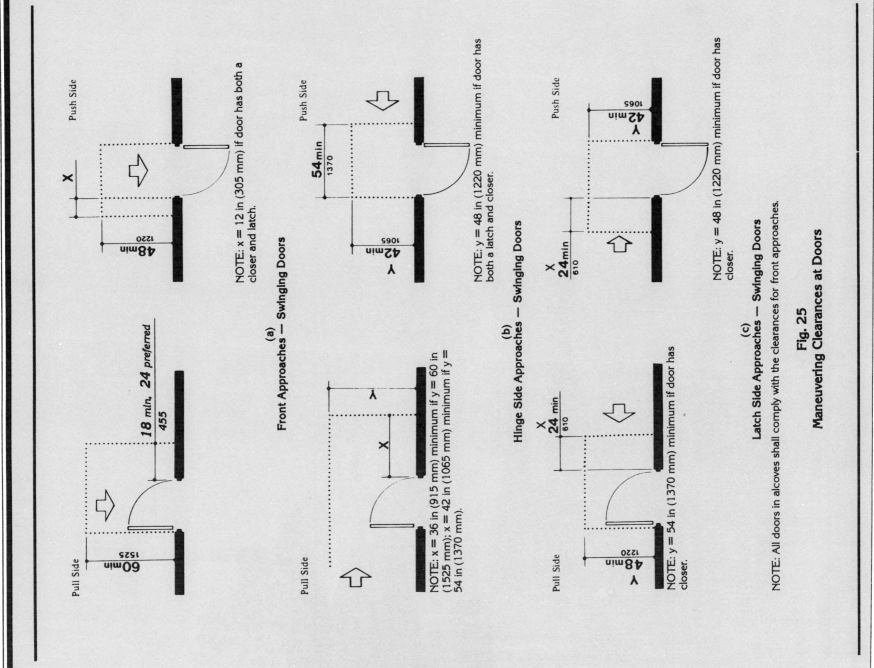

NOTE: x = 12 in (305 mm) if door has both a closer and latch.

Front Approaches — Swinging Doors

(a)

NOTE: x = 36 in (915 mm) minimum if y = 60 in (1525 mm); x = 42 in (1065 mm) minimum if y = 54 in (1370 mm).

NOTE: y = 48 in (1220 mm) minimum if door has both a latch and closer.

Hinge Side Approaches — Swinging Doors

(b)

NOTE: y = 54 in (1370 mm) minimum if door has closer.

NOTE: y = 48 in (1220 mm) minimum if door has closer.

Latch Side Approaches — Swinging Doors

(c)

NOTE: All doors in alcoves shall comply with the clearances for front approaches.

Fig. 25
Maneuvering Clearances at Doors

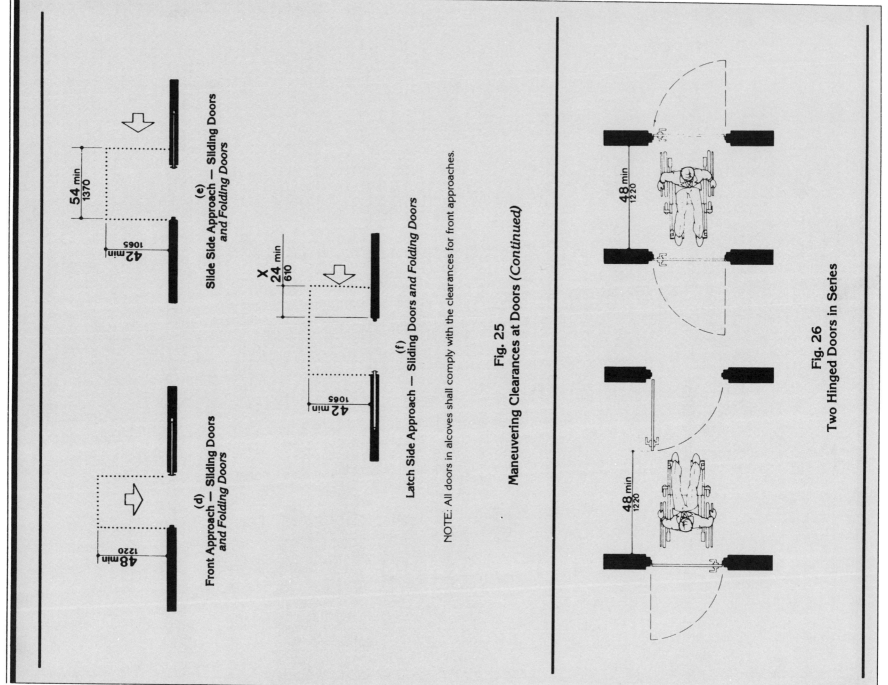

48 min
1220

Front Approach — Sliding Doors
and Folding Doors
(d)

42 min
1065

54 min
1370

Slide Side Approach — Sliding Doors
and Folding Doors
(e)

X
24 min
610

42 min
1065

Latch Side Approach — Sliding Doors and Folding Doors
(f)

NOTE: All doors in alcoves shall comply with the clearances for front approaches.

Fig. 25
Maneuvering Clearances at Doors (*Continued*)

48 min
1220

48 min
1220

Fig. 26
Two Hinged Doors in Series

4.13.12* Automatic Doors and Power-Assisted Doors. If an automatic door is used, then it shall comply with ANSI/BHMA A156.10-1985. Slowly opening, low-powered, automatic doors shall comply with ANSI A156.19-1984. Such doors shall not open to back check faster than 3 seconds and shall require no more than 15 lbf (66.6N) to stop door movement. If a power-assisted door is used, its door-opening force shall comply with 4.13.11 and its closing shall conform to the requirements in ANSI A156.19-1984.

4.14 Entrances.

4.14.1 Minimum Number. *Entrances required to be accessible by 4.1* shall be part of an accessible route complying with 4.3. Such entrances shall be connected by an accessible route to public transportation stops, to accessible parking and passenger loading zones, and to public streets or sidewalks if available (see 4.3.2(1)). They shall also be connected by an accessible route to all accessible spaces or elements within the building or facility.

4.14.2 Service Entrances. A service entrance shall not be the sole accessible entrance unless it is the only entrance to a building or facility (for example, in a factory or garage).

4.15 Drinking Fountains and Water Coolers.

4.15.1 Minimum Number. *Drinking fountains or water coolers required to be accessible by 4.1* shall comply with 4.15.

4.15.2* Spout Height. Spouts shall be no higher than 36 in (915 mm), measured from the floor or ground surfaces to the spout outlet (see Fig. 27(a)).

4.15.3 Spout Location. The spouts of drinking fountains and water coolers shall be at the front of the unit and shall direct the water flow in a trajectory that is parallel or nearly parallel to the front of the unit. The spout shall provide a flow of water at least 4 in (100 mm) high so as to allow the insertion of a cup or glass under the flow of water. *On an accessible drinking fountain with a round or oval bowl, the spout must be positioned so the flow of water is within 3 in (75 mm) of the front edge of the fountain.*

4.15.4 Controls. Controls shall comply with 4.27.4. *Unit controls shall be front mounted or side mounted near the front edge.*

4.15.5 Clearances.

(1) Wall- and post-mounted cantilevered units shall have a clear knee space between the bottom of the apron and the floor or ground at least 27 in (685 mm) high, 30 in (760 mm) wide, and 17 in to 19 in (430 mm to 485 mm) deep (see Fig. 27(a) and (b)). Such units shall also have a minimum clear floor space 30 in by 48 in (760 mm by 1220 mm) to allow a person in a wheelchair to approach the unit facing forward.

(2) Free-standing or built-in units not having a clear space under them shall have a clear floor space at least 30 in by 48 in (760 mm by 1220 mm) that allows a person in a wheelchair to make a parallel approach to the unit (see Fig. 27(c) and (d)). This clear floor space shall comply with 4.2.4.

4.16 Water Closets.

4.16.1 General. Accessible water closets shall comply with 4.16.

4.16.2 Clear Floor Space. Clear floor space for water closets not in stalls shall comply with Fig. 28. Clear floor space may be arranged to allow either a left-handed or right-handed approach.

4.16.3* Height. The height of water closets shall be 17 in to 19 in (430 mm to 485 mm), measured to the top of the toilet seat (see Fig. 29(b)). *Seats shall not be sprung to return to a lifted position.*

4.16.4* Grab Bars. Grab bars for water closets not located in stalls shall comply with 4.26 and Fig. 29. *The grab bar behind the water closet shall be 36 in (915 mm) minimum.*

4.16.5* Flush Controls. Flush controls shall be hand operated *or automatic* and shall comply with 4.27.4. Controls for flush valves shall be mounted on the wide side of toilet areas no more than 44 in (1120 mm) above the floor.

4.16.6 Dispensers. Toilet paper dispensers shall be installed within reach, as shown in Fig. 29(b). *Dispensers that control delivery, or that do not permit continuous paper flow, shall not be used.*

4.17 Toilet Stalls.

4.17.1 Location. Accessible toilet stalls shall be on an accessible route and shall meet the requirements of 4.17.

4.17.2 Water Closets. Water closets in accessible stalls shall comply with 4.16.

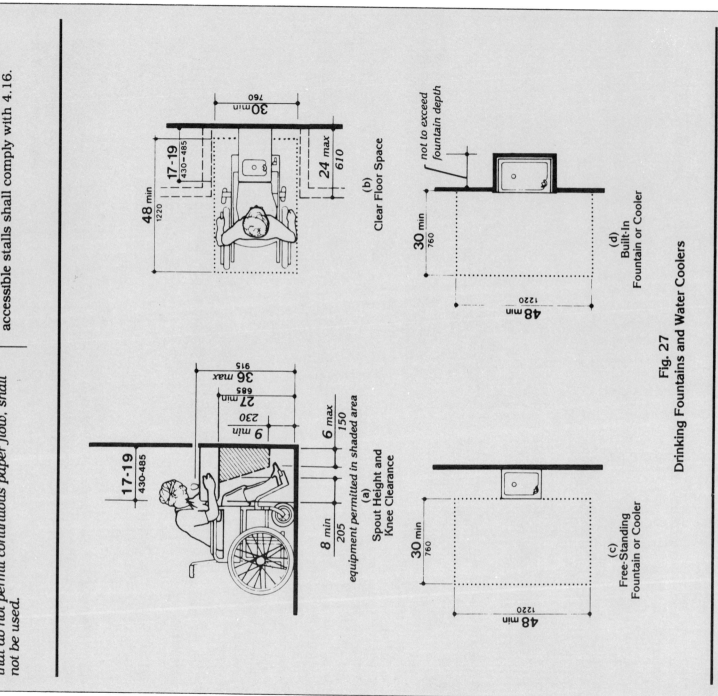

(a) Spout Height and Knee Clearance

(b) Clear Floor Space

(c) Free-Standing Fountain or Cooler

(d) Built-In Fountain or Cooler

Fig. 27
Drinking Fountains and Water Coolers

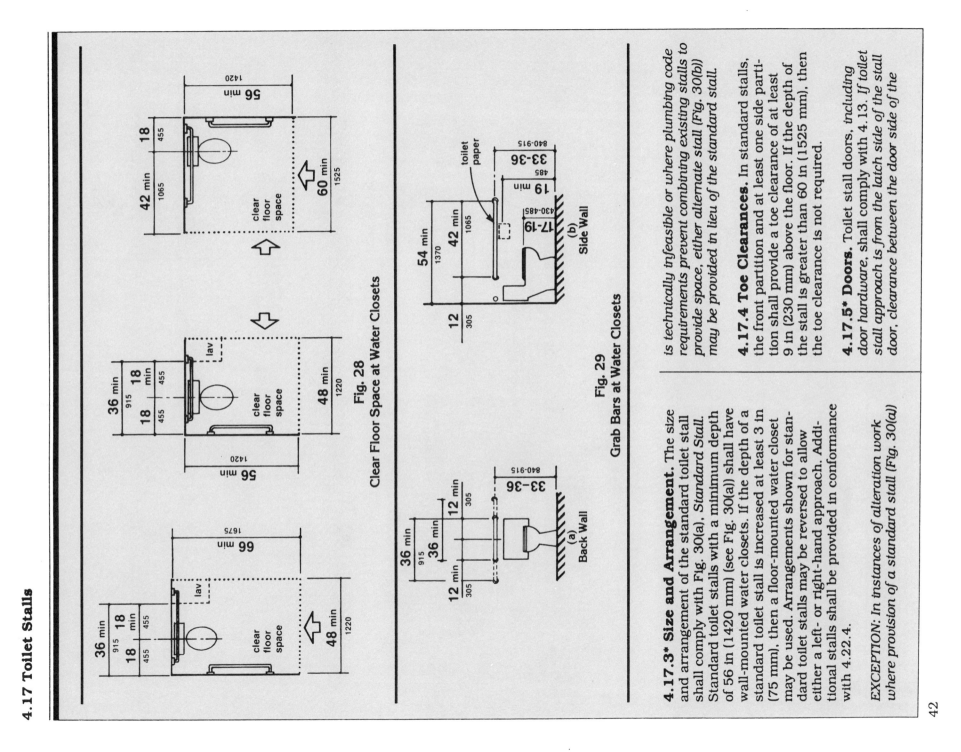

**Fig. 28
Clear Floor Space at Water Closets**

**Fig. 29
Grab Bars at Water Closets**

4.17.3* Size and Arrangement. The size and arrangement of the standard toilet stall shall comply with Fig. 30(a). *Standard Stall.* Standard toilet stalls with a minimum depth of 56 in (1420 mm) (see Fig. 30(a)) shall have wall-mounted water closets. If the depth of a standard toilet stall is increased at least 3 in (75 mm), then a floor-mounted water closet may be used. Arrangements shown for standard toilet stalls may be reversed to allow either a left- or right-hand approach. Additional stalls shall be provided in conformance with 4.22.4.

EXCEPTION: In instances of alteration work where provision of a standard stall (Fig. 30(a)

is technically infeasible or where plumbing code requirements prevent combining existing stalls to provide space, either alternate stall (Fig. 30(b)) may be provided in lieu of the standard stall.

4.17.4 Toe Clearances. In standard stalls, the front partition and at least one side partition shall provide a toe clearance of at least 9 in (230 mm) above the floor. If the depth of the stall is greater than 60 in (1525 mm), then the toe clearance is not required.

4.17.5* Doors. Toilet stall doors, *including door hardware,* shall comply with 4.13. If toilet stall approach is from the latch side of the stall door, clearance between the door side of the

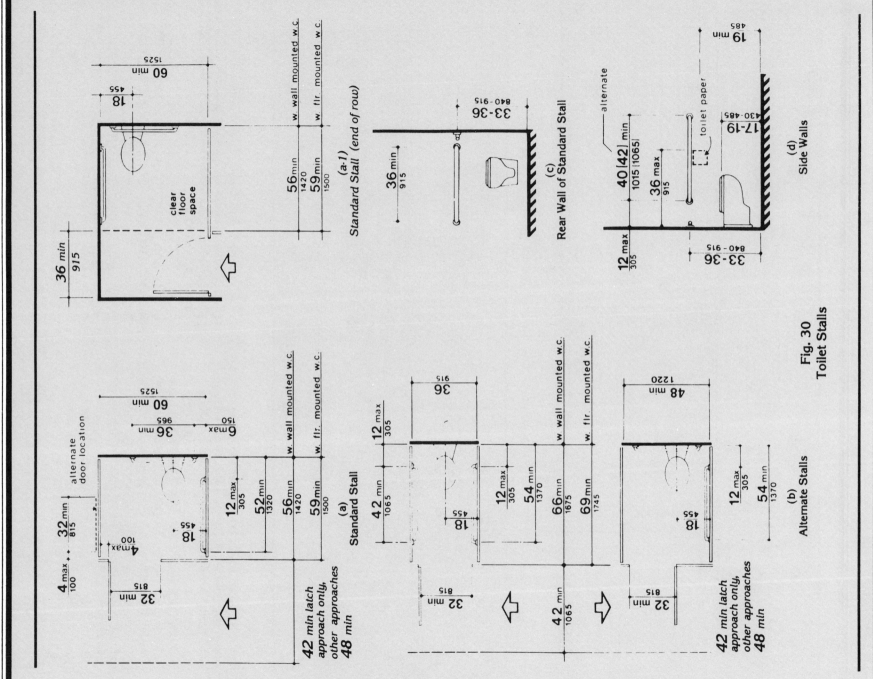

**Fig. 30
Toilet Stalls**

stall and any obstruction may be reduced to a minimum of 42 in (1065 mm) (Fig. 30).

4.17.6 Grab Bars. Grab bars complying with the length and positioning shown in Fig. 30(a), (b), (c), and (d) shall be provided. Grab bars may be mounted with any desired method as long as they have a gripping surface at the locations shown and do not obstruct the required clear floor area. Grab bars shall comply with 4.26.

4.18 Urinals.

4.18.1 General. Accessible urinals shall comply with 4.18.

4.18.2 Height. Urinals shall be stall-type or wall-hung with an elongated rim at a maximum of 17 in (430 mm) above the finish floor.

4.18.3 Clear Floor Space. A clear floor space 30 in by 48 in (760 mm by 1220 mm) shall be provided in front of urinals to allow forward approach. This clear space shall adjoin or overlap an accessible route and shall comply with 4.2.4. *Urinal shields that do not extend beyond the front edge of the urinal rim may be provided with 29 in (735 mm) clearance between them.*

4.18.4 Flush Controls. Flush controls shall be hand operated or automatic, and shall comply with 4.27.4, and shall be mounted no more than 44 in (1120 mm) above the finish floor.

4.19 Lavatories and Mirrors.

4.19.1 General. The requirements of 4.19 shall apply to lavatory fixtures, vanities, and built-in lavatories.

4.19.2 Height and Clearances. Lavatories shall be mounted with *the rim or counter surface no higher than 34 in (865 mm) above the finish floor.* Provide a clearance of at least 29 in (735 mm) above the finish floor to the bottom of the apron. Knee and toe clearance shall comply with Fig. 31.

4.19.3 Clear Floor Space. A clear floor space 30 in by 48 in (760 mm by 1220 mm) complying with 4.2.4 shall be provided in front of a lavatory to allow forward approach. Such

clear floor space shall adjoin or overlap an accessible route and shall extend a maximum of 19 in (485 mm) underneath the lavatory (see Fig. 32).

4.19.4 Exposed Pipes and Surfaces. Hot water and drain pipes under lavatories shall be insulated or otherwise *configured to protect against contact.* There shall be no sharp or abrasive surfaces under lavatories.

4.19.5 Faucets. Faucets shall comply with 4.27.4. Lever-operated, push-type, and electronically controlled mechanisms are examples of acceptable designs. *If self-closing valves are*

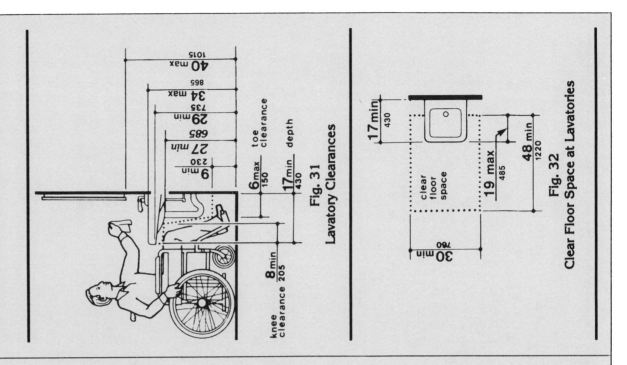

Fig. 31
Lavatory Clearances

Fig. 32
Clear Floor Space at Lavatories

used the faucet shall remain open for at least 10 seconds.

4.19.6* Mirrors. Mirrors shall be mounted with the bottom edge *of the reflecting surface* no higher than 40 in (1015 mm) *above the finish floor* (see Fig. 31).

4.20 Bathtubs.

4.20.1 General. Accessible bathtubs shall comply with 4.20.

4.20.2 Floor Space. Clear floor space in front of bathtubs shall be as shown in Fig. 33.

4.20.3 Seat. An in-tub seat or a seat at the head end of the tub shall be provided as shown in Fig. 33 and 34. The structural strength of seats and their attachments shall comply with 4.26.3. Seats shall be mounted securely and shall not slip during use.

4.20.4 Grab Bars. Grab bars complying with 4.26 shall be provided as shown in Fig. 33 and 34.

4.20.5 Controls. Faucets and other controls complying with 4.27.4 shall be located as shown in Fig. 34.

4.20.6 Shower Unit. A shower spray unit with a hose at least 60 in (1525 mm) long that can be used *both* as a fixed shower head *and* as a hand-held shower shall be provided.

4.20.7 Bathtub Enclosures. If provided, enclosures for bathtubs shall not obstruct controls or transfer from wheelchairs onto bathtub seats or into tubs. Enclosures on bathtubs shall not have tracks mounted on their rims.

4.21 Shower Stalls.

4.21.1* General. Accessible shower stalls shall comply with 4.21.

4.21.2 Size and Clearances. Except as specified in 9.1.2, shower stall size and clear floor space shall comply with Fig. 35(a) or (b). The shower stall in Fig. 35(a) shall be 36 in by 36 in (915 mm by 915 mm). Shower stalls required by 9.1.2 shall comply with Fig. 57(a)

or (b). The shower stall in Fig. 35(b) will fit into the space required for a bathtub.

4.21.3 Seat. A seat shall be provided in shower stalls 36 in by 36 in (915 mm by 915 mm) and shall be as shown in Fig. 36. The seat shall be mounted 17 in to 19 in (430 mm to 485 mm) from the bathroom floor and shall extend the full depth of the stall. In a 36 in by 36 in (915 mm by 915 mm) shower stall, the seat shall be on the wall opposite the controls. *Where a fixed seat is provided in a 30 in by 60 in minimum (760 mm by 1525 mm) shower stall, it shall be a folding type and shall be mounted on the wall adjacent to the controls as shown in Fig. 57.* The structural strength of seats and their attachments shall comply with 4.26.3.

4.21.4 Grab Bars. Grab bars complying with 4.26 shall be provided as shown in Fig. 37.

4.21.5 Controls. Faucets and other controls complying with 4.27.4 shall be located as shown in Fig. 37. In shower stalls 36 in by 36 in (915 mm by 915 mm), all controls, faucets, and the shower unit shall be mounted on the side wall opposite the seat.

4.21.6 Shower Unit. A shower spray unit with a hose at least 60 in (1525 mm) long that can be used *both* as a fixed shower head *and* as a hand-held shower shall be provided.

EXCEPTION: In unmonitored facilities where vandalism is a consideration, a fixed shower head mounted at 48 in (1220 mm) above the shower floor may be used in lieu of a hand-held shower head.

4.21.7 Curbs. If provided, curbs in shower stalls 36 in by 36 in (915 mm by 915 mm) shall be no higher than 1/2 in (13 mm). Shower stalls that are 30 in by 60 in (760 mm by 1525 mm) minimum shall not have curbs.

4.21.8 Shower Enclosures. If provided, enclosures for shower stalls shall not obstruct controls or obstruct transfer from wheelchairs onto shower seats.

4.22 Toilet Rooms.

4.22.1 Minimum Number. *Toilet facilities required to be accessible by 4.1 shall comply*

4.21 Shower Stalls

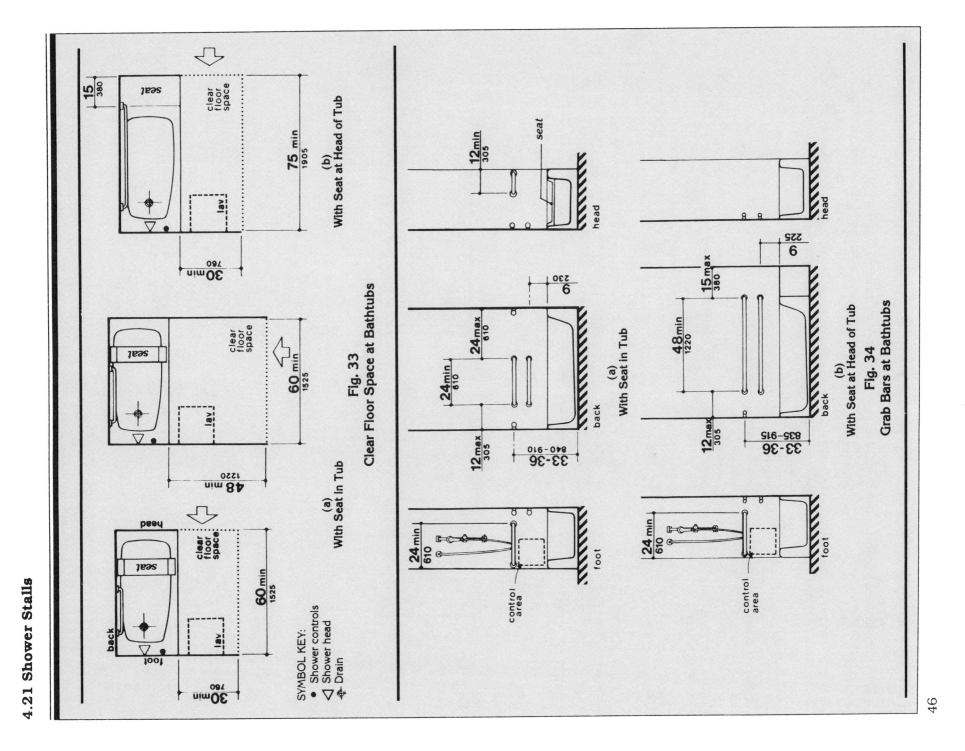

SYMBOL KEY:
● Shower controls
▽ Shower head
✛ Drain

(a)
With Seat in Tub

(b)
With Seat at Head of Tub

Fig. 33
Clear Floor Space at Bathtubs

(a)
With Seat in Tub

(b)
With Seat at Head of Tub
Fig. 34
Grab Bars at Bathtubs

with 4.22. Accessible toilet rooms shall be on an accessible route.

4.22.2 Doors. All doors to accessible toilet rooms shall comply with 4.13. Doors shall not swing into the clear floor space required for any fixture.

4.22.3* Clear Floor Space. The accessible fixtures and controls required in 4.22.4, 4.22.5, 4.22.6, and 4.22.7 shall be on an accessible route. An unobstructed turning space complying with 4.2.3 shall be provided within an accessible toilet room. The clear floor space at accessible fixtures and controls, the accessible route, and the turning space may overlap.

4.22.4 Water Closets. If toilet stalls are provided, then at least one shall be a standard

toilet stall complying with 4.17; *where 6 or more stalls are provided, in addition to the stall complying with 4.17.3, at least one stall 36 in (915 mm) wide with an outward swinging, self-closing door and parallel grab bars complying with Fig. 30(d) and 4.26 shall be provided. Water closets in such stalls shall comply with 4.16.* If water closets are not in stalls, then at least one shall comply with 4.16.

4.22.5 Urinals. If urinals are provided, *then* at least one shall comply with 4.18.

4.22.6 Lavatories and Mirrors. If lavatories and mirrors are provided, *then* at least one of each shall comply with 4.19.

4.22.7 Controls and Dispensers. If controls, dispensers, receptacles, or other

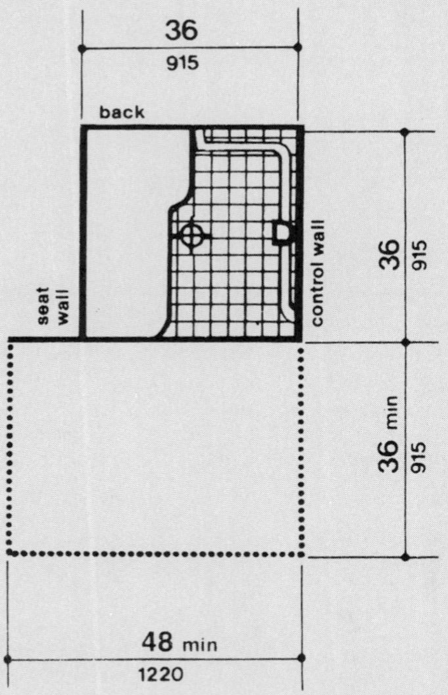

(a)
36-in by 36-in
(915-mm by 915-mm) Stall

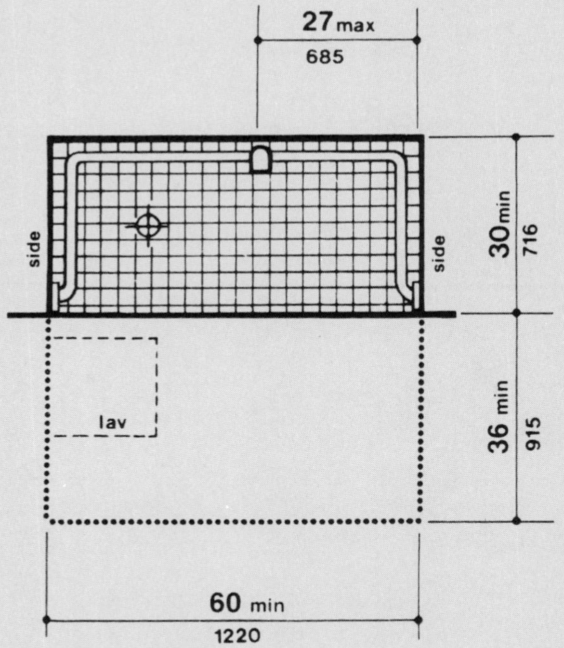

(b)
30-in by 60-in
(760-mm by 1525-mm) Stall

Fig. 35
Shower Size and Clearances

equipment are provided, *then* at least one of each shall be on an accessible route and shall comply with 4.27.

4.23 Bathrooms, Bathing Facilities, and Shower Rooms.

4.23.1 Minimum Number. Bathrooms, bathing facilities, or shower rooms *required to be accessible by 4.1* shall comply with 4.23 and shall be on an accessible route.

4.23.2 Doors. Doors to accessible bathrooms shall comply with 4.13. Doors shall not swing into the floor space required for any fixture.

4.23.3* Clear Floor Space. The accessible fixtures and controls required in 4.23.4, 4.23.5, 4.23.6, 4.23.7, 4.23.8, and 4.23.9 shall be on an accessible route. An unobstructed turning

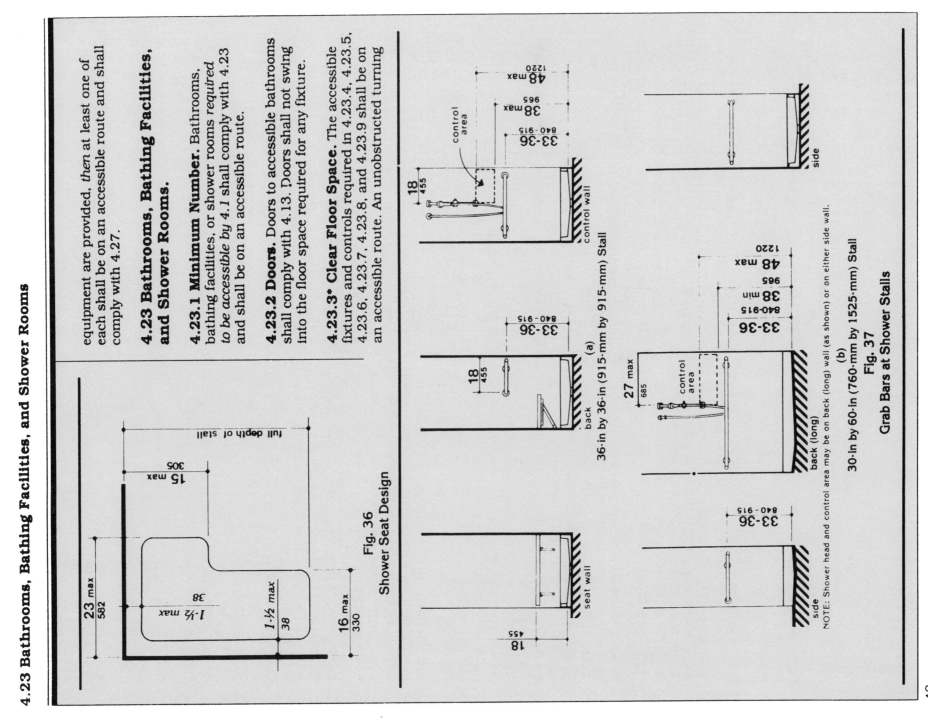

Fig. 36
Shower Seat Design

(a)
36-in by 36-in (915-mm by 915-mm) Stall

(b)
30-in by 60-in (760-mm by 1525-mm) Stall

NOTE: Shower head and control area may be on back (long) wall (as shown) or on either side wall.

Fig. 37
Grab Bars at Shower Stalls

vided underneath sinks.

4.24.4 Depth. Each sink shall be a maximum of 6-1/2 in (165 mm) deep.

4.24.5 Clear Floor Space. A clear floor space at least 30 in by 48 in (760 mm by 1220 mm) complying with 4.2.4 shall be provided in front of a sink to allow forward approach. The clear floor space shall be on an accessible route and shall extend a maximum of 19 in (485 mm) underneath the sink (see Fig. 32).

4.24.6 Exposed Pipes and Surfaces. Hot water and drain pipes exposed under sinks shall be insulated or otherwise configured so as to protect against contact. There shall be no sharp or abrasive surfaces under sinks.

4.24.7 Faucets. Faucets shall comply with 4.27.4. Lever-operated, push-type, touch-type, or electronically controlled mechanisms are acceptable designs.

4.25 Storage.

4.25.1 General. Fixed storage facilities such as cabinets, shelves, closets, and drawers required to be accessible by 4.1 shall comply with 4.25.

4.25.2 Clear Floor Space. A clear floor space at least 30 in by 48 in (760 mm by 1220 mm) complying with 4.2.4 that allows either a forward or parallel approach by a person using a wheelchair shall be provided at accessible storage facilities.

4.25.3 Height. Accessible storage spaces shall be within at least one of the reach ranges specified in 4.2.5 and 4.2.6 (see Fig. 5 and Fig. 6). Clothes rods or shelves shall be a maximum of 54 in (1370 mm) above the finish floor for a side approach. Where the distance from the wheelchair to the clothes rod or shelf exceeds 10 in (255 mm) (as in closets without accessible doors) the height and depth to the rod or shelf shall comply with Fig. 38(a) and Fig. 38(b).

4.25.4 Hardware. Hardware for accessible storage facilities shall comply with 4.27.4. Touch latches and U-shaped pulls are acceptable.

space complying with 4.2.3 shall be provided within an accessible bathroom. The clear floor spaces at fixtures and controls, the accessible route, and the turning space may overlap.

4.23.4 Water Closets. If toilet stalls are provided, then at least one shall be a standard toilet stall complying with 4.17; where 6 or more stalls are provided, in addition to the stall complying with 4.17.3, at least one stall 36 in (915 mm) wide with an outward swinging, self-closing door and parallel grab bars complying with Fig. 30(d) and 4.26 shall be provided. Water closets in such stalls shall comply with 4.16. If water closets are not in stalls, then at least one shall comply with 4.16.

4.23.5 Urinals. If urinals are provided, then at least one shall comply with 4.18.

4.23.6 Lavatories and Mirrors. If lavatories and mirrors are provided, then at least one of each shall comply with 4.19.

4.23.7 Controls and Dispensers. If controls, dispensers, receptacles, or other equipment are provided, then at least one of each shall be on an accessible route and shall comply with 4.27.

4.23.8 Bathing and Shower Facilities. If tubs or showers are provided, then at least one accessible tub that complies with 4.20 or at least one accessible shower that complies with 4.21 shall be provided.

4.23.9* Medicine Cabinets. If medicine cabinets are provided, at least one shall be located with a usable shelf no higher than 44 in (1120 mm) above the floor space. The floor space shall comply with 4.2.4.

4.24 Sinks.

4.24.1 General. Sinks required to be accessible by 4.1 shall comply with 4.24.

4.24.2 Height. Sinks shall be mounted with the counter or rim no higher than 34 in (865 mm) above the finish floor.

4.24.3 Knee Clearance. Knee clearance that is at least 27 in (685 mm) high, 30 in (760 mm) wide, and 19 in (485 mm) deep shall be pro-

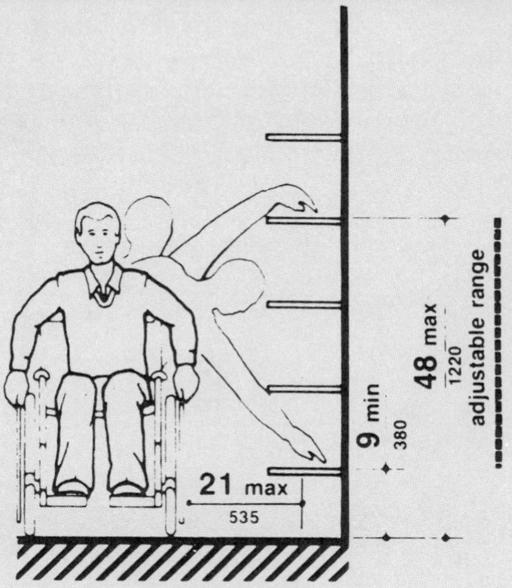

4.26 Handrails, Grab Bars, and Tub and Shower Seats

(a) Shelves

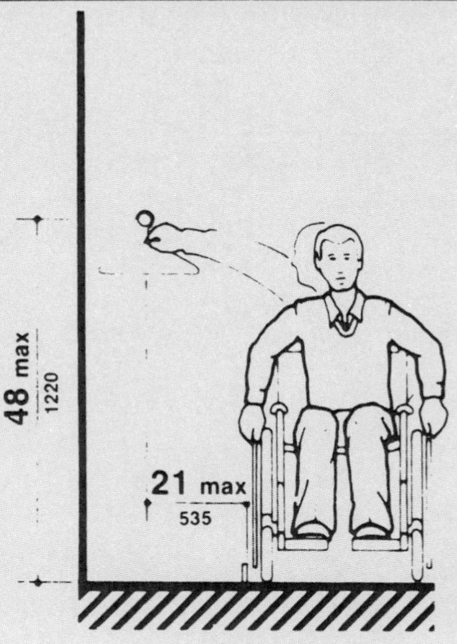

(b) Closets

Fig. 38
Storage Shelves and Closets

4.26 Handrails, Grab Bars, and Tub and Shower Seats.

4.26.1* General. All handrails, grab bars, and tub and shower seats *required to be accessible by 4.1, 4.8, 4.9, 4.16, 4.17, 4.20 or 4.21* shall comply with 4.26.

4.26.2* Size and Spacing of Grab Bars and Handrails. The diameter or width of the gripping surfaces of a handrail or grab bar shall be 1-1/4 in to 1-1/2 in (32 mm to 38 mm), or the shape shall provide an equivalent gripping surface. If handrails or grab bars are mounted adjacent to a wall, the space between the wall and the grab bar shall be 1-1/2 in (38 mm) (see Fig. 39(a), (b), (c), and (e)). Handrails may be located in a recess if the recess is a maximum of 3 in (75 mm) deep and extends at least 18 in (455 mm) above the top of the rail (see Fig. 39(d)).

4.26.3 Structural Strength. The structural strength of grab bars, tub and shower seats, fasteners, and mounting devices shall meet the following specification:

(1) Bending stress in a grab bar or seat induced by the maximum bending moment from the application of 250 lbf (1112N) shall

be less than the allowable stress for the material of the grab bar or seat.

(2) Shear stress induced in a grab bar or seat by the application of 250 lbf (1112N) shall be less than the allowable shear stress for the material of the grab bar or seat. If the connection between the grab bar or seat and its mounting bracket or other support is considered to be fully restrained, then direct and torsional shear stresses shall be totaled for the combined shear stress, which shall not exceed the allowable shear stress.

(3) Shear force induced in a fastener or mounting device from the application of 250 lbf (1112N) shall be less than the allowable lateral load of either the fastener or mounting device or the supporting structure, whichever is the smaller allowable load.

(4) Tensile force induced in a fastener by a direct tension force of 250 lbf (1112N) plus the maximum moment from the application of 250 lbf (1112N) shall be less than the allowable withdrawal load between the fastener and the supporting structure.

(5) Grab bars shall not rotate within their fittings.

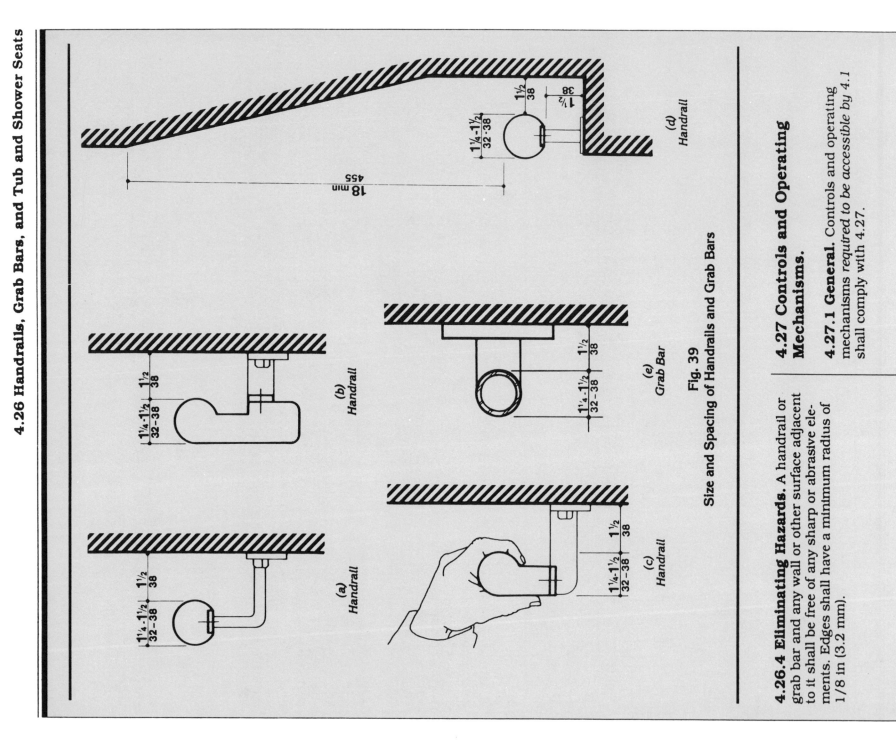

1¼-1½ 1½
32-38   38
(a)
Handrail

1¼-1½ 1½
32-38   38
(b)
Handrail

1¼-1½ 1½
32-38   38
(c)
Handrail

18 min
(455)

1¼-1½ 1½
32-38   38
(d)
Handrail

1¼-1½ 1½
32-38   38
(e)
Grab Bar

Fig. 39
Size and Spacing of Handrails and Grab Bars

4.26.4 Eliminating Hazards. A handrail or grab bar and any wall or other surface adjacent to it shall be free of any sharp or abrasive elements. Edges shall have a minimum radius of 1/8 in (3.2 mm).

4.27 Controls and Operating Mechanisms.

4.27.1 General. Controls and operating mechanisms required to be accessible by 4.1 shall comply with 4.27.

4.27.2 Clear Floor Space. Clear floor space complying with 4.2.4 that allows a forward or a parallel approach by a person using a wheelchair shall be provided at controls, dispensers, receptacles, and other operable equipment.

4.27.3* Height. The highest operable part of controls, dispensers, receptacles, and other operable equipment shall be placed within at least one of the reach ranges specified in 4.2.5 and 4.2.6. Electrical and communications system receptacles on walls shall be mounted no less than 15 in (380 mm) above the floor.

EXCEPTION: These requirements do not apply where the use of special equipment dictates otherwise or where electrical and communications systems receptacles are not normally intended for use by building occupants.

4.27.4 Operation. Controls and operating mechanisms shall be operable with one hand and shall not require tight grasping, pinching, or twisting of the wrist. The force required to activate controls shall be no greater than 5 lbf (22.2 N).

4.28 Alarms.

4.28.1 General. Alarm systems required to be accessible by 4.1 shall comply with 4.28. At a minimum, visual signal appliances shall be provided in buildings and facilities in each of the following areas: restrooms and any other general usage areas (e.g., meeting rooms), hallways, lobbies, and any other area for common use.

4.28.2* Audible Alarms. If provided, audible emergency alarms shall produce a sound that exceeds the prevailing equivalent sound level in the room or space by at least 15 dbA or exceeds any maximum sound level with a duration of 60 seconds by 5 dbA, whichever is louder. Sound levels for alarm signals shall not exceed 120 dbA.

4.28.3* Visual Alarms. Visual alarm signal appliances shall be integrated into the building or facility alarm system. If single station audible alarms are provided then single station visual alarm signals shall be provided. Visual alarm signals shall have the following minimum photometric and location features:

(1) The lamp shall be a xenon strobe type or equivalent.

(2) The color shall be clear or nominal white (i.e., unfiltered or clear filtered white light).

(3) The maximum pulse duration shall be two-tenths of one second (0.2 sec) with a maximum duty cycle of 40 percent. The pulse duration is defined as the time interval between initial and final points of 10 percent of maximum signal.

(4) The intensity shall be a minimum of 75 candela.

(5) The flash rate shall be a minimum of 1 Hz and a maximum of 3 Hz.

(6) The appliance shall be placed 80 in (2030 mm) above the highest floor level within the space or 6 in (152 mm) below the ceiling, whichever is lower.

(7) In general, no place in any room or space required to have a visual signal appliance shall be more than 50 ft (15 m) from the signal (in the horizontal plane). In large rooms and spaces exceeding 100 ft (30 m) across, without obstructions 6 ft (2 m) above the finish floor, such as auditoriums, devices may be placed around the perimeter, spaced a maximum 100 ft (30 m) apart, in lieu of suspending appliances from the ceiling.

(8) No place in common corridors or hallways in which visual alarm signalling appliances are required shall be more than 50 ft (15 m) from the signal.

4.28.4* Auxiliary Alarms. Units and sleeping accommodations shall have a visual alarm connected to the building emergency alarm system or shall have a standard 110-volt electrical receptacle into which such an alarm can be connected and a means by which a signal from the building emergency alarm system can trigger such an auxiliary alarm. When visual alarms are in place the signal shall be visible in all areas of the unit or room. Instructions for use of the auxiliary alarm or receptacle shall be provided.

4.29 Detectable Warnings.

4.29.1 General. Detectable warnings required by 4.1 and 4.7 shall comply with 4.29.

4.29.2* Detectable Warnings on Walking Surfaces. Detectable warnings shall consist of raised truncated domes with a diameter of nominal 0.9 in (23 mm), a height of nominal 0.2 in (5 mm) and a center-to-center spacing of nominal 2.35 in (60 mm) and shall contrast visually with adjoining surfaces, either light-on-dark, or dark-on-light.

The material used to provide contrast shall be an integral part of the walking surface. Detectable warnings used on interior surfaces shall differ from adjoining walking surfaces in resiliency or sound-on-cane contact.

4.29.3 Detectable Warnings on Doors To Hazardous Areas. (Reserved).

4.29.4 Detectable Warnings at Stairs. (Reserved).

4.29.5 Detectable Warnings at Hazardous Vehicular Areas. If a walk crosses or adjoins a vehicular way, and the walking surfaces are not separated by curbs, railings, or other elements between the pedestrian areas and vehicular areas, the boundary between the areas shall be defined by a continuous detectable warning which is 36 in (915 mm) wide, complying with 4.29.2.

4.29.6 Detectable Warnings at Reflecting Pools. The edges of reflecting pools shall be protected by railings, walls, curbs, or detectable warnings complying with 4.29.2.

4.29.7 Standardization. (Reserved).

4.30 Signage.

4.30.1* General. Signage required to be accessible by 4.1 shall comply with the applicable provisions of 4.30.

4.30.2* Character Proportion. Letters and numbers on signs shall have a width-to-height ratio between 3:5 and 1:1 and a stroke-width-to-height ratio between 1:5 and 1:10.

4.30.3 Character Height. Characters and numbers on signs shall be sized according to the viewing distance from which they are to be read. The minimum height is measured using an upper case X. Lower case characters are permitted.

Height Above Finished Floor	Minimum Character Height
Suspended or Projected Overhead in compliance with 4.4.2	3 in. (75 mm) minimum

4.30.4* Raised and Brailled Characters and Pictorial Symbol Signs (Pictograms). Letters and numerals shall be raised 1/32 in (0.8 mm) minimum, upper case, sans serif or simple serif type and shall be accompanied with Grade 2 Braille. Raised characters shall be at least 5/8 in (16 mm) high, but no higher than 2 in (50 mm). Pictograms shall be accompanied by the equivalent verbal description placed directly below the pictogram. The border dimension of the pictogram shall be 6 in (152 mm) minimum in height.

4.30.5* Finish and Contrast. The characters and background of signs shall be eggshell, matte, or other non-glare finish. Characters and symbols shall contrast with their background — either light characters on a dark background or dark characters on a light background.

4.30.6 Mounting Location and Height. Where permanent identification is provided for rooms and spaces, signs shall be installed on the wall adjacent to the latch side of the door. Where there is no wall space to the latch side of the door, including at double leaf doors, signs shall be placed on the nearest adjacent wall. Mounting height shall be 60 in (1525 mm) above the finish floor to the centerline of the sign. Mounting location for such signage shall be so that a person may approach within 3 in (76 mm) of signage without encountering protruding objects or standing within the swing of a door.

4.30.7* Symbols of Accessibility.

(1) Facilities and elements required to be identified as accessible by 4.1 shall use the international symbol of accessibility. The

symbol shall be displayed as shown in Fig. 43(a) and (b).

(2) Volume Control Telephones. Telephones required to have a volume control by 4.1.3(17)(b) shall be identified by a sign containing a depiction of a telephone handset with radiating sound waves.

(3) Text Telephones. Text telephones required by 4.1.3 (17)(c) shall be identified by the international TDD symbol (Fig 43(c)). In addition, if a facility has a public text telephone, directional signage indicating the location of the nearest text telephone shall be placed adjacent to all banks of telephones which do not contain a text telephone. Such directional signage shall include the international TDD symbol. If a facility has no banks of telephones, the directional signage shall be provided at the entrance (e.g., in a building directory).

(4) Assistive Listening Systems. In assembly areas where permanently installed assistive listening systems are required by 4.1.3(19)(b) the availability of such systems shall be identified with signage that includes the international symbol of access for hearing loss (Fig 43(d)).

4.30.8* Illumination Levels. *(Reserved).*

4.31 Telephones.

4.31.1 General. Public telephones required to be accessible by 4.1 shall comply with 4.31.

4.31.2 Clear Floor or Ground Space. A clear floor or ground space at least 30 in by 48 in (760 mm by 1220 mm) that allows either a forward or parallel approach by a person using a wheelchair shall be provided at telephones (see Fig. 44). The clear floor or ground space shall comply with 4.2.4. Bases, enclosures, and fixed seats shall not impede approaches to telephones by people who use wheelchairs.

4.31.3* Mounting Height. The highest operable part of the telephone shall be within the reach ranges specified in 4.2.5 or 4.2.6.

4.31.4 Protruding Objects. *Telephones shall comply with 4.4.*

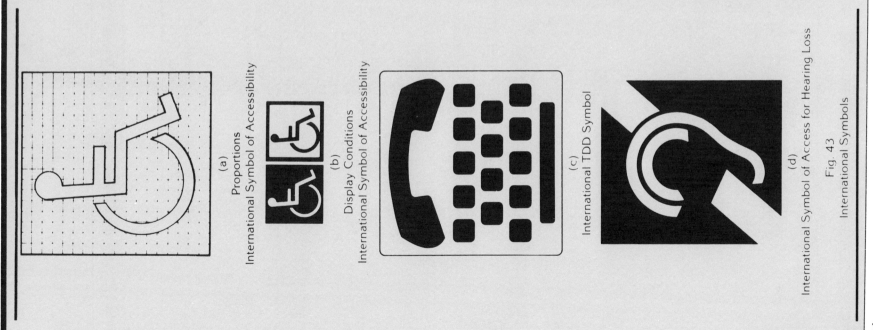

(a)
Proportions
International Symbol of Accessibility

(b)
Display Conditions
International Symbol of Accessibility

(c)
International TDD Symbol

(d)
International Symbol of Access for Hearing Loss

Fig. 43
International Symbols

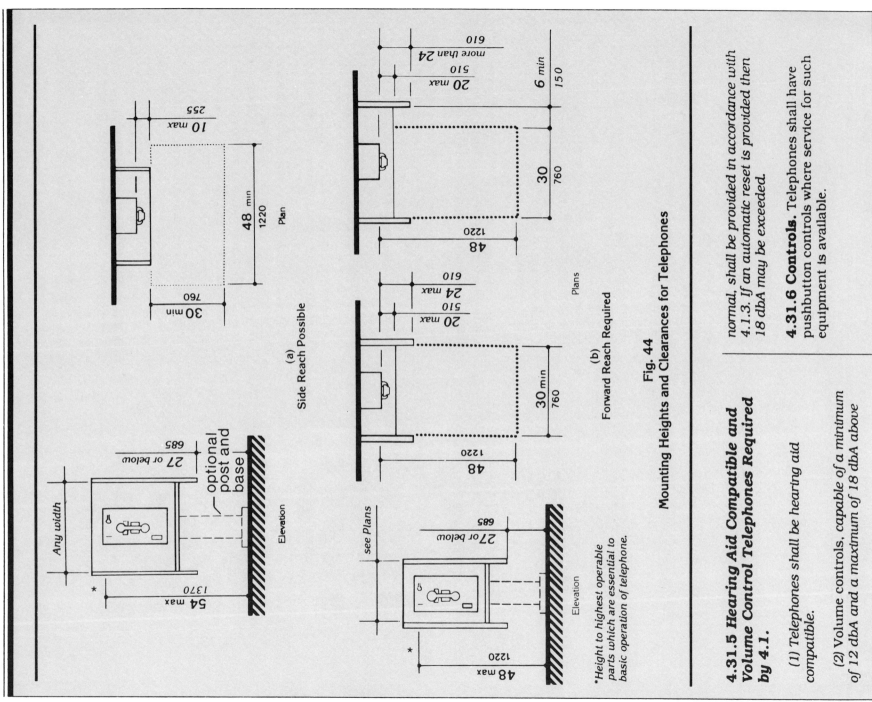

(a)

Side Reach Possible

(b)

Forward Reach Required

Fig. 44

Mounting Heights and Clearances for Telephones

*Height to highest operable parts which are essential to basic operation of telephone.

4.31.5 Hearing Aid Compatible and Volume Control Telephones Required by 4.1.

(1) Telephones shall be hearing aid compatible.

(2) Volume controls, capable of a minimum of 12 dbA and a maximum of 18 dbA above

normal, shall be provided in accordance with 4.1.3. If an automatic reset is provided then 18 dbA may be exceeded.

4.31.6 Controls. Telephones shall have pushbutton controls where service for such equipment is available.

4.31.7 Telephone Books. Telephone books, if provided, shall be located in a position that complies with the reach ranges specified in 4.2.5 and 4.2.6.

4.31.8 Cord Length. The cord from the telephone to the handset shall be at least 29 in (735 mm) long.

4.31.9* Text Telephones Required by 4.1.

(1) Text telephones used with a pay telephone shall be permanently affixed within, or adjacent to, the telephone enclosure. If an acoustic coupler is used, the telephone cord shall be sufficiently long to allow connection of the text telephone and the telephone receiver.

(2) Pay telephones designed to accommodate a portable text telephone shall be equipped with a shelf and an electrical outlet within or adjacent to the telephone enclosure. The telephone handset shall be capable of being placed flush on the surface of the shelf. The shelf shall be capable of accommodating a text telephone and shall have 6 in (152 mm) minimum vertical clearance in the area where the text telephone is to be placed.

(3) Equivalent facilitation may be provided. For example, a portable text telephone may be made available in a hotel at the registration desk if it is available on a 24-hour basis for use with nearby public pay telephones. In this instance, at least one pay telephone shall comply with paragraph 2 of this section. In addition, if an acoustic coupler is used, the telephone handset cord shall be sufficiently long so as to allow connection of the text telephone and the telephone receiver. Directional signage shall be provided and shall comply with 4.30.7.

4.32 Fixed or Built-in Seating and Tables.

4.32.1 Minimum Number. Fixed or built-in seating or tables required to be accessible by 4.1 shall comply with 4.32.

4.32.2 Seating. If seating spaces for people in wheelchairs are provided at fixed tables or counters, clear floor space complying with 4.2.4 shall be provided. Such clear floor space shall not overlap knee space by more than 19 in (485 mm) (see Fig. 45).

4.32.3 Knee Clearances. If seating for people in wheelchairs is provided at tables or counters, knee spaces at least 27 in (685 mm) high, 30 in (760 mm) wide, and 19 in (485 mm) deep shall be provided (see Fig. 45).

4.32.4* Height of Tables or Counters. The tops of *accessible* tables and *counters* shall be from 28 to 34 in (710 mm to 865 mm) *above the finish floor or ground.*

4.33 Assembly Areas.

4.33.1 Minimum Number. *Assembly and associated areas required to be accessible by 4.1 shall comply with 4.33.*

4.33.2* Size of Wheelchair Locations. Each wheelchair location shall provide minimum clear ground or floor spaces as shown in Fig. 46.

4.33.3* Placement of Wheelchair Locations. Wheelchair areas shall be an integral part of any fixed seating plan and shall be provided so as to provide people with physical disabilities a choice of admission prices and lines of sight comparable to those for members of the general public. They shall adjoin an accessible route that also serves as a means of egress in case of emergency. At least one companion fixed seat shall be provided next to each wheelchair seating area. When the seating capacity exceeds 300, wheelchair spaces shall be provided in more than one location. Readily removable seats may be installed in wheelchair spaces when the spaces are not required to accommodate wheelchair users.

EXCEPTION: Accessible viewing positions may be clustered for bleachers, balconies, and other areas having sight lines that require slopes of greater than 5 percent. Equivalent accessible viewing positions may be located on levels having accessible egress.

4.33.4 Surfaces. The ground or floor at wheelchair locations shall be level and shall comply with 4.5.

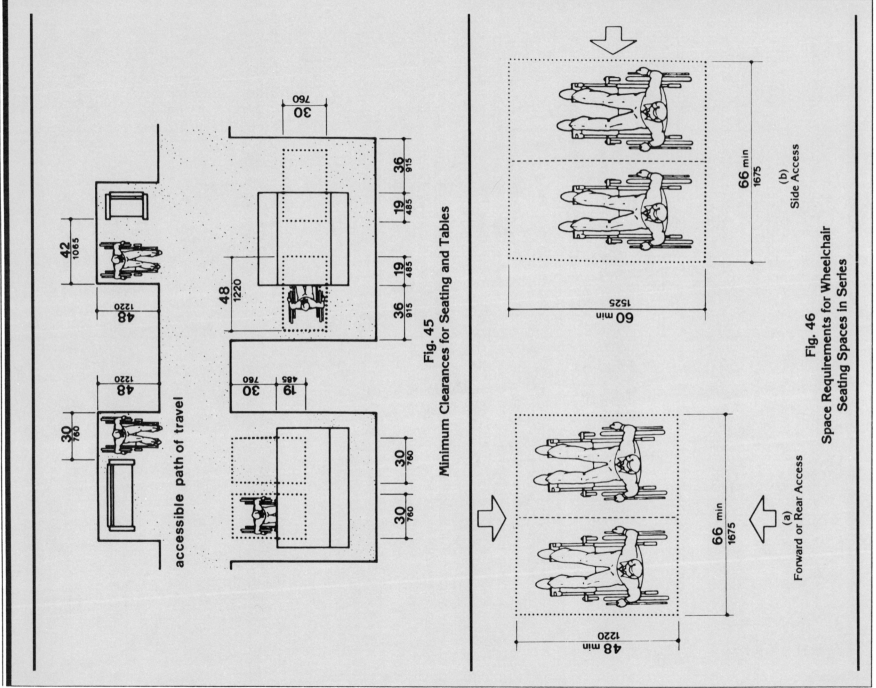

accessible path of travel

Fig. 45
Minimum Clearances for Seating and Tables

Fig. 46
Space Requirements for Wheelchair
Seating Spaces in Series

(a)
Forward or Rear Access

(b)
Side Access

4.35 Dressing and Fitting Rooms.

4.35.1 General. Dressing and fitting rooms required to be accessible by 4.1 shall comply with 4.35 and shall be on an accessible route.

4.35.2 Clear Floor Space. A clear floor space allowing a person using a wheelchair to make a 180-degree turn shall be provided in every accessible dressing room entered through a swinging or sliding door. No door shall swing into any part of the turning space. Turning space shall not be required in a private dressing room entered through a curtained opening at least 32 in (815 mm) wide if clear floor space complying with section 4.2 renders the dressing room usable by a person using a wheelchair.

4.35.3 Doors. All doors to accessible dressing rooms shall be in compliance with section 4.13.

4.35.4 Bench. Every accessible dressing room shall have a 24 in by 48 in (610 mm by 1220 mm) bench fixed to the wall along the longer dimension. The bench shall be mounted 17 in to 19 in (430 mm to 485 mm) above the finish floor. Clear floor space shall be provided alongside the bench to allow a person using a wheelchair to make a parallel transfer onto the bench. The structural strength of the bench and attachments shall comply with 4.26.3. Where installed in conjunction with showers, swimming pools, or other wet locations, water shall not accumulate upon the surface of the bench and the bench shall have a slip-resistant surface.

4.35.5 Mirror. Where mirrors are provided in dressing rooms of the same use, then in an accessible dressing room, a full-length mirror, measuring at least 18 in wide by 54 in high (460 mm by 1370 mm), shall be mounted in a position affording a view to a person on the bench as well as to a person in a standing position.

NOTE: Sections 4.1.1 through 4.1.7 and sections 5 through 10 are different from ANSI A117.1 in their entirety and are printed in standard type.

4.33.5 Access to Performing Areas.
An accessible route shall connect wheelchair seating locations with performing areas, including stages, arena floors, dressing rooms, locker rooms, and other spaces used by performers.

4.33.6* Placement of Listening Systems.
If the listening system provided serves individual fixed seats, then such seats shall be located within a 50 ft (15 m) viewing distance of the stage or playing area and shall have a complete view of the stage or playing area.

4.33.7* Types of Listening Systems.
Assistive listening systems (ALS) are intended to augment standard public address and audio systems by providing signals which can be received directly by persons with special receivers or their own hearing aids and which eliminate or filter background noise. The type of assistive listening system appropriate for a particular application depends on the characteristics of the setting, the nature of the program, and the intended audience. Magnetic induction loops, infra-red and radio frequency systems are types of listening systems which are appropriate for various applications.

4.34 Automated Teller Machines.

4.34.1 General. Each machine required to be accessible by 4.1.3 shall be on an accessible route and shall comply with 4.34.

4.34.2 Controls. Controls for user activation shall comply with the requirements of 4.27.

4.34.3 Clearances and Reach Range. Free standing or built-in units not having a clear space under them shall comply with 4.27.2 and 4.27.3 and provide for a parallel approach and both a forward and side reach to the unit allowing a person in a wheelchair to access the controls and dispensers.

4.34.4 Equipment for Persons with Vision Impairments.
Instructions and all information for use shall be made accessible to and independently usable by persons with vision impairments.

5. RESTAURANTS AND CAFETERIAS.

5.1* General. Except as specified or modified in this section, restaurants and cafeterias shall comply with the requirements of 4.1 to 4.35. Where fixed tables (or dining counters where food is consumed but there is no service) are provided, at least 5 percent, but not less than one, of the fixed tables (or a portion of the dining counter) shall be accessible and shall comply with 4.32 as required in 4.1.3(18). In establishments where separate areas are designated for smoking and non-smoking patrons, the required number of accessible fixed tables (or counters) shall be proportionally distributed between the smoking and non-smoking areas. In new construction, and where practicable in alterations, accessible fixed tables (or counters) shall be distributed throughout the space or facility.

5.2 Counters and Bars. Where food or drink is served at counters exceeding 34 in (865 mm) in height for consumption by customers seated on stools or standing at the counter, a portion of the main counter which is 60 in (1525 mm) in length minimum shall be provided in compliance with 4.32 or service shall be available at accessible tables within the same area.

5.3 Access Aisles. All accessible fixed tables shall be accessible by means of an access aisle at least 36 in (915 mm) clear between parallel edges of tables or between a wall and the table edges.

5.4 Dining Areas. In new construction, all dining areas, including raised or sunken dining areas, loggias, and outdoor seating areas, shall be accessible. In non-elevator buildings, an accessible means of vertical access to the mezzanine is not required under the following conditions: 1) the area of mezzanine seating measures no more than 33 percent of the area of the total accessible seating area; 2) the same services and decor are provided in an accessible space usable by the general public; and, 3) the accessible areas are not restricted to use by people with disabilities. In alterations, accessibility to raised or sunken dining areas, or to all parts of outdoor seating areas is not required provided that the same services and decor are provided in an accessible space usable by the general public and are not restricted to use by people with disabilities.

5.5 Food Service Lines. Food service lines shall have a minimum clear width of 36 in (915 mm), with a preferred clear width of 42 in (1065 mm) to allow passage around a person using a wheelchair. Tray slides shall be mounted no higher than 34 in (865 mm) above the floor (see Fig. 53). If self-service shelves

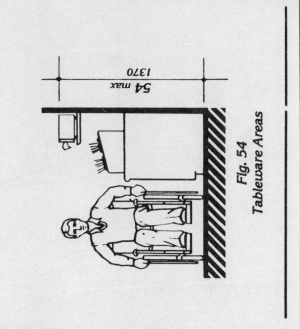

36 min
915

34 max
865

Fig. 53
Food Service Lines

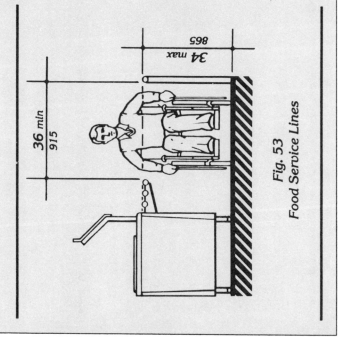

54 max
1370

Fig. 54
Tableware Areas

are provided, at least 50 percent of each type must be within reach ranges specified in 4.2.5 and 4.2.6.

5.6 Tableware and Condiment Areas.
Self-service shelves and dispensing devices for tableware, dishware, condiments, food and beverages shall be installed to comply with 4.2 (see Fig. 54).

5.7 Raised Platforms.
In banquet rooms or spaces where a head table or speaker's lectern is located on a raised platform, the platform shall be accessible in compliance with 4.8 or 4.11. Open edges of a raised platform shall be protected by placement of tables or by a curb.

5.8 Vending Machines and Other Equipment.
Spaces for vending machines and other equipment shall comply with 4.2 and shall be located on an accessible route.

5.9 Quiet Areas.
(Reserved).

6. MEDICAL CARE FACILITIES.

6.1 General.
Medical care facilities included in this section are those in which people receive physical or medical treatment or care and where persons may need assistance in responding to an emergency and where the period of stay may exceed twenty-four hours. In addition to the requirements of 4.1 through 4.35, medical care facilities and buildings shall comply with 6.

(1) Hospitals - general purpose hospitals, psychiatric facilities, detoxification facilities — At least 10 percent of patient bedrooms and toilets, and all public use and common use areas are required to be designed and constructed to be accessible.

(2) Hospitals and rehabilitation facilities that specialize in treating conditions that affect mobility, or units within either that specialize in treating conditions that affect mobility — All patient bedrooms and toilets, and all public use and common use areas are required to be designed and constructed to be accessible.

(3) Long term care facilities, nursing homes — At least 50 percent of patient bedrooms and toilets, and all public use and common use areas are required to be designed and constructed to be accessible.

(4) Alterations to patient bedrooms.

(a) When patient bedrooms are being added or altered as part of a planned renovation of an entire wing, a department, or other discrete area of an existing medical facility, a percentage of the patient bedrooms that are being added or altered shall comply with 6.3. The percentage of accessible rooms provided shall be consistent with the percentage of rooms required to be accessible by the applicable requirements of 6.1(1), 6.1(2), or 6.1(3), until the number of accessible patient bedrooms in the facility equals the overall number that would be required if the facility were newly constructed. (For example, if 20 patient bedrooms are being altered in the obstetrics department of a hospital, 2 of the altered rooms must be made accessible. If, within the same hospital, 20 patient bedrooms are being altered in a unit that specializes in treating mobility impairments, all of the altered rooms must be made accessible.) Where toilet/bath rooms are part of patient bedrooms which are added or altered and required to be accessible, each such patient toilet/bathroom shall comply with 6.4.

(b) When patient bedrooms are being added or altered individually, and not as part of an alteration of the entire area, the altered patient bedrooms shall comply with 6.3, unless either: a) the number of accessible patient bedrooms provided in the department or area containing the altered patient bedroom equals the number of accessible patient bedrooms that would be required if the percentage requirements of 6.1(1), 6.1(2), or 6.1(3) were applied to that department or area; or b) the number of accessible patient bedrooms in the facility equals the overall number that would be required if the facility were newly constructed. Where toilet/bathrooms are part of patient bedrooms which are added or altered and required to be accessible, each such toilet/bathroom shall comply with 6.4.

6.2 Entrances. At least one accessible entrance that complies with 4.14 shall be protected from the weather by canopy or roof overhang. Such entrances shall incorporate a passenger loading zone that complies with 4.6.6.

6.3 Patient Bedrooms. Provide accessible patient bedrooms in compliance with 4.1 through 4.35. Accessible patient bedrooms shall comply with the following:

(1) Each bedroom shall have a door that complies with 4.13.

EXCEPTION: Entry doors to acute care hospital bedrooms for in-patients shall be exempted from the requirement in 4.13.6 for maneuvering space at the latch side of the door if the door is at least 44 in (1120 mm) wide.

(2) Each bedroom shall have adequate space to provide a maneuvering space that complies with 4.2.3. In rooms with 2 beds, it is preferable that this space be located between beds.

(3) Each bedroom shall have adequate space to provide a minimum clear floor space of 36 in (915 mm) along each side of the bed and to provide an accessible route complying with 4.3.3 to each side of each bed.

6.4 Patient Toilet Rooms. Where toilet/bath rooms are provided as a part of a patient bedroom, each patient bedroom that is required to be accessible shall have an accessible toilet/bath room that complies with 4.22 or 4.23 and shall be on an accessible route.

7. BUSINESS AND MERCANTILE.

7.1 General. In addition to the requirements of 4.1 to 4.35, the design of all areas used for business transactions with the public shall comply with 7.

7.2 Sales and Service Counters, Teller Windows, Information Counters.

(1) In department stores and miscellaneous retail stores where counters have cash registers and are provided for sales or distribution of goods or services to the public, at least one of each type shall have a portion of the counter which is at least 36 in (915 mm) in length with a maximum height of 36 in (915 mm) above the finish floor. It shall be on an accessible route complying with 4.3. The accessible counters must be dispersed throughout the building or facility. In alterations where it is technically infeasible to provide an accessible counter, an auxiliary counter meeting these requirements may be provided.

(2) At ticketing counters, teller stations in a bank, registration counters in hotels and motels, box office ticket counters, and other counters that may not have a cash register but at which goods or services are sold or distributed, either:

(i) a portion of the main counter which is a minimum of 36 in (915 mm) in length shall be provided with a maximum height of 36 in (915 mm); or

(ii) an auxiliary counter with a maximum height of 36 in (915 mm) in close proximity to the main counter shall be provided; or

(iii) equivalent facilitation shall be provided (e.g., at a hotel registration counter, equivalent facilitation might consist of:

(1) provision of a folding shelf attached to the main counter on which an individual with disabilities can write, and (2) use of the space on the side of the counter or at the concierge desk, for handing materials back and forth).

All accessible sales and service counters shall be on an accessible route complying with 4.3.

(3)* Assistive Listening Devices. (Reserved)

7.3* Check-out Aisles.

(1) In new construction, accessible check-out aisles shall be provided in conformance with the table below:

Total Check-out Aisles of Each Design	Minimum Number of Accessible Check-out Aisles (of each design)
1 – 4	1
5 – 8	2
9 – 15	3
over 15	3, plus 20% of additional aisles

EXCEPTION: In new construction, where the selling space is under 5000 square feet, only one check-out aisle is required to be accessible.

EXCEPTION: In alterations, at least one check-out aisle shall be accessible in facilities under 5000 square feet of selling space. In facilities of 5000 or more square feet of selling space, at least one of each design of check-out aisle shall be made accessible when altered until the number of accessible check-out aisles of each design equals the number required in new construction.

Examples of check-out aisles of different "design" include those which are specifically designed to serve different functions. Different "design" includes but is not limited to the following features - length of belt or no belt; or permanent signage designating the aisle as an express lane.

(2) Clear aisle width for accessible check-out aisles shall comply with 4.2.1 and maximum adjoining counter height shall not exceed 38 in (965 mm) above the finish floor. The top of the lip shall not exceed 40 in (1015 mm) above the finish floor.

(3) Signage identifying accessible check-out aisles shall comply with 4.30.7 and shall be mounted above the check-out aisle in the same location where the check-out number or type of check-out is displayed.

7.4 Security Bollards. Any device used to prevent the removal of shopping carts from store premises shall not prevent access or egress to people in wheelchairs. An alternate

entry that is equally convenient to that provided for the ambulatory population is acceptable.

8. LIBRARIES.

8.1 General. In addition to the requirements of 4.1 to 4.35, the design of all public areas of a library shall comply with 8, including reading and study areas, stacks, reference rooms, reserve areas, and special facilities or collections.

8.2 Reading and Study Areas. At least 5 percent or a minimum of one of each element of fixed seating, tables, or study carrels shall comply with 4.2 and 4.32. Clearances between fixed accessible tables and between study carrels shall comply with 4.3.

8.3 Check-Out Areas. At least one lane at each check-out area shall comply with 7.2(1). Any traffic control or book security gates or turnstiles shall comply with 4.13.

8.4 Card Catalogs and Magazine Displays. Minimum clear aisle space at card catalogs and magazine displays shall comply with Fig. 55. Maximum reach height shall comply with 4.2, with a height of 48 in (1220 mm) preferred irrespective of approach allowed.

8.5 Stacks. Minimum clear aisle width between stacks shall comply with 4.3, with a minimum clear aisle width of 42 in (1065 mm) preferred where possible. Shelf height in stack areas is unrestricted (see Fig. 56).

9. ACCESSIBLE TRANSIENT LODGING.

(1) Except as specified in the special technical provisions of this section, accessible transient lodging shall comply with the applicable requirements of 4.1 through 4.35. Transient lodging includes facilities or portions thereof used for sleeping accommodations, when not classed as a medical care facility.

9.1 Hotels, Motels, Inns, Boarding Houses, Dormitories, Resorts and Other Similar Places of Transient Lodging.

9.1.1 General. All public use and common use areas are required to be designed and constructed to comply with section 4 (Accessible Elements and Spaces: Scope and Technical Requirements).

EXCEPTION: Sections 9.1 through 9.4 do not apply to an establishment located within a building that contains not more than five rooms for rent or hire and that is actually occupied by the proprietor of such establishment as the residence of such proprietor.

9.1.2 Accessible Units, Sleeping Rooms, and Suites. Accessible sleeping rooms or suites that comply with the requirements of 9.2 (Requirements for Accessible Units, Sleeping Rooms, and Suites) shall be provided in conformance with the table below. In addition, in hotels, of 50 or more sleeping rooms or suites, additional accessible sleeping rooms or suites that include a roll-in shower shall also be provided in conformance with the table below. Such accommodations shall comply with the requirements of 9.2, 4.21, and Figure 57(a) or (b).

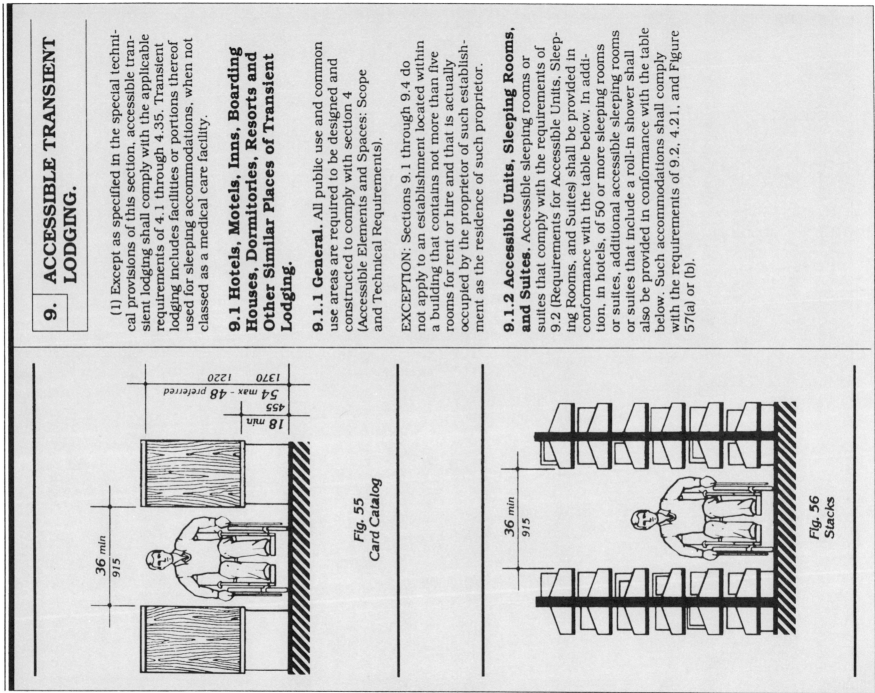

Fig. 55
Card Catalog

Fig. 56
Stacks

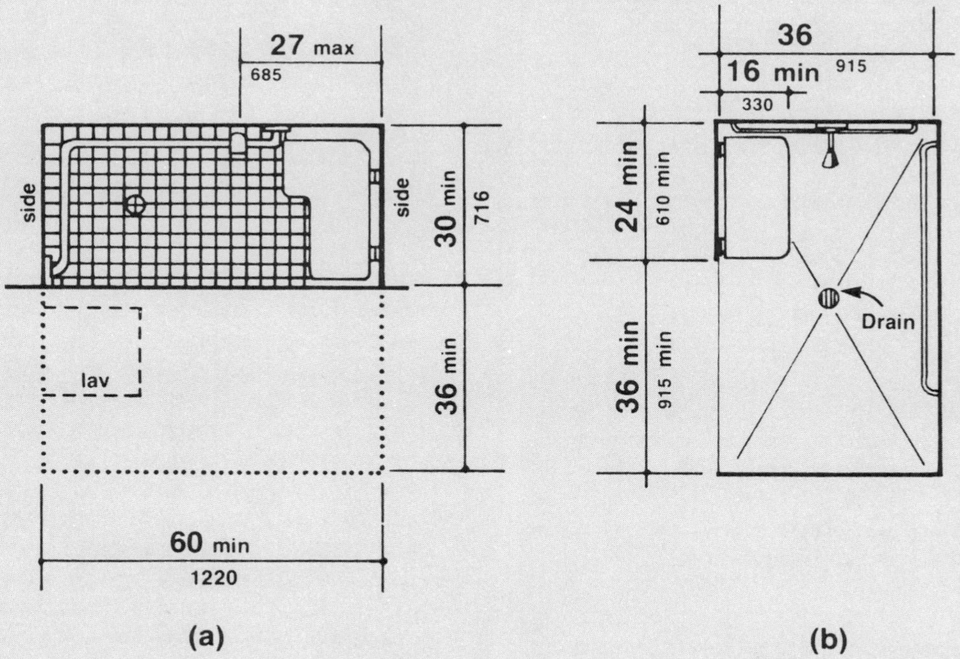

(a)

(b)

Fig. 57
Roll-in Shower with Folding Seat

and suites that comply with 9.3 (Visual Alarms, Notification Devices, and Telephones) shall be provided in conformance with the following table:

Number of Elements	Accessible Elements
1 to 25	1
26 to 50	2
51 to 75	3
76 to 100	4
101 to 150	5
151 to 200	6
201 to 300	7
301 to 400	8
401 to 500	9
501 to 1000	2% of total
1001 and over	20 plus 1 for each 100 over 1000

Number of Rooms	Accessible Rooms	Rooms with Roll-in Showers
1 to 25	1	
26 to 50	2	
51 to 75	3	1
76 to 100	4	1
101 to 150	5	2
151 to 200	6	2
201 to 300	7	3
301 to 400	8	4
401 to 500	9	4 plus one for each additional 100 over 400
501 to 1000	2% of total	
1001 and over	20 plus 1 for each 100 over 1000	

9.1.3 Sleeping Accommodations for Persons with Hearing Impairments.

In addition to those accessible sleeping rooms and suites required by 9.1.2, sleeping rooms

accessible route complying with 4.3 and have the following accessible elements and spaces.

(1) Accessible sleeping rooms shall have a 36 in (915 mm) clear width maneuvering space located along both sides of a bed, except that where two beds are provided, this requirement can be met by providing a 36 in (915 mm) wide maneuvering space located between the two beds.

(2) An accessible route complying with 4.3 shall connect all accessible spaces and elements, including telephones, within the unit, sleeping room, or suite. This is not intended to require an elevator in multi-story units as long as the spaces identified in 9.2.2(6) and (7) are on accessible levels and the accessible sleeping area is suitable for dual occupancy.

(3) Doors and doorways designed to allow passage into and within all sleeping rooms, suites or other covered units shall comply with 4.13.

(4) If fixed or built-in storage facilities such as cabinets, shelves, closets, and drawers are provided in accessible spaces, at least one of each type provided shall contain storage space complying with 4.25. Additional storage may be provided outside of the dimensions required by 4.25.

(5) All controls in accessible units, sleeping rooms, and suites shall comply with 4.27.

(6) Where provided as part of an accessible unit, sleeping room, or suite, the following spaces shall be accessible and shall be on an accessible route:

(a) the living area.

(b) the dining area.

(c) at least one sleeping area.

(d) patios, terraces, or balconies.

EXCEPTION: The requirements of 4.13.8 and 4.3.8 do not apply where it is necessary to utilize a higher door threshold or a change in level to protect the integrity of the unit from wind/water damage. Where this exception results in patios, terraces or balconies that are not at an accessible level, equivalent facilitation

9.1.4 Classes of Sleeping Accommodations.

(1) In order to provide persons with disabilities a range of options equivalent to those available to other persons served by the facility, sleeping rooms and suites required to be accessible by 9.1.2 shall be dispersed among the various classes of sleeping accommodations available to patrons of the place of transient lodging. Factors to be considered include room size, cost, amenities provided, and the number of beds provided.

(2) Equivalent Facilitation. For purposes of this section, it shall be deemed equivalent facilitation if the operator of a facility elects to limit construction of accessible rooms to those intended for multiple occupancy, provided that such rooms are made available at the cost of a single-occupancy room to an individual with disabilities who requests a single-occupancy room.

9.1.5. Alterations to Accessible Units, Sleeping Rooms, and Suites. When sleeping rooms are being altered in an existing facility, or portion thereof, subject to the requirements of this section, at least one sleeping room or suite that complies with the requirements of 9.2 (Requirements for Accessible Units, Sleeping Rooms, and Suites) shall be provided for each 25 sleeping rooms, or fraction thereof, of rooms being altered until the number of such rooms provided equals the number of such rooms required to be accessible with 9.1.2. In addition, at least one sleeping room or suite that complies with the requirements of 9.3 (Visual Alarms, Notification Devices, and Telephones) shall be provided for each 25 sleeping rooms, or fraction thereof, of rooms being altered until the number of such rooms equals the number required to be accessible by 9.1.3.

9.2 Requirements for Accessible Units, Sleeping Rooms and Suites.

9.2.1 General. Units, sleeping rooms, and suites required to be accessible by 9.1 shall comply with 9.2.

9.2.2 Minimum Requirements. An accessible unit, sleeping room or suite shall be on an

shall be provided. (E.g., equivalent facilitation at a hotel patio or balcony might consist of providing raised decking or a ramp to provide accessibility.)

(e) at least one full bathroom (i.e., one with a water closet, a lavatory, and a bathtub or shower).

(f) If only half baths are provided, at least one half bath.

(g) carports, garages or parking spaces.

(7) Kitchens, Kitchenettes, or Wet Bars. When provided as accessory to a sleeping room or suite, kitchens, kitchenettes, wet bars, or similar amenities shall be accessible. Clear floor space for a front or parallel approach to cabinets, counters, sinks, and appliances shall be provided to comply with 4.2.4. Countertops and sinks shall be mounted at a maximum height of 34 in (865 mm) above the floor. At least fifty percent of shelf space in cabinets or refrigerator/freezers shall be within the reach ranges of 4.2.5 or 4.2.6 and space shall be designed to allow for the operation of cabinet and/or appliance doors so that all cabinets and appliances are accessible and usable. Controls and operating mechanisms shall comply with 4.27.

(8) Sleeping room accommodations for persons with hearing impairments required by 9.1 and complying with 9.3 shall be provided in the accessible sleeping room or suite.

9.3 Visual Alarms, Notification Devices and Telephones.

9.3.1 General. In sleeping rooms required to comply with this section, auxiliary visual alarms shall be provided and shall comply with 4.28.4. Visual notification devices shall also be provided in units, sleeping rooms and suites to alert room occupants of incoming telephone calls and a door knock or bell. Notification devices shall not be connected to auxiliary visual alarm signal appliances. Permanently installed telephones shall have volume controls complying with 4.31.5; an accessible electrical outlet within 4 ft (1220 mm) of a telephone connection shall be provided to facilitate the use of a text telephone.

9.3.2 Equivalent Facilitation. For purposes of this section, equivalent facilitation shall include the installation of electrical outlets (including outlets connected to a facility's central alarm system) and telephone wiring in sleeping rooms and suites to enable persons with hearing impairments to utilize portable visual alarms and communication devices provided by the operator of the facility.

9.4 Other Sleeping Rooms and Suites.
Doors and doorways designed to allow passage into and within all sleeping units or other covered units shall comply with 4.13.5.

9.5 Transient Lodging in Homeless Shelters, Halfway Houses, Transient Group Homes, and Other Social Service Establishments.

9.5.1 New Construction. In new construction all public use and common use areas are required to be designed and constructed to comply with section 4. At least one of each type of amenity (such as washers, dryers and similar equipment installed for the use of occupants) in each common area shall be accessible and shall be located on an accessible route to any accessible unit or sleeping accommodation.

EXCEPTION. Where elevators are not provided as allowed in 4.1.3(5), accessible amenities are not required on inaccessible floors as long as one of each type is provided in common areas on accessible floors.

9.5.2 Alterations.

(1) Social service establishments which are not homeless shelters:

(a) The provisions of 9.5.3 and 9.1.5 shall apply to sleeping rooms and beds.

(b) Alteration of other areas shall be consistent with the new construction provisions of 9.5.1.

(2) Homeless shelters. If the following elements are altered, the following requirements apply:

10. TRANSPORTATION FACILITIES.

10.1 General. Every station, bus stop, bus stop pad, terminal, building or other transportation facility, shall comply with the applicable provisions of 4.1 through 4.35, sections 5 through 9, and the applicable provisions of this section. The exceptions for elevators in 4.1.3(5), exception 1 and 4.1.6(1)(k) do not apply to a terminal, depot, or other station used for specified public transportation, or an airport passenger terminal, or facilities subject to Title II.

10.2 Bus Stops and Terminals.

10.2.1 New Construction.

(1) Where new bus stop pads are constructed at bus stops, bays or other areas where a lift or ramp is to be deployed, they shall have a firm, stable surface; a minimum clear length of 96 inches (measured from the curb or vehicle roadway edge) and a minimum clear width of 60 inches (measured parallel to the vehicle roadway) to the maximum extent allowed by legal or site constraints; and shall be connected to streets, sidewalks or pedestrian paths by an accessible route complying with 4.3 and 4.4. The slope of the pad parallel to the roadway shall, to the extent practicable, be the same as the roadway. For water drainage, a maximum slope of 1:50 (2%) perpendicular to the roadway is allowed.

(2) Where provided, new or replaced bus shelters shall be installed or positioned so as to permit a wheelchair or mobility aid user to enter from the public way and to reach a location, having a minimum clear floor area of 30 inches by 48 inches, entirely within the perimeter of the shelter. Such shelters shall be connected by an accessible route to the boarding area provided under paragraph (1) of this section.

(3) Where provided, all new bus route identification signs shall comply with 4.30.5. In addition, to the maximum extent practicable, all new bus route identification signs shall comply with 4.30.2 and 4.30.3. Signs

(a) at least one public entrance shall allow a person with mobility impairments to approach, enter and exit including a minimum clear door width of 32 in (815 mm).

(b) sleeping space for homeless persons as provided in the scoping provisions of 9.1.2 shall include doors to the sleeping area with a minimum clear width of 32 in (815 mm) and maneuvering space around the beds for persons with mobility impairments complying with 9.2.2(1).

(c) at least one toilet room for each gender or one unisex toilet room shall have a minimum clear door width of 32 in (815 mm), minimum turning space complying with 4.2.3, one water closet complying with 4.16, one lavatory complying with 4.19 and the door shall have a privacy latch; and, if provided, at least one tub or shower shall comply with 4.20 or 4.21, respectively.

(d) at least one common area which a person with mobility impairments can use including approach, enter and exit including a minimum clear door width of 32 in (815 mm).

(e) at least one route connecting elements (a), (b), (c) and (d) which a person with mobility impairments can use including minimum clear width of 36 in (915 mm), passing space complying with 4.3.4, turning space complying with 4.2.3 and changes in levels complying with 4.3.8.

(f) homeless shelters can comply with the provisions of (a)-(e) by providing the above elements on one accessible floor.

9.5.3. Accessible Sleeping Accommodations in New Construction.

Accessible sleeping rooms shall be provided in conformance with the table in 9.1.2 and shall comply with 9.2 Accessible Units, Sleeping Rooms and Suites (where the items are provided). Additional sleeping rooms that comply with 9.3 Sleeping Accommodations for Persons with Hearing Impairments shall be provided in conformance with the table provided in 9.1.3.

In facilities with multi-bed rooms or spaces, a percentage of the beds equal to the table provided in 9.1.2 shall comply with 9.2.2(1).

that are sized to the maximum dimensions permitted under legitimate local, state or federal regulations or ordinances shall be considered in compliance with 4.30.2 and 4.30.3 for purposes of this section.

EXCEPTION: Bus schedules, timetables, or maps that are posted at the bus stop or bus bay are not required to comply with this provision.

10.2.2 Bus Stop Siting and Alterations.

(1) Bus stop sites shall be chosen such that, to the maximum extent practicable, the areas where lifts or ramps are to be deployed comply with section 10.2.1(1) and (2).

(2) When new bus route identification signs are installed or old signs are replaced, they shall comply with the requirements of 10.2.1(3).

10.3 Fixed Facilities and Stations.

10.3.1 New Construction. New stations in rapid rail, light rail, commuter rail, intercity bus, intercity rail, high speed rail, and other fixed guideway systems (e.g., automated guideway transit, monorails, etc.) shall comply with the following provisions, as applicable:

(1) Elements such as ramps, elevators or other circulation devices, fare vending or other ticketing areas, and fare collection areas shall be placed to minimize the distance which wheelchair users and other persons who cannot negotiate steps may have to travel compared to the general public. The circulation path, including an accessible entrance and an accessible route, for persons with disabilities shall, to the maximum extent practicable, coincide with the circulation path for the general public. Where the circulation path is different, signage complying with 4.30.1, 4.30.2, 4.30.3, 4.30.5, and 4.30.7(1) shall be provided to indicate direction to and identify the accessible entrance and accessible route.

(2) In lieu of compliance with 4.1.3(8), at least one entrance to each station shall comply with 4.14. Entrances. If different entrances to a station serve different transportation fixed routes or groups of fixed routes, at least one entrance serving each group or route shall

comply with 4.14. Entrances. All accessible entrances shall, to the maximum extent practicable, coincide with those used by the majority of the general public.

(3) Direct connections to commercial, retail, or residential facilities shall have an accessible route complying with 4.3 from the point of connection to boarding platforms and all transportation system elements used by the public. Any elements provided to facilitate future direct connections shall be on an accessible route connecting boarding platforms and all transportation system elements used by the public.

(4) Where signs are provided at entrances to stations identifying the station or the entrance, or both, at least one sign at each entrance shall comply with 4.30.4 and 4.30.6. Such signs shall be placed in uniform locations at entrances within the transit system to the maximum extent practicable.

EXCEPTION: Where the station has no defined entrance, but signage is provided, then the accessible signage shall be placed in a central location.

(5) Stations covered by this section shall have identification signs complying with 4.30.1, 4.30.2, 4.30.3, and 4.30.5. Signs shall be placed at frequent intervals and shall be clearly visible from within the vehicle on both sides when not obstructed by another train. When station identification signs are placed close to vehicle windows (i.e., on the side opposite from boarding) each shall have the top of the highest letter or symbol below the top of the vehicle window and the bottom of the lowest letter or symbol above the horizontal mid-line of the vehicle window.

(6) Lists of stations, routes, or destinations served by the station and located on boarding areas, platforms, or mezzanines shall comply with 4.30.1, 4.30.2, 4.30.3, and 4.30.5. A minimum of one sign identifying the specific station and complying with 4.30.4 and 4.30.6 shall be provided on each platform or boarding area. All signs referenced in this paragraph shall, to the maximum extent practicable, be placed in uniform locations within the transit system.

(7)* Automatic fare vending, collection and adjustment (e.g., add-fare) systems shall comply with 4.34.2, 4.34.3, and 4.34.4. At each accessible entrance such devices shall be located on an accessible route. If self-service fare collection devices are provided for the use of the general public, at least one accessible device for entering, and at least one for exiting, unless one device serves both functions, shall be provided at each accessible point of entry or exit. Accessible fare collection devices shall have a minimum clear opening width of 32 inches; shall permit passage of a wheelchair; and, where provided, coin or card slots and controls necessary for operation shall comply with 4.27. Gates which must be pushed open by wheelchair or mobility aid users shall have a smooth continuous surface extending from 2 inches above the floor to 27 inches above the floor and shall comply with 4.13. Where the circulation path does not coincide with that used by the general public, accessible fare collection systems shall be located at or adjacent to the accessible point of entry or exit.

(8) Platform edges bordering a drop-off and not protected by platform screens or guard rails shall have a detectable warning. Such detectable warnings shall comply with 4.29.2 and shall be 24 inches wide running the full length of the platform drop-off.

(9) In stations covered by this section, rail-to-platform height in new stations shall be coordinated with the floor height of new vehicles so that the vertical difference, measured when the vehicle is at rest, is within plus or minus 5/8 inch under normal passenger load conditions. For rapid rail, light rail, commuter rail, high speed rail, and intercity rail systems in new stations, the horizontal gap, measured when the new vehicle is at rest, shall be no greater than 3 inches. For slow moving automated guideway "people mover" transit systems, the horizontal gap in new stations shall be no greater than 1 inch.

EXCEPTION 1: Existing vehicles operating in new stations may have a vertical difference with respect to the new platform within plus or minus 1-1/2 inches.

EXCEPTION 2: In light rail, commuter rail and intercity rail systems where it is not operation-

ally or structurally feasible to meet the horizontal gap or vertical difference requirements, mini-high platforms, car-borne or platform-mounted lifts, ramps or bridge plates, or similar manually deployed devices, meeting the applicable requirements of 36 CFR part 1192, or 49 CFR part 38 shall suffice.

(10) Stations shall not be designed or constructed so as to require persons with disabilities to board or alight from a vehicle at a location other than one used by the general public.

(11) Illumination levels in the areas where signage is located shall be uniform and shall minimize glare on signs. Lighting along circulation routes shall be of a type and configuration to provide uniform illumination.

(12) Text Telephones: The following shall be provided in accordance with 4.31.9:

(a) If an interior public pay telephone is provided in a transit facility (as defined by the Department of Transportation) at least one interior public text telephone shall be provided in the station.

(b) Where four or more public pay telephones serve a particular entrance to a rail station and at least one is in an interior location, at least one interior public text telephone shall be provided to serve that entrance. Compliance with this section constitutes compliance with section 4.1.3(17)(c).

(13) Where it is necessary to cross tracks to reach boarding platforms, the route surface shall be level and flush with the rail top at the outer edge and between the rails, except for a maximum 2-1/2 inch gap on the inner edge of each rail to permit passage of wheel flanges. Such crossings shall comply with 4.29.5. Where gap reduction is not practicable, an above-grade or below-grade accessible route shall be provided.

(14) Where public address systems are provided to convey information to the public in terminals, stations, or other fixed facilities, a means of conveying the same or equivalent information to persons with hearing loss or who are deaf shall be provided.

10.3.2 Existing Facilities: Key Stations.

(1) Rapid, light and commuter rail key stations, as defined under criteria established by the Department of Transportation in subpart C of 49 CFR part 37 and existing intercity rail stations shall provide at least one accessible route from an accessible entrance to those areas necessary for use of the transportation system.

(2) The accessible route required by 10.3.2(1) shall include the features specified in 10.3.1 (1), (4)-(9), (11)-(15), and (17)-(19).

(3) Where technical infeasibility in existing stations requires the accessible route to lead from the public way to a paid area of the transit system, an accessible fare collection system, complying with 10.3.1(7), shall be provided along such accessible route.

(4) In light rail, rapid rail and commuter rail key stations, the platform or a portion thereof and the vehicle floor shall be coordinated so that the vertical difference, measured when the vehicle is at rest, is within plus or minus 1-1/2 inches under all normal passenger load conditions, and the horizontal gap, measured when the vehicle is at rest, is no greater than 3 inches for at least one door of each vehicle or car required to be accessible by 49 CFR part 37.

EXCEPTION 1: Existing vehicles retrofitted to meet the requirements of 49 CFR 37.93 (one-car-per-train rule) shall be coordinated with the platform such that, for at least one door, the vertical difference between the vehicle floor and the platform, measured when the vehicle is at rest with 50% normal passenger capacity, is within plus or minus 2 inches and the horizontal gap is no greater than 4 inches.

EXCEPTION 2: Where it is not structurally or operationally feasible to meet the horizontal gap or vertical difference requirements, mini-high platforms, car-borne or platform mounted lifts, ramps or bridge plates, or similar manually deployed devices, meeting the applicable requirements of 36 CFR part 1192, or 49 CFR part 38, shall suffice.

(15) Where clocks are provided for use by the general public, the clock face shall be uncluttered so that its elements are clearly visible. Hands, numerals, and/or digits shall contrast with the background either light-on-dark or dark-on-light. Where clocks are mounted overhead, numerals and/or digits shall comply with 4.30.3. Clocks shall be placed in uniform locations throughout the facility and system to the maximum extent practicable.

(16) Where provided in below grade stations, escalators shall have a minimum clear width of 32 inches. At the top and bottom of each escalator run, at least two contiguous treads shall be level beyond the comb plate before the risers begin to form. All escalator treads shall be marked by a strip of clearly contrasting color, 2 inches in width, placed parallel to and on the nose of each step. The strip shall be of a material that is at least as slip resistant as the remainder of the tread. The edge of the tread shall be apparent from both ascending and descending directions.

(17) Where provided, elevators shall be glazed or have transparent panels to allow an unobstructed view both in to and out of the car. Elevators shall comply with 4.10.

EXCEPTION: Elevator cars with a clear floor area in which a 60 inch diameter circle can be inscribed may be substituted for the minimum car dimensions of 4.10. Fig. 22.

(18) Where provided, ticketing areas shall permit persons with disabilities to obtain a ticket and check baggage and shall comply with 7.2.

(19) Where provided, baggage check-in and retrieval systems shall be on an accessible route complying with 4.3, and shall have space immediately adjacent complying with 4.2. If unattended security barriers are provided, at least one gate shall comply with 4.13. Gates which must be pushed open by wheelchair or mobility aid users shall have a smooth continuous surface extending from 2 inches above the floor to 27 inches above the floor.

(5) New direct connections to commercial, retail, or residential facilities shall, to the maximum extent feasible, have an accessible route complying with 4.3 from the point of connection to boarding platforms and all transportation system elements used by the public. Any elements provided to facilitate future direct connections shall be on an accessible route connecting boarding platforms and all transportation system elements used by the public.

10.3.3 Existing Facilities: Alterations.

(1) For the purpose of complying with 4.1.6(2) Alterations to an Area Containing a Primary Function, an area of primary function shall be as defined by applicable provisions of 49 CFR 37.43(c) [Department of Transportation's ADA Rule] or 28 CFR 36.403 [Department of Justice's ADA Rule].

10.4. Airports.

10.4.1 New Construction.

(1) Elements such as ramps, elevators or other vertical circulation devices, ticketing areas, security checkpoints, or passenger waiting areas shall be placed to minimize the distance which wheelchair users and other persons who cannot negotiate steps may have to travel compared to the general public.

(2) The circulation path, including an accessible entrance and an accessible route, for persons with disabilities shall, to the maximum extent practicable, coincide with the circulation path for the general public. Where the circulation path is different, directional signage complying with 4.30.1, 4.30.2, 4.30.3 and 4.30.5 shall be provided which indicates the location of the nearest accessible entrance and its accessible route.

(3) Ticketing areas shall permit persons with disabilities to obtain a ticket and check baggage and shall comply with 7.2.

(4) Where public pay telephones are provided, and at least one is at an interior location, a public text telephone shall be provided in compliance with 4.31.9. Additionally, if four or more public pay telephones are located in any of the following locations, at least one public text telephone shall also be provided in that location:

(a) a main terminal outside the security areas;

(b) a concourse within the security areas; or

(c) a baggage claim area in a terminal.

Compliance with this section constitutes compliance with section 4.1.3(17)(c).

(5) Baggage check-in and retrieval systems shall be on an accessible route complying with 4.3, and shall have space immediately adjacent complying with 4.2.4. If unattended security barriers are provided, at least one gate shall comply with 4.13. Gates which must be pushed open by wheelchair or mobility aid users shall have a smooth continuous surface extending from 2 inches above the floor to 27 inches above the floor.

(6) Terminal information systems which broadcast information to the general public through a public address system shall provide a means to provide the same or equivalent information to persons with a hearing loss or who are deaf. Such methods may include, but are not limited to, visual paging systems using video monitors and computer technology. For persons with certain types of hearing loss such methods may include, but are not limited to, an assistive listening system complying with 4.33.7.

(7) Where clocks are provided for use by the general public the clock face shall be uncluttered so that its elements are clearly visible. Hands, numerals, and/or digits shall contrast with their background either light-on-dark or dark-on-light. Where clocks are mounted overhead, numerals and/or digits shall comply with 4.30.3. Clocks shall be placed in uniform locations throughout the facility to the maximum extent practicable.

(8) Security Systems. [Reserved]

10.5 Boat and Ferry Docks. [Reserved]

APPENDIX

This appendix contains materials of an advisory nature and provides additional information that should help the reader to understand the minimum requirements of the guidelines or to design buildings or facilities for greater accessibility. The paragraph numbers correspond to the sections or paragraphs of the guideline to which the material relates and are therefore not consecutive (for example, A4.2.1 contains additional information relevant to 4.2.1). Sections of the guidelines for which additional material appears in this appendix have been indicated by an asterisk. Nothing in this appendix shall in any way obviate any obligation to comply with the requirements of the guidelines itself.

A2.2 Equivalent Facilitation. Specific examples of equivalent facilitation are found in the following sections:

4.1.6(3)(c)	Elevators in Alterations
4.31.9	Text Telephones
7.2	Sales and Service Counters, Teller Windows, Information Counters
9.1.4	Classes of Sleeping Accommodations
9.2.2(6)(d)	Requirements for Accessible Units, Sleeping Rooms, and Suites

A4.1.1 Application.

A4.1.1(3) Areas Used Only by Employees as Work Areas. Where there are a series of individual work stations of the same type (e.g., laboratories, service counters, ticket booths), 5%, but not less than one, of each type of work station should be constructed so that an individual with disabilities can maneuver within the work stations. Rooms housing individual offices in a typical office building must meet the requirements of the guidelines concerning doors, accessible routes, etc. but do not need to allow for maneuvering space around individual desks. Modifications required to permit maneuvering within the work area may be accomplished as a reasonable accommodation to individual employees with disabilities under Title I of the ADA. Consideration should also be given to placing shelves in employee work areas at a convenient height for accessibility or installing commercially available shelving that is adjustable so that reasonable accommodations can be made in the future.

If work stations are made accessible they should comply with the applicable provisions of 4.2 through 4.35.

A4.1.2 Accessible Sites and Exterior Facilities: New Construction.

A4.1.2(5)(e) Valet Parking. Valet parking is not always usable by individuals with disabilities. For instance, an individual may use a type of vehicle controls that render the regular controls inoperable or the driver's seat in a van may be removed. In these situations, another person cannot park the vehicle. It is recommended that some self-parking spaces be provided at valet parking facilities for individuals whose vehicles cannot be parked by another person and that such spaces be located on an accessible route to the entrance of the facility.

A4.1.3 Accessible Buildings: New Construction.

A4.1.3(5) Only full passenger elevators are covered by the accessibility provisions of 4.10. Materials and equipment hoists, freight elevators not intended for passenger use, dumbwaiters, and construction elevators are not covered by these guidelines. If a building is exempt from the elevator requirement, it is not necessary to provide a platform lift or other means of vertical access in lieu of an elevator.

Under Exception 4, platform lifts are allowed where existing conditions make it impractical to install a ramp or elevator. Such conditions generally occur where it is essential to provide access to small raised or lowered areas where space may not be available for a ramp. Examples include, but are not limited to, raised pharmacy platforms, commercial offices raised above a sales floor, or radio and news booths.

A4.1.3(9) Supervised automatic sprinkler systems have built in signals for monitoring features of the system such as the opening and closing of water control valves, the power supplies for needed pumps, water tank levels, and for indicating conditions that will impair the satisfactory operation of the sprinkler system.

A4.2 Space Allowances and Reach Ranges

A4.2 Space Allowances and Reach Ranges.

A4.2.1 Wheelchair Passage Width.

(1) Space Requirements for Wheelchairs. Many persons who use wheelchairs need a 30 in (760 mm) clear opening width for doorways, gates, and the like, when the latter are entered head-on. If the person is unfamiliar with a building, if competing traffic is heavy, if sudden or frequent movements are needed, or if the wheelchair must be turned at an opening, then greater clear widths are needed. For most situations, the addition of an inch of leeway on either side is sufficient. Thus, a minimum clear width of 32 in (815 mm) will provide adequate clearance. However, when an opening or a restriction in a passageway is more than 24 in (610 mm) long, it is essentially a passageway and must be at least 36 in (915 mm) wide.

(2) Space Requirements for Use of Walking Aids. Although people who use walking aids can maneuver through clear width openings of 32 in (815 mm), they need 36 in (915 mm) wide passageways and walks for comfortable gaits. Crutch tips, often extending down at a wide angle, are a hazard in narrow passageways where they might not be seen by other pedestrians. Thus, the 36 in (915 mm) width provides a safety allowance both for the person with a disability and for others.

(3) Space Requirements for Passing. Able-bodied persons in winter clothing, walking

Fig. A1
Minimum Passage Width for One Wheelchair and One Ambulatory Person

Because of these monitoring features, supervised automatic sprinkler systems have a high level of satisfactory performance and response to fire conditions.

A4.1.3(10) *If an odd number of drinking fountains is provided on a floor, the requirement in 4.1.3(10)(b) may be met by rounding down the odd number to an even number and calculating 50% of the even number. When more than one drinking fountain on a floor is required to comply with 4.15, those fountains should be dispersed to allow wheelchair users convenient access. For example, in a large facility such as a convention center that has water fountains at several locations on a floor, the accessible water fountains should be located so that wheelchair users do not have to travel a greater distance than other people to use a drinking fountain.*

A4.1.3(17)(b) *In addition to the requirements of section 4.1.3(17)(b), the installation of additional volume controls is encouraged. Volume controls may be installed on any telephone.*

A4.1.3(19)(a) *Readily removable or folding seating units may be installed in lieu of providing an open space for wheelchair users. Folding seating units are usually two fixed seats that can be easily folded into a fixed center bar to allow for one or two open spaces for wheelchair users when necessary. These units are more easily adapted than removable seats which generally require the seat to be removed in advance by the facility management.*

Either a sign or a marker placed on seating with removable or folding arm rests is required by this section. Consideration should be given for ensuring identification of such seats in a darkened theater. For example, a marker which contrasts (light on dark or dark on light) and which also reflects light could be placed on the side of such seating so as to be visible in a lighted auditorium and also to reflect light from a flashlight.

A4.1.6 Accessible Buildings: Alterations.

A4.1.6(1)(h) *When an entrance is being altered, it is preferable that those entrances being altered be made accessible to the extent feasible.*

A4.2 Space Allowances and Reach Ranges

straight ahead with arms swinging, need 32 in (815 mm) of width, which includes 2 in (50 mm) on either side for sway, and another 1 in (25 mm) tolerance on either side for clearing nearby objects or other pedestrians. Almost all wheelchair users and those who use walking aids can also manage within this 32 in (815 mm) width for short distances. Thus, two streams of traffic can pass in 64 in (1625 mm) in a comfortable flow. Sixty inches (1525 mm) provides a minimum width for a somewhat more restricted flow. If the clear width is less than 60 in (1525 mm), two wheelchair users will not be able to pass but will have to seek a wider place for passing. Forty-eight inches (1220 mm) is the minimum width needed for an ambulatory person to pass a nonambulatory or semi-ambulatory person. Within this 48 in (1220 mm) width, the ambulatory person will have to twist to pass a wheelchair user, a person with a *service animal*, or a

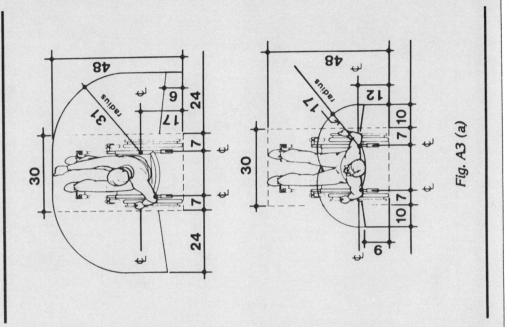

Fig. A3 (a)

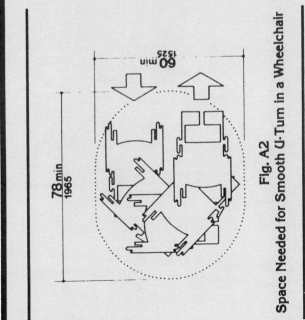

Fig. A2
Space Needed for Smooth U-Turn in a Wheelchair

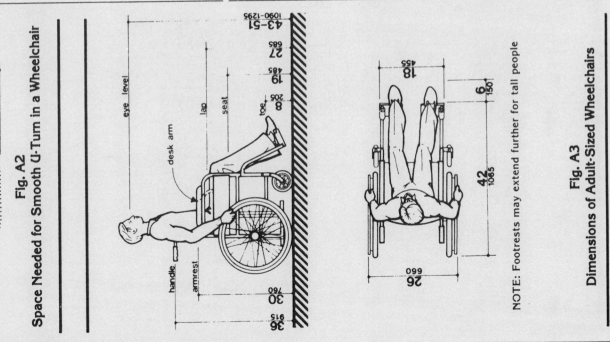

NOTE: Footrests may extend further for tall people

Fig. A3
Dimensions of Adult-Sized Wheelchairs

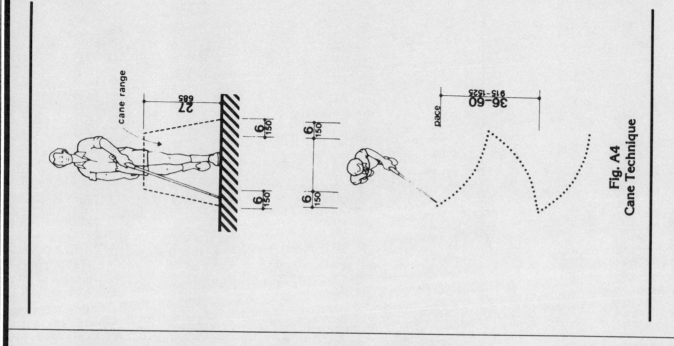

Fig. A4
Cane Technique

A4.3.10 Egress. Because people with disabilities may visit, be employed or be a resident in any building, emergency management plans with specific provisions to ensure their safe evacuation also play an essential role in fire safety and life safety.

A4.3.11.3 Stairway Width. *A 48 inch (1220 mm) wide exit stairway is needed to allow assisted evacuation (e.g., carrying a person in a wheelchair) without encroaching on the exit path for ambulatory persons.*

semi-ambulatory person. There will be little leeway for swaying or missteps (see Fig. A1).

A4.2.3 Wheelchair Turning Space.
These guidelines specify a minimum space of 60 in (1525 mm) diameter or a 60 in by 60 in (1525 mm by 1525 mm) T-shaped space for a pivoting 180-degree turn of a wheelchair. This space is usually satisfactory for turning around, but many people will not be able to turn without repeated tries and bumping into surrounding objects. The space shown in Fig. A2 will allow most wheelchair users to complete U-turns without difficulty.

A4.2.4 Clear Floor or Ground Space for Wheelchairs. The wheelchair and user shown in Fig. A3 represent typical dimensions for a large adult male. The space requirements in this *guideline* are based upon maneuvering clearances that will accommodate most wheelchairs. Fig. A3 provides a uniform reference for design not covered by this *guideline.*

A4.2.5 & A4.2.6 Reach. *Reach ranges for persons seated in wheelchairs may be further clarified by Fig. A3(a). These drawings approximate in the plan view the information shown in Fig. 4, 5, and 6.*

A4.3 Accessible Route.

A4.3.1 General.

(1) Travel Distances. Many people with mobility impairments can move at only very slow speeds; for many, traveling 200 ft (61 m) could take about 2 minutes. This assumes a rate of about 1.5 ft/s (455 mm/s) on level ground. It also assumes that the traveler would move continuously. However, on trips over 100 ft (30 m), disabled people are apt to rest frequently, which substantially increases their trip times. Resting periods of 2 minutes for every 100 ft (30 m) can be used to estimate travel times for people with severely limited stamina. In inclement weather, slow progress and resting can greatly increase a disabled person's exposure to the elements.

(2) Sites. Level, indirect routes or those with running slopes lower than 1:20 can sometimes provide more convenience than direct routes with maximum allowable slopes or with ramps.

A4.3.11.4 Two-way Communication. *It is essential that emergency communication not be dependent on voice communications alone because the safety of people with hearing or speech impairments could be jeopardized. The visible signal requirement could be satisfied with something as simple as a button in the area of rescue assistance that lights, indicating that help is on the way, when the message is answered at the point of entry.*

A4.4 Protruding Objects.

A4.4.1 General. *Service animals are trained to recognize and avoid hazards. However, most people with severe impairments of vision use the long cane as an aid to mobility.* The two principal cane techniques are the touch technique, where the cane arcs from side to side and touches points outside both shoulders; and the diagonal technique, where the cane is held in a stationary position diagonally across the body with the cane tip touching or just above the ground at a point outside one shoulder and the handle or grip extending to a point outside the other shoulder. The touch technique is used primarily in uncontrolled areas, while the diagonal technique is used primarily in certain limited, controlled, and familiar environments. Cane users are often trained to use both techniques.

Potential hazardous objects are noticed only if they fall within the detection range of canes (see Fig. A4). Visually impaired people walking toward an object can detect an overhang if its lowest surface is not higher than 27 in (685 mm). When walking alongside protruding objects, they cannot detect overhangs. Since proper cane and service animal techniques keep people away from the edge of a path or from walls, a slight overhang of no more than 4 in (100 mm) is not hazardous.

A4.5 Ground and Floor Surfaces.

A4.5.1 General. *People who have difficulty walking or maintaining balance or who use crutches, canes, or walkers, and those with restricted gaits are particularly sensitive to slipping and tripping hazards. For such people, a stable and regular surface is necessary for safe walking, particularly on stairs. Wheelchairs can be propelled most easily on surfaces that are hard, stable, and regular. Soft loose* surfaces such as shag carpet, loose sand or gravel, wet clay, and irregular surfaces such as cobblestones can significantly impede wheelchair movement.

Slip resistance is based on the frictional force necessary to keep a shoe heel or crutch tip from slipping on a walking surface under conditions likely to be found on the surface. *While the _dynamic_ coefficient of friction during walking varies in a complex and non-uniform way, the _static_ coefficient of friction, which can be measured in several ways, provides a close approximation of the slip resistance of a surface. Contrary to popular belief, some slippage is _necessary_ to walking, especially for persons with restricted gaits; a truly "non-slip" surface could not be negotiated.*

The Occupational Safety and Health Administration recommends that walking surfaces have a static coefficient of friction of 0.5. A research project sponsored by the Architectural and Transportation Barriers Compliance Board (Access Board) conducted tests with persons with disabilities and concluded that a higher coefficient of friction was needed by such persons. A static coefficient of friction of 0.6 is recommended for accessible routes and 0.8 for ramps.

It is recognized that the coefficient of friction varies considerably due to the presence of contaminants, water, floor finishes, and other factors not under the control of the designer or builder and not subject to design and construction guidelines and that compliance would be difficult to measure on the building site. Nevertheless, many common building materials suitable for flooring are now labeled with information on the static coefficient of friction. While it may not be possible to compare one product directly with another, or to guarantee a constant measure, builders and designers are encouraged to specify materials with appropriate values. As more products include information on slip resistance, improved uniformity in measurement and specification is likely. The Access Board's advisory guidelines on Slip Resistant Surfaces provides additional information on this subject.

Cross slopes on walks and ground or floor surfaces can cause considerable difficulty in propelling a wheelchair in a straight line.

A4.5.3 Carpet. Much more needs to be done in developing both quantitative and qualitative criteria for carpeting (i.e., problems associated with texture and weave need to be studied). However, certain functional characteristics are well established. When both carpet and padding are used, it is desirable to have minimum movement (preferably none) between the floor and the pad and the pad and the carpet which would allow the carpet to hump or warp. In heavily trafficked areas, a thick, soft (plush) pad or cushion, particularly in combination with long carpet pile, makes it difficult for individuals in wheelchairs and those with other ambulatory disabilities to get about. Firm carpeting can be achieved through proper selection and combination of pad and carpet, sometimes with the elimination of the pad or cushion, and with proper installation. Carpeting designed with a weave that causes a zig-zag effect when wheeled across is strongly discouraged

A4.6 Parking and Passenger Loading Zones.

A4.6.3 Parking Spaces. The increasing use of vans with side-mounted lifts or ramps by persons with disabilities has necessitated some revisions in specifications for parking spaces and adjacent access aisles. The typical accessible parking space is 96 in (2440 mm) wide with an adjacent 60 in (1525 mm) access aisle. However, this aisle does not permit lifts or ramps to be deployed and still leave room for a person using a wheelchair or other mobility aid to exit the lift platform or ramp. In tests conducted with actual lift/van/wheelchair combinations, (under a Board-sponsored Accessible Parking and Loading Zones Project) researchers found that a space and aisle totaling almost 204 in (5180 mm) wide was needed to deploy a lift and exit conveniently. The "van accessible" parking space required by these guidelines provides a 96 in (2440 mm) wide space with a 96 in (2440 mm) adjacent access aisle which is just wide enough to maneuver and exit from a side mounted lift. If a 96 in (2440 mm) access aisle is placed between two spaces, two "van accessible" spaces are created. Alternatively, if the wide access aisle is provided at the end of a row (an area often unused), it may be possible to provide the wide access aisle without additional space (see Fig. A5(a)).

A sign is needed to alert van users to the presence of the wider aisle, but the space is not intended to be restricted only to vans.

"Universal" Parking Space Design. An alternative to the provision of a percentage of spaces with a wide aisle, and the associated need to include additional signage, is the use of what has been called the "universal" parking space design. Under this design, all accessible spaces are 132 in (3350 mm) wide with a 60 in (1525 mm) access aisle (see Fig. A5(b)). One

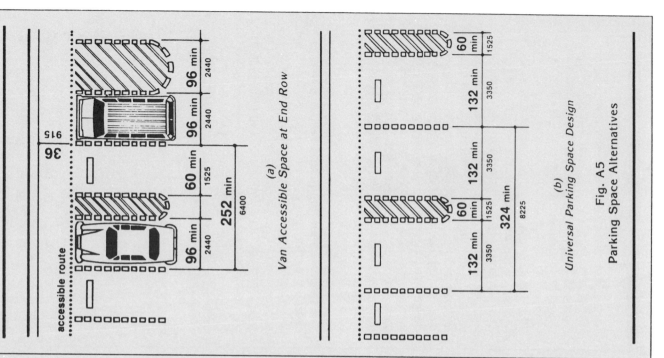

accessible route

96 min — 2440 | 60 min — 1525 | 252 min — 6400 | 96 min — 2440 | 96 min — 2440

36 / 915

(a)

Van Accessible Space at End Row

132 min — 3350 | 60 min — 1525 | 132 min — 3350 | 60 min — 1525 | 132 min — 3350

324 min — 8225

(b)

Universal Parking Space Design

Fig. A5
Parking Space Alternatives

advantage to this design is that no additional signage is needed because all spaces can accommodate a van with a side-mounted lift or ramp. Also, there is no competition between cars and vans for spaces since all spaces can accommodate either. Furthermore, the wider space permits vehicles to park to one side or the other within the 132 in (3350 mm) space to allow persons to exit and enter the vehicle on either the driver or passenger side, although, in some cases, this would require exiting or entering without a marked access aisle.

An essential consideration for any design is having the access aisle level with the parking space. Since a person with a disability, using a lift or ramp, must maneuver within the access aisle, the aisle cannot include a ramp or sloped area. The access aisle must be connected to an accessible route to the appropriate accessible entrance of a building or facility. The parking access aisle must either blend with the accessible route or have a curb ramp complying with 4.7. Such a curb ramp opening must be located within the access aisle boundaries, not within the parking space boundaries. Unfortunately, many facilities are designed with a ramp that is blocked when any vehicle parks in the accessible space. Also, the required dimensions of the access aisle cannot be restricted by planters, curbs or wheel stops.

A4.6.4 Signage. Signs designating parking places for disabled people can be seen from a driver's seat if the signs are mounted high enough above the ground and located at the front of a parking space.

A4.6.5 Vertical Clearance. High-top vans, which disabled people or transportation services often use, require higher clearances in parking garages than automobiles.

A4.8 Ramps.

A4.8.1 General. Ramps are essential for wheelchair users if elevators or lifts are not available to connect different levels. However, some people who use walking aids have difficulty with ramps and prefer stairs.

A4.8.2 Slope and Rise. *Ramp slopes between 1:16 and 1:20 are preferred. The ability to manage an incline is related to both its slope and its length. Wheelchair users with*

disabilities affecting their arms or with low stamina have serious difficulty using inclines. Most ambulatory people and most people who use wheelchairs can manage a slope of 1:16. Many people cannot manage a slope of 1:12 for 30 ft (9 m).

A4.8.4 Landings. *Level landings are essential toward maintaining an aggregate slope that complies with these guidelines. A ramp landing that is not level causes individuals using wheelchairs to tip backward or bottom out when the ramp is approached.*

A4.8.5 Handrails. The requirements for stair and ramp handrails in this guideline are for adults. When children are principal users in a building or facility, a second set of handrails at an appropriate height can assist them and aid in preventing accidents.

A4.9 Stairs.

A4.9.1 Minimum Number. *Only interior and exterior stairs connecting levels that are not connected by an elevator, ramp, or other accessible means of vertical access have to comply with 4.9.*

A4.10 Elevators.

A4.10.6 Door Protective and Reopening Device. The required door reopening device would hold the door open for 20 seconds if the doorway remains obstructed. After 20 seconds, the door may begin to close. However, if designed in accordance with *ASME A17.1-1990,* the door closing movement could still be stopped if a person or object exerts sufficient force at any point on the door edge.

A4.10.7 Door and Signal Timing for Hall Calls. This paragraph allows variation in the location of call buttons, advance time for warning signals, and the door-holding period used to meet the time requirement.

A4.10.12 Car Controls. Industry-wide standardization of elevator control panel design would make all elevators significantly more convenient for use by people with severe visual impairments. In many cases, it will be possible to locate the highest control on elevator panels within 48 in (1220 mm) from the floor.

A4.10.13 Car Position Indicators. A spe- cial button may be provided that would activate the audible signal within the given elevator only for the desired trip, rather than maintaining the audible signal in constant operation.

A4.10.14 Emergency Communications. A device that requires no handset is easier to use by people who have difficulty reaching. Also, small handles on handset compartment doors are not usable by people who have difficulty grasping.

Ideally, emergency two-way communication systems should provide both voice and visual display intercommunication so that persons with hearing impairments and persons with vision impairments can receive information regarding the status of a rescue. A voice inter- communication system cannot be the only means of communication because it is not accessible to people with speech and hearing impairments. While a voice intercommunication system is not required, at a minimum, the system should provide both an audio and visual indication that a rescue is on the way.

A4.11 Platform Lifts *(Wheelchair Lifts).*

A4.11.2 Other Requirements. *Inclined stairway chairlifts, and inclined and vertical platform lifts (wheelchair lifts) are available for short-distance, vertical transportation of people with disabilities. Care should be taken in selecting lifts as some lifts are not equally suitable for use by both wheelchair users and semi-ambulatory individuals.*

A4.12 Windows.

A4.12.1 General. *Windows intended to be operated by occupants in accessible spaces should comply with 4.12.*

A4.12.2 Window Hardware. *Windows requiring pushing, pulling, or lifting to open (for example, double-hung, sliding, or casement and awning units without cranks) should require no more than 5 lbf (22.2 N) to open or close. Locks, cranks, and other window hardware should comply with 4.27.*

A4.13 Doors.

A4.13.8 Thresholds at Doorways. Thresh- olds and surface height changes in doorways are particularly inconvenient for wheelchair users who also have low stamina or restric- tions in arm movement because complex maneuvering is required to get over the level change while operating the door.

A4.13.9 Door Hardware. Some disabled persons must push against a door with their chair or walker to open it. Applied kickplates on doors with closers can reduce required maintenance by withstanding abuse from wheelchairs and canes. To be effective, they should cover the door width, less approxi- mately 2 in (51 mm), up to a height of 16 in (405 mm) from its bottom edge and be cen- tered across the *width of the door.*

A4.13.10 Door Closers. Closers with de- layed action features give a person more time to maneuver through doorways. They are par- ticularly useful on frequently used interior doors such as entrances to toilet rooms.

A4.13.11 Door Opening Force. Although most people with disabilities can exert at least 5 lbf (22.2N), both pushing and pulling from a stationary position, a few people with severe disabilities cannot exert 3 lbf (13.13N). Al- though some people cannot manage the allow- able forces in this guideline and many others have difficulty, door closers must have certain minimum closing forces to close doors satisfac- torily. Forces for pushing or pulling doors open are measured with a push-pull scale under the following conditions:

(1) Hinged doors: Force applied perpen- dicular to the door at the door opener or 30 in (760 mm) from the hinged side, whichever is farther from the hinge.

(2) Sliding or folding doors: Force applied parallel to the door at the door pull or latch.

(3) Application of force: Apply force gradually so that the applied force does not exceed the resistance of the door. In high-rise buildings, air-pressure differentials may require a modifi- cation of this specification in order to meet the functional intent.

A4.13.12 Automatic Doors and Power-Assisted Doors.
Sliding automatic doors do not need guard rails and are more convenient for wheelchair users and visually impaired people to use. If slowly opening automatic doors can be reactivated before their closing cycle is completed, they will be more convenient in busy doorways.

A4.15 Drinking Fountains and Water Coolers.

A4.15.2 Spout Height. *Two drinking fountains, mounted side by side or on a single post, are usable by people with disabilities and people who find it difficult to bend over.*

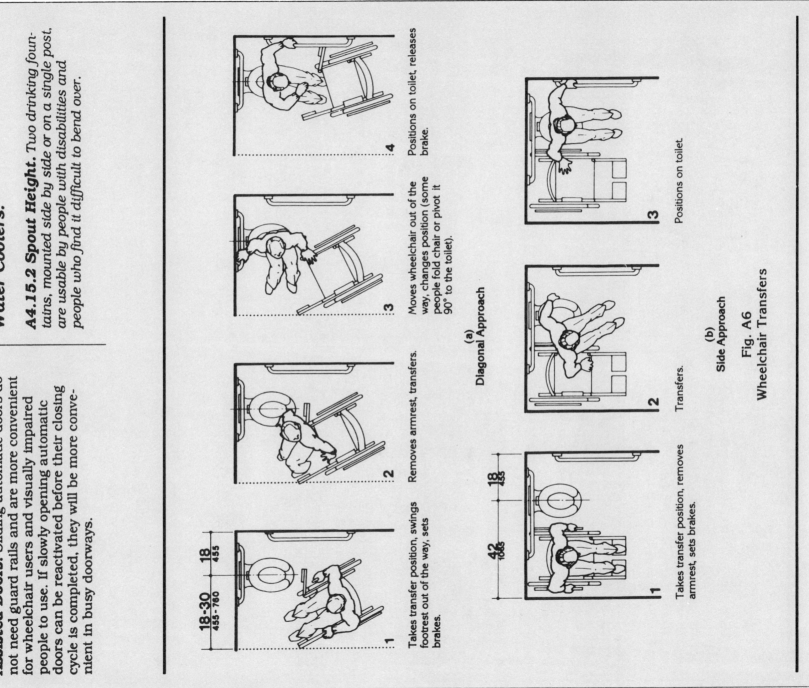

Takes transfer position, swings footrest out of the way, sets brakes.

Removes armrest, transfers.

Moves wheelchair out of the way, changes position (some people fold chair or pivot it 90° to the toilet).

Positions on toilet, releases brake.

(a)
Diagonal Approach

Takes transfer position, removes armrest, sets brakes.

Transfers.

Positions on toilet

(b)
Side Approach

Fig. A6
Wheelchair Transfers

A4.16 Water Closets.

A4.16.3 Height. Height preferences for toilet seats vary considerably among disabled people. Higher seat heights may be an advantage to some ambulatory disabled people, but are often a disadvantage for wheelchair users and others. Toilet seats 18 in (455 mm) high seem to be a reasonable compromise. Thick seats and filler rings are available to adapt standard fixtures to these requirements.

A4.16.4 Grab Bars. Fig. A6(a) and (b) show the diagonal and side approaches most commonly used to transfer from a wheelchair to a water closet. Some wheelchair users can transfer from the front of the toilet while others use a 90-degree approach. Most people who use the two additional approaches can also use either the diagonal approach or the side approach.

A4.16.5 Flush Controls. Flush valves and related plumbing can be located behind walls or to the side of the toilet, or a toilet seat lid can be obtained by special order with controls mounted on the right side. If administrative authorities require flush controls for flush valves to be located in a position that conflicts with the location of the rear grab bar, then that bar may be split or shifted toward the wide side of the toilet area.

A4.17 Toilet Stalls.

A4.17.3 Size and Arrangement. *This section requires use of the 60 in (1525 mm) standard stall [Figure 30(a)] and permits the 36 in (915 mm) or 48 in (1220 mm) wide alternate stall [Figure 30(b)] only in alterations where provision of the standard stall is technically infeasible or where local plumbing codes prohibit reduction in the number of fixtures. A standard stall provides a clear space on one side of the water closet to enable persons who use wheelchairs to perform a side or diagonal transfer from the wheelchair to the water closet. However, some persons with disabilities who use mobility aids such as walkers, canes or crutches*

are better able to use the two parallel grab bars in the 36 in (915 mm) wide alternate stall to achieve a standing position.

In large toilet rooms, where six or more toilet stalls are provided, it is therefore required that a 36 in (915 mm) wide stall with parallel grab bars be provided in addition to the standard stall required in new construction. The 36 in (915 mm) width is necessary to achieve proper use of the grab bars; wider stalls would position the grab bars too far apart to be easily used and narrower stalls would position the grab bars too close to the water closet. Since the stall is primarily intended for use by persons using canes, crutches and walkers, rather than wheelchairs, the length of the stall could be conventional. The door, however, must swing outward to ensure a usable space for people who use crutches or walkers.

A4.17.5 Doors. To make it easier for wheelchair users to close toilet stall doors, doors can be provided with closers, spring hinges, or a pull bar mounted on the inside surface of the door near the hinge side.

A4.19 Lavatories and Mirrors.

A4.19.6 Mirrors. If mirrors are to be used by both ambulatory people and wheelchair users, then they must be at least 74 in (1880 mm) high at their topmost edge. A single full length mirror can accommodate all people, including children.

A4.21 Shower Stalls.

A4.21.1 General. Shower stalls that are 36 in by 36 in (915 mm by 915 mm) wide provide additional safety to people who have difficulty maintaining balance because all grab bars and walls are within easy reach. Seated people use the walls of 36 in by 36 in (915 mm by 915 mm) showers for back support. Shower stalls that are 60 in (1525 mm) wide and have no curb may increase usability of a bathroom by wheelchair users because the shower area provides additional maneuvering space.

A4.22 Toilet Rooms.

A4.22.3 Clear Floor Space. *In many small facilities, single-user restrooms may be the only* facilities provided for all building users. In addition, the guidelines allow the use of "unisex" or "family" accessible toilet rooms in alterations when technical infeasibility can be demonstrated. Experience has shown that the provision of accessible "unisex" or single-user restrooms is a reasonable way to provide access for wheelchair users and any attendants, especially when attendants are of the opposite sex. Since these facilities have proven so useful, it is often considered advantageous to install a "unisex" toilet room in new facilities in addition to making the multi-stall restrooms accessible, especially in shopping malls, large auditoriums, and convention centers.

Figure 28 (section 4.16) provides minimum clear floor space dimensions for toilets in accessible "unisex" toilet rooms. The dotted lines designate the minimum clear floor space, depending on the direction of approach, required for wheelchair users to transfer onto the water closet. The dimensions of 48 in (1220 mm) and 60 in (1525 mm), respectively, correspond to the two common transfer space required for the two common transfer approaches utilized by wheelchair users (see Fig. A6). It is important to keep in mind that the placement of the lavatory to the immediate side of the water closet will preclude the side approach transfer illustrated in Figure A6(b).

To accommodate the side transfer, the space adjacent to the water closet must remain clear of obstruction for 42 in (1065 mm) from the centerline of the toilet (Figure 28) and the lavatory must not be located within this clear space. A turning circle or T-turn, the clear floor space at the lavatory, and maneuvering space at the door must be considered when determining the possible wall locations. A privacy latch or other accessible means of ensuring privacy during use should be provided at the door.

RECOMMENDATIONS:

1. In new construction, accessible single-user restrooms may be desirable in some situations because they can accommodate a wide variety of building users. However, they cannot be used in lieu of making the multi-stall toilet rooms accessible as required.

2. Where strict compliance to the guidelines for accessible toilet facilities is technically infeasible in the alteration of existing facilities, accessible "unisex" toilets are a reasonable alternative.

3. In designing accessible single-user restrooms, the provisions of adequate space to allow a side transfer will provide accommodation to the largest number of wheelchair users.

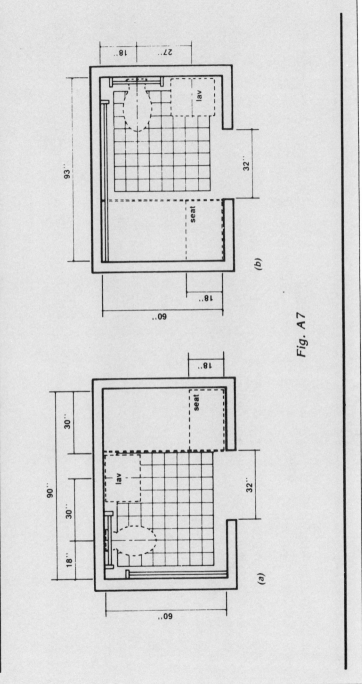

Fig. A7

A4.23 Bathrooms, Bathing Facilities, and Shower Rooms.

A4.23.3 Clear Floor Space. *Figure A7 shows two possible configurations of a toilet room with a roll-in shower. The specific shower shown is designed to fit exactly within the dimensions of a standard bathtub. Since the shower does not have a lip, the floor space can be used for required maneuvering space. This would permit a toilet room to be smaller than would be permitted with a bathtub and still provide enough floor space to be considered accessible. This design can provide accessibility in facilities where space is at a premium (i.e. hotels and medical care facilities). The alternate roll-in shower (Fig. 57b) also provides sufficient room for the "T-turn" and does not require plumbing to be on more than one wall.*

A4.23.9 Medicine Cabinets. Other alternatives for storing medical and personal care items are very useful to disabled people. Shelves, drawers, and floor-mounted cabinets can be provided within the reach ranges of disabled people.

A4.26 Handrails, Grab Bars, and Tub and Shower Seats.

A4.26.1 General. Many disabled people rely heavily upon grab bars and handrails to maintain balance and prevent serious falls. Many people brace their forearms between supports and walls to give them more leverage and stability in maintaining balance or for lifting. The grab bar clearance of 1-1/2 in (38 mm) required in this guideline is a safety clearance to prevent injuries resulting from arms slipping through the openings. It also provides adequate gripping room.

A4.26.2 Size and Spacing of Grab Bars and Handrails. This specification allows for alternate shapes of handrails as long as they allow an opposing grip similar to that provided by a circular section of 1-1/4 in to 1-1/2 in (32 mm to 38 mm).

A4.27 Controls and Operating Mechanisms.

A4.27.3 Height. *Fig. A8 further illustrates*

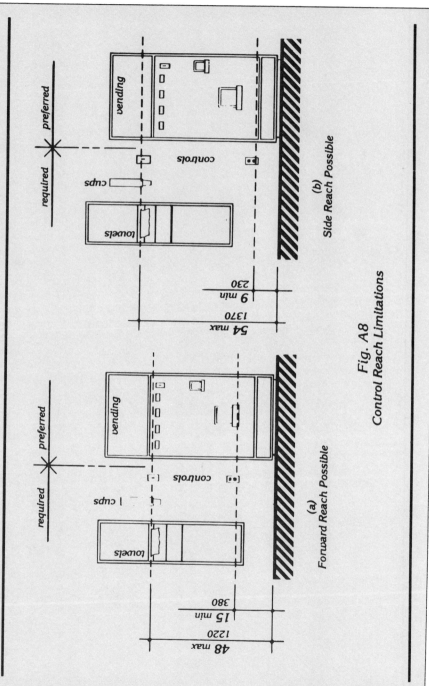

Fig. A8
Control Reach Limitations

mandatory and advisory control mounting height provisions for typical equipment.

Electrical receptacles installed to serve individual appliances and not intended for regular or frequent use by building occupants are not required to be mounted within the specified reach ranges. Examples would be receptacles installed specifically for wall-mounted clocks, refrigerators, and microwave ovens.

A4.28 Alarms.

A4.28.2 Audible Alarms. Audible emergency signals must have an intensity and frequency that can attract the attention of individuals who have partial hearing loss. People over 60 years of age generally have difficulty perceiving frequencies higher than 10,000 Hz. An alarm signal which has a periodic element to its signal, such as single stroke bells (clang-pause-clang-pause), hi-low (up-down-up-down) and fast whoop (on-off-on-off) are best. Avoid continuous or reverberating tones. Select a signal which has a sound characterized by three or four clear tones without a great deal of "noise" in between.

A4.28.3 Visual Alarms. The specifications in this section do not preclude the use of zoned or coded alarm systems.

A4.28.4 Auxiliary Alarms. Locating visual emergency alarms in rooms where persons who are deaf may work or reside alone can ensure that they will always be warned when an emergency alarm is activated. To be effective, such devices must be located and oriented so that they will spread signals and reflections throughout a space or raise the overall light level sharply. However, visual alarms alone are not necessarily the best means to alert sleepers. A study conducted by Underwriters Laboratory (UL) concluded that a flashing light more than seven times brighter was required (110 candela v. 15 candela, at the same distance) to awaken sleepers as was needed to alert awake subjects in a normal daytime illuminated room.

For hotel and other rooms where people are likely to be asleep, a signal-activated vibrator placed between mattress and box spring or under a pillow was found by UL to be much more effective in alerting sleepers. Many readily available devices are sound-activated so that they could respond to an alarm clock, clock .

radio, wake-up telephone call or room smoke detector. Activation by a building alarm system can either be accomplished by a separate circuit activating an auditory alarm which would, in turn, trigger the vibrator or by a signal transmitted through the ordinary 110-volt outlet. Transmission of signals through the power line is relatively simple and is the basis of common, inexpensive remote light control systems sold in many department and electronic stores for home use. So-called "wireless" intercoms operate on the same principal.

A4.29 Detectable Warnings.

A4.29.2 Detectable Warnings on Walking Surfaces. *The material used to provide contrast should contrast by at least 70%. Contrast in percent is determined by:*

$$Contrast = [(B_1 - B_2)/B_1] \times 100$$

where B_1 = light reflectance value (LRV) of the lighter area
and B_2 = light reflectance value (LRV) of the darker area.

Note that in any application both white and black are never absolute; thus, B_1 never equals 100 and B_2 is always greater than 0.

A4.30 Signage.

A4.30.1 General. In building complexes where finding locations independently on a routine basis may be a necessity (for example, college campuses), tactile maps or prerecorded instructions can be very helpful to visually impaired people. Several maps and auditory instructions have been developed and tested for specific applications. The type of map or instructions used must be based on the information to be communicated, which depends highly on the type of buildings or users.

Landmarks that can easily be distinguished by visually impaired individuals are useful as orientation cues. Such cues include changes in illumination level, bright colors, unique patterns, wall murals, location of special equipment or other architectural features.

Many people with disabilities have limitations in movement of their heads and reduced peripheral vision. Thus, signage positioned perpendicular to the path of travel is easiest for them to notice. People can generally distinguish signage within an angle of 30 degrees to either side of the centerlines of their faces without moving their heads.

A4.30.2 Character Proportion. The legibility of printed characters is a function of the viewing distance, character height, the ratio of the stroke width to the height of the character, the contrast of color between character and background, and print font. The size of characters must be based upon the intended viewing distance. A severely nearsighted person may have to be much closer to recognize a character of a given size than a person with normal visual acuity.

A4.30.4 Raised and Brailled Characters and Pictorial Symbol Signs (Pictograms). The standard dimensions for literary Braille are as follows:

Dot diameter	.059 in.
Inter-dot spacing	.090 in.
Horizontal separation between cells	.241 in.
Vertical separation between cells	.395 in.

Raised borders around signs containing raised characters may make them confusing to read unless the border is set far away from the characters. Accessible signage with descriptive materials about public buildings, monuments, and objects of cultural interest may not provide sufficiently detailed and meaningful information. Interpretive guides, audio tape devices, or other methods may be more effective in presenting such information.

A4.30.5 Finish and Contrast. An eggshell finish (11 to 19 degree gloss on 60 degree glossimeter) is recommended. Research indicates that signs are more legible for persons with low vision when characters contrast with their background by at least 70 percent. Contrast in percent shall be determined by:

$$\text{Contrast} = [(B_1 - B_2)/B_1] \times 100$$

where B_1 = light reflectance value (LRV) of the lighter area
and B_2 = light reflectance value (LRV) of the darker area.

Note that in any application both white and black are never absolute; thus, B_1 never equals 100 and B_2 is always greater than 0.

The greatest readability is usually achieved through the use of light-colored characters or symbols on a dark background.

A4.30.7 Symbols of Accessibility for Different Types of Listening Systems. Paragraph 4 of this section requires signage indicating the availability of an assistive listening system. An appropriate message should be displayed with the international symbol of access for hearing loss since this symbol conveys general accessibility for people with hearing loss. Some suggestions are:

INFRARED
ASSISTIVE LISTENING SYSTEM
AVAILABLE
——PLEASE ASK——

AUDIO LOOP IN USE
TURN T-SWITCH FOR
BETTER HEARING
——OR ASK FOR HELP——

FM
ASSISTIVE LISTENING
SYSTEM AVAILABLE
——PLEASE ASK——

The symbol may be used to notify persons of the availability of other auxiliary aids and services such as: real time captioning, captioned note taking, sign language interpreters, and oral interpreters.

A4.30.8 Illumination Levels. Illumination levels on the sign surface shall be in the 100 to 300 lux range (10 to 30 footcandles) and shall be uniform over the sign surface. Signs shall be located such that the illumination level on the surface of the sign is not significantly exceeded by the ambient light or visible bright lighting source behind or in front of the sign.

A4.31 Telephones.

A4.31.3 Mounting Height. In localities
where the dial-tone first system is in operation, calls can be placed at a coin telephone through the operator without inserting coins. The operator button is located at a height of 46 in (1170 mm) if the coin slot of the telephone is at 54 in (1370 mm). A generally available public telephone with a coin slot mounted lower on the equipment would allow universal installation of telephones at a height of 48 in (1220 mm) or less to all operable parts.

A4.31.9 Text Telephones. *A public text
telephone may be an integrated text telephone pay phone unit or a conventional portable text telephone that is permanently affixed within, or adjacent to, the telephone enclosure. In order to be usable with a pay phone, a text telephone which is not a single integrated text telephone pay phone unit will require a shelf large enough (10 in (255mm) wide by 10 in (255 mm) deep with a 6 in (150 mm) vertical clearance minimum) to accommodate the device, an electrical outlet, and a power cord. Movable or portable text telephones may be used to provide equivalent facilitation. A text telephone should be readily available so that a person using it may access the text telephone easily and conveniently. As currently designed pocket-type text telephones for personal use do not accommodate a wide range of users. Such devices would not be considered substantially equivalent to conventional text telephones. However, in the future as technology develops this could change.*

A4.32 Fixed or Built-in Seating and Tables.

A4.32.4 Height of Tables or Counters.
Different types of work require different table or counter heights for comfort and optimal performance. Light detailed work such as writing requires a *table or counter* close to elbow height for a standing person. Heavy manual work such as rolling dough requires *a counter or table* height about 10 in (255 mm) below elbow height for a standing person. This principle of *high/low table or counter heights* also applies for seated persons; however, the limiting condition for seated manual work is clearance under the *table or counter.*

Table A1 shows convenient *counter heights* for seated persons. The great variety of heights for comfort and optimal performance indicates a need for alternatives or a compromise in height if people who stand and people who sit will be using the same counter area.

Table A1
Convenient Heights of Tables and Counters for Seated People[1]

Conditions of Use	Short Women in mm		Tall Men in mm	
Seated in a wheelchair:				
Manual work—				
Desk or removeable				
armrests	26	660	30	760
Fixed, full-size armrests[2]	32[3]	815	32[3]	815
Light detailed work:				
Desk or removable				
armrests	29	735	34	865
Fixed, full-size armrests[2]	32[3]	815	34	865
Seated in a 16-in. (405-mm)				
High chair:				
Manual work	26	660	27	685
Light detailed work	28	710	31	785

[1] All dimensions are based on a work-surface thickness of 1 1/2 in (38 mm) and a clearance of 1 1/2 in (38 mm) between legs and the underside of a work surface.

[2] This type of wheelchair arm does not interfere with the positioning of a wheelchair under a work surface.

[3] This dimension is limited by the height of the armrests: a lower height would be preferable. Some people in this group prefer lower work surfaces, which require positioning the wheelchair back from the edge of the counter.

A4.33 Assembly Areas.

A4.33.2 Size of Wheelchair Locations.
Spaces large enough for two wheelchairs allow people who are coming to a performance together to sit together.

A4.33.3 Placement of Wheelchair Locations. The location of wheelchair areas can be planned so that a variety of positions

Table A2. Summary of Assistive Listening Devices

within the seating area are provided. This will allow choice in viewing and price categories.

Building/life safety codes set minimum distances between rows of fixed seats with consideration of the number of seats in a row, the exit aisle width and arrangement, and the location of exit doors. "Continental" seating, with a greater number of seats per row and a commensurate increase in row spacing and exit doors, facilitates emergency egress for all people and increases ease of access to mid-row seats especially for people who walk with difficulty. Consideration of this positive attribute of "continental" seating should be included along with all other factors in the design of fixed seating areas.

Table A2. Summary of Assistive Listening Devices

System	Advantages	Disadvantages	Typical Applications
Induction Loop Transmitter: Transducer wired to induction loop around listening area. Receiver: Self-contained induction receiver or personal hearing aid with telecoil.	Cost-Effective Low Maintenance Easy to use Unobtrusive May be possible to integrate into existing public address system. Some hearing aids can function as receivers.	Signal spills over to adjacent rooms. Susceptible to electrical interference. Limited portability Inconsistent signal strength. Head position affects signal strength. Lack of standards for induction coil performance.	Meeting areas Theaters Churches and Temples Conference rooms Classrooms TV viewing
FM Transmitter: Flashlight-sized worn by speaker. Receiver: With personal hearing aid via DAI or induction neck-loop and telecoil; or self-contained with earphone(s).	Highly portable Different channels allow use by different groups within the same room. High user mobility Variable for large range of hearing losses.	High cost of receivers Equipment fragile Equipment obtrusive High maintenance Expensive to maintain Custom fitting to individual user may be required.	Classrooms Tour groups Meeting areas Outdoor events One-on-one
Infrared Transmitter: Emitter in line-of-sight with receiver. Receiver: Self-contained. Or with personal hearing aid via DAI or induction neckloop and telecoil.	Easy to use Insures privacy or confidentiality Moderate cost Can often be integrated into existing public address system.	Line-of-sight required between emitter and receiver. Ineffective outdoors Limited portability Requires installation	Theaters Churches and Temples Auditoriums Meetings requiring confidentiality TV viewing

Source: Rehab Brief, National Institute on Disability and Rehabilitation Research, Washington, DC, Vol. XII, No. 10, (1990).

New York has also adopted a detailed technical specification which may be useful.

A5.0 Restaurants and Cafeterias.

A5.1 General. Dining counters (where there is no service) are typically found in small carry-out restaurants, bakeries, or coffee shops and may only be a narrow eating surface attached to a wall. This section requires that where such a dining counter is provided, a portion of the counter shall be at the required accessible height.

A7.0 Business and Mercantile.

A7.2(3) Assistive Listening Devices. At all sales and service counters, teller windows, box offices, and information kiosks where a physical barrier separates service personnel and customers, it is recommended that at least one permanently installed assistive listening device complying with 4.33 be provided at each location or series. Where assistive listening devices are installed, signage should be provided identifying those stations which are so equipped.

A7.3 Check-out Aisles. Section 7.2 refers to counters without aisles; section 7.3 concerns check-out aisles. A counter without an aisle (7.2) can be approached from more than one direction such as in a convenience store. In order to use a check-out aisle (7.3), customers must enter a defined area (an aisle) at a particular point, pay for goods, and exit at a particular point.

A10.3 Fixed Facilities and Stations.

A10.3.1(7) Route Signs. One means of making control buttons on fare vending machines usable by persons with vision impairments is to raise them above the surrounding surface. Those activated by a mechanical motion are likely to be more detectable. If farecard vending, collection, and adjustment devices are designed to accommodate farecards having one tactually distinctive corner, then a person who has a vision impairment will insert the card with greater ease. Token collection devices that are designed to accommodate tokens which are perforated can allow a person to distinguish more readily between tokens and common coins. Thoughtful placement of accessible gates and fare vending machines in relation to inaccessible devices will make their use and detection easier for all persons with disabilities.

A4.33.6 Placement of Listening Systems. A distance of 50 ft (15 m) allows a person to distinguish performers' facial expressions.

A4.33.7 Types of Listening Systems. An assistive listening system appropriate for an assembly area for a group of persons or where the specific individuals are not known in advance, such as a playhouse, lecture hall or movie theater, may be different from the system appropriate for a particular individual provided as an auxiliary aid or as part of a reasonable accommodation. The appropriate device for an individual is the type that individual can use, whereas the appropriate system for an assembly area will necessarily be geared toward the "average" or aggregate needs of various individuals. A listening system that can be used from any seat in a seating area is the most flexible way to meet this specification. Earphone jacks with variable volume controls can benefit only people who have slight hearing loss and do not help people who use hearing aids. At the present time, magnetic induction loops are the most feasible type of listening system for people who use hearing aids equipped with "T-coils," but people without hearing aids or those with hearing aids not equipped with inductive pick-ups cannot use them without special receivers. Radio frequency systems can be extremely effective and inexpensive. People without hearing aids can use them, but people with hearing aids need a special receiver to use them as they are presently designed. If hearing aids had a jack to allow a by-pass of microphones, then radio frequency systems would be suitable for people with and without hearing aids. Some listening systems may be subject to interference from other equipment and feedback from hearing aids of people who are using the systems. Such interference can be controlled by careful engineering design that anticipates feedback sources in the surrounding area.

Table A2, reprinted from a National Institute of Disability and Rehabilitation Research "Rehab Brief," shows some of the advantages and disadvantages of different types of assistive listening systems. In addition, the Architectural and Transportation Barriers Compliance Board (Access Board) has published a pamphlet on Assistive Listening Systems which lists demonstration centers across the country where technical assistance can be obtained in selecting and installing appropriate systems. The state of

Appendix 3
Scenario Solutions

CHAPTER 4 SOLUTIONS

CURB RAMPS

As shown in Figure S4–1, textured surfaces can be affixed to the curb ramp using the proscribed configuration (4.7.7). This would be readily discernible by anyone using a cane as a navigational aid. Several manufacturers are making textured surface products available for this use. Note that the curb ramps have flared sides rather than a returned curb. This is an essential feature where pedestrians are likely to traverse the ramp parallel to the sidewalk, as in a downtown area (4.7.5). As this book goes to press, the use of textured surfaces has been put on reserve by the ATBCB.

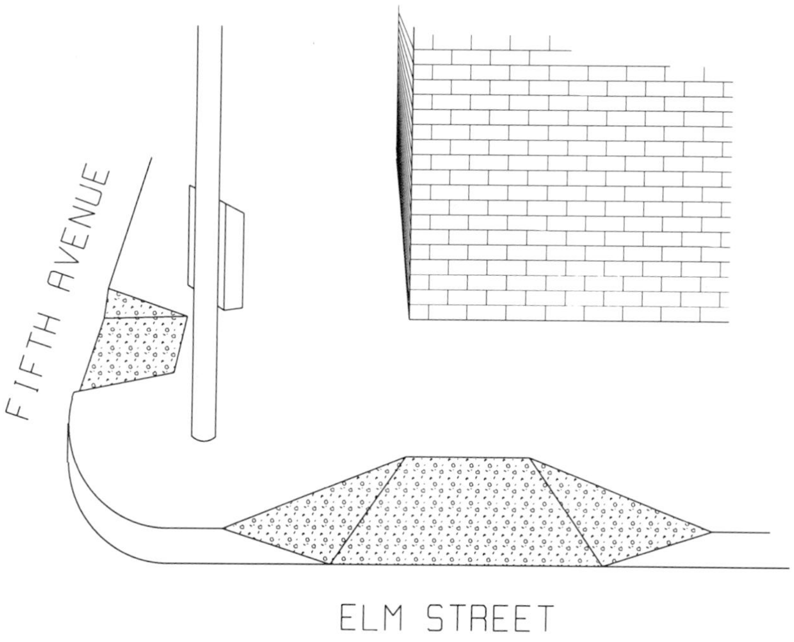
FIFTH AVENUE
ELM STREET

FIGURE S4–1.

SIGNAGE FOR ACCESSIBLE PARKING

The parking lot as depicted in Figure 4–2 has a few problems. ADAAG calls for 8 accessible parking spaces in a public parking lot that has 301 to 400 slots, but it also requires that one in every eight spaces be "van accessible" (4.1.2). Therefore one of the eight accessible spaces must have a wider access aisle to comply with this (see Figure S4–2a for proper access aisle width). The remaining spaces are satisfactory as shown, in that they are 96 inches and have the necessary 60-inch access aisle (4.6.3). As an alternative to providing two types of accessible spaces, a designer might opt to use the universal parking space design if space permits (A4.6.3). This suggests that all accessible spaces be 132 inches with a 60-inch access aisle, making them available to both van and car drivers.

Another problem in Figure 4–2 concerns signage. Stenciling the access symbol on the pavement does not meet the guidelines (4.6.4). Signage depicting the International Symbol of Accessibility should be posted on a stanchion high enough to be visible from the driver's seat (A4.6.4).

In terms of the accessible route, only one curb ramp is allotted from the accessible spaces to the sidewalk that serves the shopping mall. Unfortunately this circumstance requires that people using these spaces go behind parked cars to reach the curb

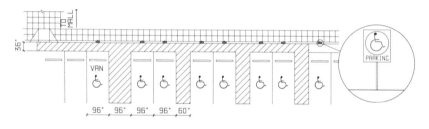

FIGURE S4–2b.

ramp, putting themselves in danger. A more sensitive design, shown in Figure S4-2a, involves installing curb ramps at each access aisle, thereby allowing users to reach the accessible route without endangering themselves. A less expensive alternative, depicted in Figure S4-2b, may be used in new construction or when restriping is done, though it is not feasible in many existing lots. The designer could leave a 36-inch access aisle between the sidewalk and the parking slots. Wheel blocks at the head of each slot will prohibit cars from entering the access aisle. This would allow the installation of only one curb ramp (using a flared side configuration) since users at any of the accessible slots would be able to reach the curb ramp directly by way of the access aisle.

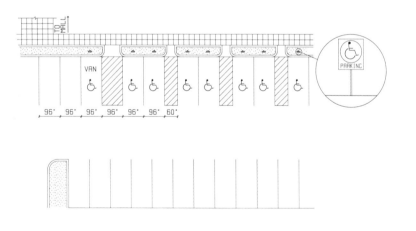

FIGURE S4–2a.

PARKING AREAS

In the outdoor lot the accessible parking spaces are not the closest ones to the main entrance (4.6.2). Even though they are 156 inches wide, which is adequate for a 96-inch space plus the 60-inch access aisle, they do not have the markings to designate the access aisle. Striping is not actually required by ADAAG, but it creates better visual identification for drivers. In addition, adequate signage is not provided to alert drivers to these spaces (4.6.4). Correcting these barriers will present no specific problems for the client since there is adequate room for configuring the parking spaces accordingly, as shown in Figure S4–3.

This solves only part of the problem, however, since the pedestrian route to the main entrance is not accessible (4.3.2).

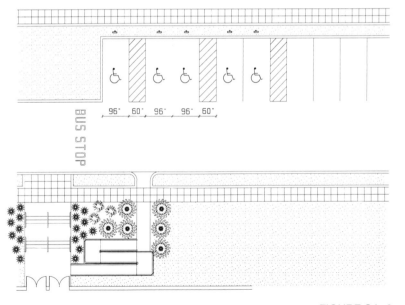

BUS STOP

96" 60" 96" 96" 60"

FIGURE S4–3.

Even if a person in a wheelchair could negotiate the parking lot, he would then have to cross the driveway to the sidewalk, which has no curb ramp (4.7). Likewise, anyone alighting at the public drop-off point would face the same curb problem. Once up the curb, pedestrians face two sets of stairs without ramps before reaching the main entry (4.3.8). To resolve these problems, the designer should first decide how long the ramp must be, based on the 1:12 ratio requirement (4.8.2). Six stairs would require a ramp of 36 to 42 feet to achieve the necessary elevation. Obviously this cannot be done on a straight run, so turnbacks with landings must be utilized (4.8.4). Where the ramp meets the sidewalk a curb ramp should be installed (4.7). Although textured surfaces are usually desirable at curb ramps, in this case it is unnecessary. People with visual disabilities are more likely to use the stairs and cross at the curb, while the curb ramp will be used primarily by people with mobility disabilities. Handrails should be provided for both stairs (4.9.4) and ramps (4.8.5), a safety feature for all users. For aesthetic purposes the area around the ramp can be graded and planted.

In Figure 4–4 two major barriers can be seen in the indoor parking area. First, the accessible spaces are not the closest ones to the accessible entrance (4.6.2) and they do not conform to the adjacent access aisle requirements (4.6.3). Second, the curb ramp situated at the entrance deck to the elevators is blocked by a parking space, precluding wheelchair users access to the elevator lobby (4.7.8). This is an excellent example of the need for both technical guidelines *and* sensitivity. The original designer of the parking area followed the regulations for ramps, but did not consider the amount of access space required for a wheelchair user to successfully approach the ramp. In fact, no parking space should have been outlined there at all.

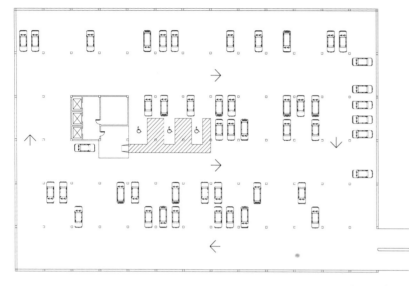

FIGURE S4–4.

Figure S4–4 shows a reconfiguration of the parking area to address the two barriers described above. One strategy for creating three accessible spaces in close proximity to the elevator deck is to relocate the curb ramp (eliminating the need to remove the parking space in front of the ramp). In this way an accessible route can be made directly from the spaces to the ramp without necessitating entry into the traffic areas of the parking lot. Using the accessible route may necessitate going behind parked cars in the accessible spaces, but people who use these spaces are more likely to be sensitive to the need for caution where pedestrians with disabilities are concerned. The designer must work around the structural columns in order to achieve the necessary access aisle width for the accessible

spaces. Remember that vertical signs must be placed at accessible parking spaces (4.6.4).

EXTERIOR DOORS

Since the doors at the Central Avenue entrance are already accessible, one solution is to install signage at the Main Street exterior entrance notifying users of the accessible entrance on Central (4.30.7). The set of three interior steps should be ramped at a 1:12 ratio (4.8.2) as shown in Figure S4–5a, requiring a 19½-foot ramp with handrails on both sides (4.8.5). The doors opening into the hall on both sides make it difficult to decide on which

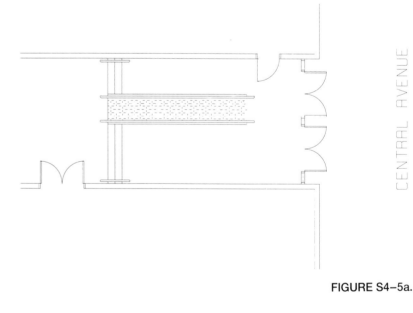

FIGURE S4–5a.

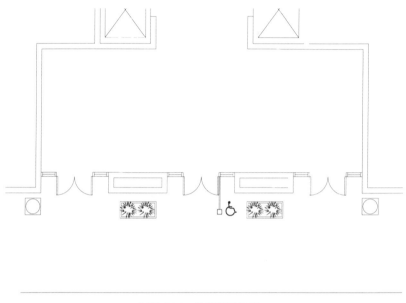

MAIN STREET

FIGURE S4–5b.

switch on a 30-inch-high railing to open one set of door leaves (4.13.12), as shown in Figure S4–5b. The railing should extend far enough from the building front so that a person in a wheelchair would be clear of the swinging doors, allowing for either front or side approaches. The railing extending out might pose a problem for an individual with a visual impairment. To avoid this, it should have a curved corner in the front that extends to the ground so it is detectable with a cane. Existing planters along the face of the building may be pulled out flush with the lamp stanchions to provide an alerting mechanism to anyone with a cane, inducing that person to walk clear of the building front.

side of the stairs the ramp should be placed. Because the management office has more traffic than the retail store, it seems appropriate to ramp the right center of the staircase. The existing stairs already have handrails and are therefore in compliance with ADAAG (4.9.4).

Another possible (and less costly) solution would involve the use of the Main Street entrance (in which case signage would be needed on Central Avenue to indicate the accessible entrance at Main). Although the management does not wish to make any alterations at this entrance that would detract from the historical significance of the building, one could install an automatic door

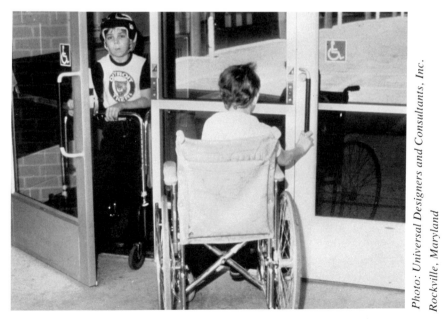

Photo: Universal Designers and Consultants, Inc. Rockville, Maryland

FIGURE S4–6.

MANEUVERING CLEARANCE

Because it is impossible for a person with a mobility aid (such as a walker, crutches, or a wheelchair) to open a door that swings out while directly in front of it, he or she must first move to a position adjacent to the latch side of the door. A minimum of 18 inches, and preferably 24 inches, should be allowed at the latch side for maneuvering clearance (4.13.6). Using the existing exterior frame, this clearance can be accomplished by replacing the two sidelights with one large glass panel between the doors, as shown in Figure S4–6. Note the change in door handles to a more accessible style and the addition of the accessibility symbol. (See Figure S4–6 on page 187.)

C H A P T E R 5 S O L U T I O N S

ELEVATORS AND SIGNAGE

1. Nothing should be placed on the floor under the call buttons, and anything mounted beneath call buttons should not project more than 4 inches (4.10.3). In this situation simply removing the ash urns to walls without call buttons will achieve accessibility (see Figure S5–1a). The ash urn is not only an obstacle to individuals with visual impairments, but also impedes those using wheelchairs. Call buttons should be mounted on the wall vertically with the "up" button on top, centered at 42 inches AFF (above finish floor), and buttons should be raised or flush, not indented (4.10.3). Audio bells should signal with one or two rings before the elevator doors open, indicating which cab is answering the call and the direction it is going (4.10.4). These should be accompanied by visual signals to alert individuals with

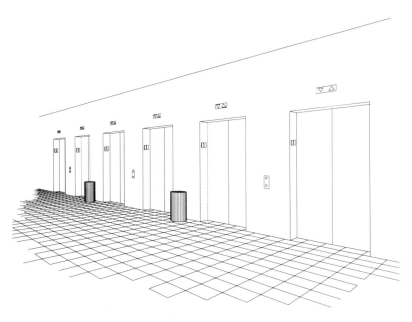

FIGURE S5–1a.

hearing impairments (4.10.4). The minimum amount of time that the elevator door remains open should be determined by the distance from the call buttons to the cab, but should not be less than 3 seconds (4.10.7, 4.10.8). This allows ample time for anyone, with or without a disability, to reach the appropriate elevator car. In addition, the door should be equipped to stop and reopen automatically if the doorway becomes obstructed by an object or person who catches the door as it is closing (4.10.6). The interior cab buttons should have raised characters and Braille (4.10.12). Also in new construction or major alterations, care should be given to the placement and function of the emergency communications (4.10.14). Raised and Braille floor identification plates should also appear at a 60-inch-high level on both sides of the hoistway to identify each floor when the elevator opens (4.10.5). In the elevator lobby at each floor there should be signage indicating which direction to turn for specific office numbers, as shown in Figure S5–1b (4.30).

2. If room identification varies in terms of placement or style, or is nonexistent, then people with visual disabilities must rely on others. This problem can be alleviated easily by providing consistent room identification (4.30). Figure S5–1c shows the appropriate location of signage outside of offices and permanent rooms. Consistent cueing is an essential design component that allows a person with a visual disability to navigate through the world of the sighted, and failing to use adequate signage or plac-

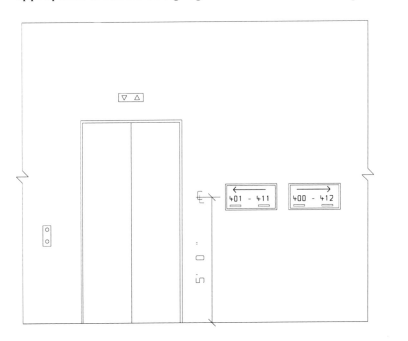

FIGURE S5–1b.

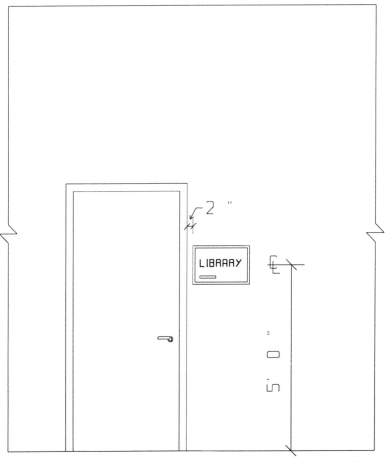

FIGURE S5–1c.

ing it in an unexpected position creates a situation in which the person is no longer able to be independent.

Regarding signage, it should be pointed out that people with visual impairments can utilize a variety of tools and cues to help them maintain their independence. Some of the possibilities are discussed in the ADAAG Appendix (A4.30.1).

STAIRWAYS

The stairs have overhanging stair treads that can easily catch the toes of someone using a walking aid or someone who has trouble bending his or her knees. Instead the risers should be slanted or a radius rounded nosing should be used to eliminate the overhanging nosing on the treads (4.9.3). Figure S5–2 shows this and other changes. The stairs should have a handrail on both sides of the stairway to accommodate those with strength in only one side of the body, and handrails should extend 12 inches beyond the top and bottom risers (4.9.4). Note that the handrail returns smoothly to the post. In addition, the door at the top of the stairs should have a levered handle rather than a knob to enable those with limited dexterity to easily open the door (4.13.9). Signage should indicate the floor number on the wall to the latch side of the door (4.30.6).

This scenario identifies a situation in which sensitivity is definitely lacking, though not necessarily on the part of the designer. Elderly people often have disabilities, and should therefore be accommodated on the ground floor of a building if possible, or in a building with elevators, to minimize their inconvenience and

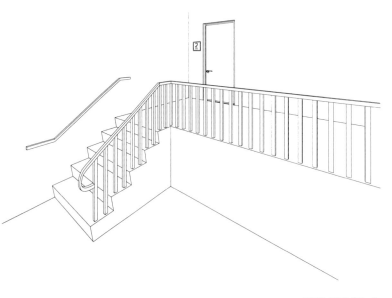

FIGURE S5–2.

possible accidents. Especially important is adequate signage (4.30); no one wants to walk in the wrong direction, particularly when walking is difficult. Designers can act as advocates for the elderly by educating their clients about the limitations of this group during the design phase of the project, if the circumstance calls for such intervention.

TELEPHONES

For people who are deaf or hearing impaired, the major concern in telephones is the provision of volume control and, of course, signage indicating this provision (4.30.7). It is required that 25 percent, but never less than one, of all public telephones be equipped with volume control and accompanying signage (4.1.3, 4.30.7). Because some people with auditory disabilities also use wheelchairs or are of short stature, a bank of two or more phones must have at least one that is properly positioned to be accessible with the highest operable part of the instrument at 48 inches or lower, and this phone should be equipped with volume control as well. Figure S5–3a depicts a telephone at the proper height, and Figure S5–3b illustrates the appropriate signage for volume control.

**Telephone Handset
Amplification Symbol**

FIGURE S5–3b.

FIGURE S5–3a.

GROUND AND FLOOR SURFACES

Because the lobby floor has but one carpet pattern throughout, it does not provide directional cues that partially sighted visitors can use to indicate paths leading to specific locations. Changing the floor pattern, color, or ground surface to indicate paths of travel can provide the necessary cues, as shown in Figure S5-4,

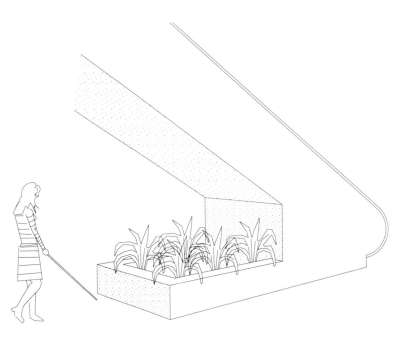

FIGURE S5-5.

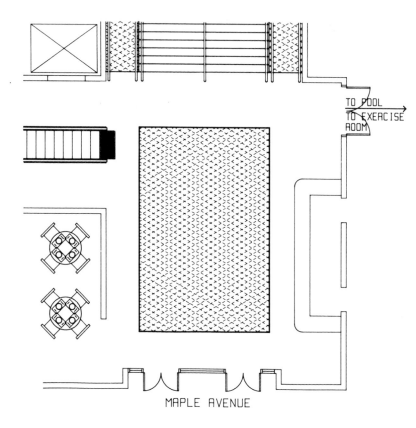

FIGURE S5-4.

where the patterned carpet is surrounded by a nonslip floor surface. Floor coverings should comply with the guidelines in 4.5. Additionally, large contrasting signage (4.30.5) as well as raised and Braille characters (4.30.4) should be used to indicate areas of interest to the public. Visitors who are blind must rely on signage, or seek assistance from staff members (an alternate method adhering to the guidelines of the ADA). Finally, some sort of a barrier that is detectable with a cane must be installed underneath the escalator to prevent individuals from bumping their heads on the underside (4.4.2). Figure S5-5 depicts one solution.

FIGURE S5–6.

DRINKING FOUNTAINS

The existing fountain should be replaced by a desk type unit that permits forward approach from the wheelchair (see Figure S5–6). The spout should be at the front of the fixture directing the flow of water nearly parallel to the front, and the controls on the front or side should be mounted for easy access (4.15). Fortunately the existing fountain was recessed so that it did not present a hazard to people with sight disabilities (4.4), thus making the retrofitting less expensive than it might have been had repositioning been necessary.

ALARMS

Wherever the local code says an audible alarm should be placed, a visual alarm must also appear. In this case an existing audible alarm in the elevator lobby should be supplemented with a visual alarm (4.28.3). However, because auditory alarms are able to send signals farther than visual alarms, it is imperative that extra visual alarms be included in as many areas as needed to be readily discernible. Figure S5–7 shows visual alarms strategically placed in the systems furniture area, in the conference room, and in the restrooms in addition to the elevator lobby. More than one is used in the systems area because of the

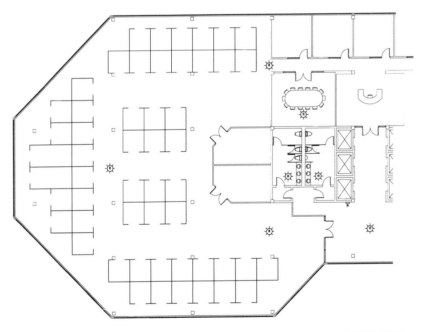

FIGURE S5–7.

ADAAG requirement regarding large spaces (4.28.3). In the event that an employee who is deaf is hired in the future and occupies one of the hard offices (permanent walls), he or she may request a visual alarm as a reasonable accommodation under Title I (A4.28.4). Additionally, evacuation plans should be implemented to assist employees with mobility disabilities.

BATHROOMS

1. If local requirements do not permit reconfiguration, a unisex accessible bathroom would be an acceptable alternative solution (4.1.6). Signage at the inaccessible bathroom should indicate the location of the nearest accessible facility (4.30). If local codes do not present a problem, then the most practical and economical way to provide an accessible stall would be to combine two of the stalls into one larger one, complete with grab bars and a toilet positioned to allow for wheelchair transfer and adequate turning radius, as shown in Figure S5–8a (4.17.3, 4.22.4). In this example the bathroom is large enough to allow for adequate maneuvering clearance, though this is not always the case in alterations. Kick clearances of 9 inches under stall partitions and/or lavatory base cabinets will increase maneuvering space if it is impossible to enlarge the room (4.17.4, 4.19.2). This 9-inch space is necessary to accommodate the footrest on a wheelchair, which extends forward several inches. (Figure S5–8b depicts a small restroom where this might be useful.)

Figure 5–8 shows the vanity counter to be 27 inches deep. According to ADAAG, this is acceptable since the tap sets

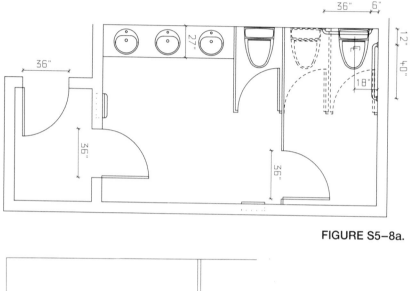

FIGURE S5–8a.

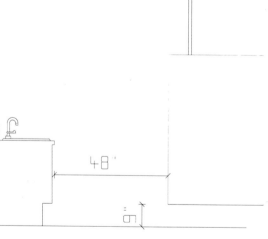

FIGURE S5–8b.

would be close enough to allow forward reach over an obstruction (4.2.5). The top surface of the counter (shown in Figure 5–9) is acceptable at 34 inches AFF, but this leaves only 26 inches of knee clearance. At least one sink should be adapted to allow 29 inches AFF for knee clearance, with the top surface no higher than 34 inches AFF (4.22.6). (This is illustrated in Figure S5–9 along with the remainder of the solutions for this problem.) In addition, the drain and hot-water pipes under an accessible sink should be insulated to protect against contact with the legs of a person in a wheelchair (4.19.4). This also provides an extra safety measure for small children. The tap sets, too, should be automatic or easily turned by minimal grasping effort to accommodate people with dexterity problems (4.19.5). The mirror is appropriately placed with the bottom edge at 40 inches AFF (4.19.6).

In Figure 5–9 the paper towel dispenser is shown at 60 inches AFF. Wall-mounted accessories should be at a height of 48 inches to allow for forward or side reach for individuals in wheelchairs (4.2.5, 4.2.6). It is also helpful to place paper towel dispensers next to accessible sinks, since it is difficult to rotate the wheels of a wheelchair with wet hands. Recessing the dispensers is appropriate so they do not become a hazard (4.4).

One other barrier that should be addressed involves the entrance to the bathroom. There is not adequate clearance at the latch side of the door (4.13.6). The appropriate change is shown in Figure S5–8a.

2. Interior doors should require no more than 5 lbf. to operate (4.13.11). The outer door to the bathroom, while wide enough to allow wheelchair entry, still precludes many people from entering because it is too heavy. Once inside the vestibule, there is inadequate space for pulling open the second door. The vestibule should be enlarged to 48 inches plus the width of the second door, and both doors should open into the bathroom (4.13.7), as shown in Figure S5–10. The remainder of the bathroom is in compliance with accessibility guidelines.

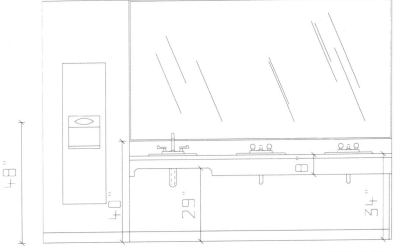

FIGURE S5–9.

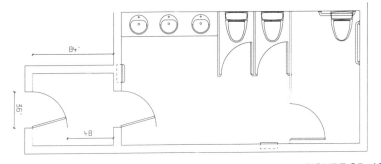

FIGURE S5–10.

3. The vestibule is large enough to accommodate the turning radius of a wheelchair, but the bench obstructs the clear floor space needed to effect a turn, making it impossible to enter (4.22.3). Removing the bench to another wall, as shown in Figure S5–11, will allow wheelchair users greater maneuverability in entering the restroom. However, a right angle foyer creates a much more difficult egress because the doors must be pulled toward the wheelchair user. A straight run would be preferable whenever possible. The paper towel dispenser protrudes into the path of travel and creates a potential hazard for both wheelchair users and people who are blind (4.4.1). An appropriate solution would be to recess the paper towel dispenser. Also, moving it closer to the sinks would be useful, particularly for wheelchair users who would have difficulty turning the wheels with wet hands. One toilet stall has already been made accessible in accordance with ADAAG.

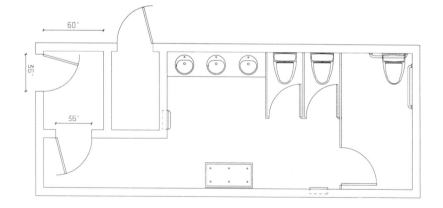

FIGURE S5–11.

INTERIOR STAIRS AND RAMPS

1. Ramping this stairway is technically infeasible, since a 28-foot ramp would be needed to provide the appropriate slope of 1:12 (4.8.2). Where an accessible element is technically infeasible, some alternative method must be used for achieving accessibility to the extent that it is possible (4.1.6). In this case, an evacuation plan must be developed within each individual office whereby employees are assigned to assist their coworkers with disabilities in effecting a safe evacuation. This alternative accommodation is within the mandate of the ADA. However, the infeasibility of a ramp does not preclude making other accessible changes. Handrails should be installed on the stairs to assist people with visual impairments, individuals with mobility disabilities who are ambulatory, and indeed, anyone trying to safely descend the stairs (4.9.4). Adequate signage should indicate where accessible exits are located (4.30). The levered handle on the door complies with accessibility requirements for door hardware (4.13.9).

2. A slope of 10 degrees is too severe to meet the 1:12 ratio (4.8.2). The ramp must be feathered to achieve the proper slope (see Figure S5–13). A 60-inch-deep flat landing is necessary at

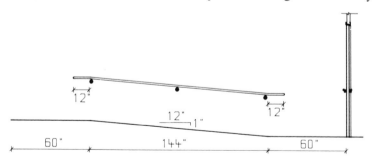

FIGURE S5–13.

the top and bottom of the ramp so that a person in a wheelchair can open both the interior and egress doors (4.8.4). Handrails of 1½-inch diameter (4.26) should be affixed on both sides of the ramp, with clear space of 1½ inches between the wall and the handrail. The handrails should extend 12 inches beyond the top and bottom of the ramp (4.8.5). Again, signage indicating exits, and especially accessible exits, is crucial (4.30).

ELEVATOR LOBBY LEADING TO A ROOF

Because this is the only access to the roof garden, it must be retrofitted to comply with the ADA mandate. It would not be feasible to ramp the staircase, since the 1:12 requirement for ramps would dictate a 12-foot ramp in this situation. Because this would intrude on the elevator lobby, an alternative measure must be taken. Figures S5-14 and S5-15 illustrate a possible solution. A wheelchair lift should be installed to the right of the stairway where the drop is now protected by a handrail (4.11, A4.11.2). Handrails must be used on both sides of the existing staircase (4.9.4). A ramp should be installed to negotiate both

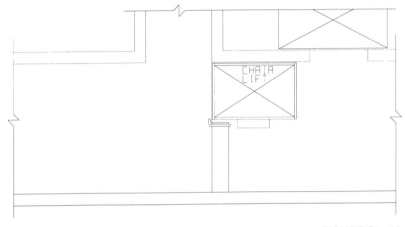

FIGURE S5-15.

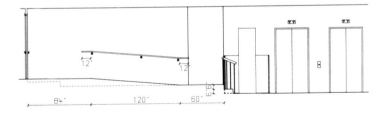

FIGURE S5-14.

the 6-inch riser to the landing as well as the 4-inch curb beneath the egress door (4.8). A 60-inch landing will be needed at the bottom of the ramp (4.8.4); this is the minimum depth allowable by ADAAG. A landing will be necessary at the top of the ramp as well, though here an 84-inch landing is advisable to allow clearance for the door swing, particularly since there are not 18 inches of maneuvering clearance to the latch side of the door. If a 60-inch landing were used, it would require a wheelchair user to back up with the rear wheels on the ramp to effect a door opening, which is extremely precarious. Designers should be sure to evaluate each situation separately to create the most sensitive solution. The 60-inch landing suggested in ADAAG may not always be appropriate, unless of course the architectural configuration allows no other solution. Finally, a 1:12 ramp must be installed on the outside of the door to give access to the garden (4.8.2).

C H A P T E R 6 S O L U T I O N S

INTERIOR OF A BANK

Although it is too heavy for some people in wheelchairs to use comfortably (and for many ambulatory people as well), the initial entry door is acceptable at 10 lbf. because the guidelines on this issue are currently reserved (4.13.11). A consensus determination of the proper pulling force must be established with respect to air pressure that could cause entry doors to swing open. The interior entry door, on the other hand, must be adjusted to a maximum of 5 lbf. (4.13.11). The vestibule poses a problem in that the 6-foot length does not accommodate a wheelchair plus the door swing (4.13.7). Enlarging this vestibule to 7 feet would eliminate this barrier, as shown in Figure S6–1.

The interior of the bank is spacious and allows for good traffic flow and adequate turning radius for wheelchairs. However, the deposit/withdrawal desk is too high at 42 inches, and a portion of it should provide an extended writing surface no more than 34 inches high, with a clear knee space of 27 inches AFF. Likewise, the teller window should have at least one station lowered to 34 inches. These solutions follow the guidelines for fixed tables (4.32.3, 4.32.4) rather than that for service counters and teller windows (7.2). The latter guideline suggests a counter with a maximum height of 36 inches and does not mention knee space. In this particular situation the appropriate ADAAG solution (7.2) does not provide the sensitivity needed to comfortably accommodate people in wheelchairs, and as an experienced designer you realize that the regulations will not always provide the best solution for every situation. Remember, your decisions should be based on awareness of needs as much as technical knowledge. Regarding the carpet, it meets the guidelines (4.5.3) and should cause no difficulty for wheelchair users. If these modifications can be accomplished in a readily achievable fashion, then they must be immediately addressed. If not, then cus-

tomer assistance should be provided by the bank employees as an alternate service. For instance, the clerk at the desk in front of the vault could assist customers with their banking needs.

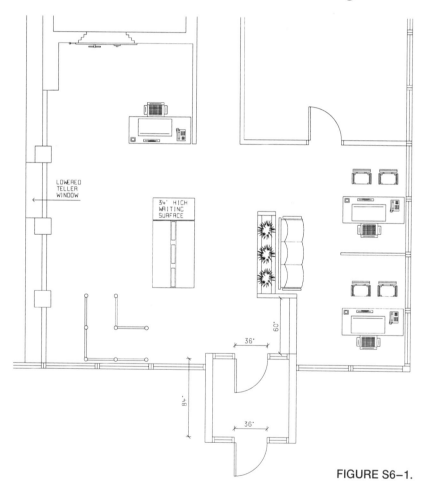

FIGURE S6–1.

TRANSIENT LODGING

1. First, it should be noted that transient lodging must comply with 4.1 through 4.35, and all of the barrier solutions mentioned below are cited in section 9, entitled "Accessible Transient Lodging." Although door width was considered for this room, dimensions for many other elements were neglected. For the sake of clarity, we will divide the solution into two sections: one dealing with the entry/bathroom area, and the other with the sleeping area. The solutions are depicted in Figure S6–2.

The door to the room is an accessible width (4.13.5). However, a minimum of 18 inches, preferably 24 inches, maneuvering clearance must be provided to the latch side of the door for egress (4.13.6). Consequently, the closet should be relocated to

acquire the extra space. Inside the bathroom the main problem is insufficient space. Once the wheelchair moves in, there is not adequate turning space (4.2.3) and the user would find it difficult to shut the door. Also there is no side access to the toilet (4.16.2) and the bathtub does not have a seat (4.20.3). Extra space is gained by cantilevering the sink and relocating the toilet, which is positioned to allow for a side approach. In addition, replacing the tub with a shower reduces space needs and provides the extra room needed for the closet. Grab bars must be installed for both the toilet and shower (4.16.4, 4.21.4), as well as a pull-down shower seat and adjustable shower head (4.21.3, 4.21.6). Note that ADAAG requires roll-in showers in a certain number of accessible rooms in larger hotels (9.1.2). Since knee clearance at the lavatory is only 27 inches AFF, the apron must be adjusted to allow a minimum of 29 inches AFF to the bottom of the apron (4.19.2). The drainpipe and hot water pipe should also be insulated (4.19.4). Finally, the tap sets should be retrofitted with lever-type handles for the ease and comfort of people with dexterity disabilities (4.19.5).

In the sleeping area there is insufficient space to move around the beds or to reach the drapery controls. Because of the room size, the only way to achieve accessibility is to change from a two-bed room to a one-bed room. In this way the necessary clearance space of 36 inches can be provided along both sides of the bed (9.2.2). This also allows adequate space for reaching the drapery controls (4.27.2). If the controls are placed on the side of the window farthest from the television with the armchair at the opposite end of the window, then there will be adequate floor space for an individual to view the television while sitting in a wheelchair. Providing enough space to maneuver in the room can make people much more comfortable, which is one of

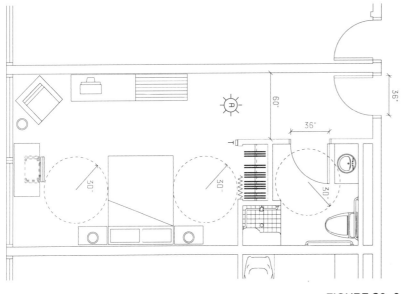

FIGURE S6–2.

the goals of universal design.

Several other problems must be addressed in the room. The thermostat control is clearly too high (4.27.3), as is the clothes rod (4.25.3). The appropriate height for these depends on whether approach is from the front or the side. Adequate knee clearance was not considered for the writing desk, which is both too low and too narrow. It should be at least 27 inches AFF and 30 inches wide (4.32.3). Since the room is more spacious with only one bed, the desk can be moved to the window, leaving space for a suitcase rack. The drawer pulls on the desk and the dresser should be altered to a more accessible style because many people have difficulty with manual dexterity, as Mr. Connors does (4.25.4). As a final note, the designer should recommend that the hotel management consider alterations in a larger room to provide a two-bed accessible room as well.

2. As for the provisions for people with auditory disabilities, the major concerns are alarm systems and communication systems (9.3). Auxiliary visual alarms (strobes) must be provided in sleeping rooms (4.28.4), or alternatively, signal-activated vibrators may be used on mattresses (A4.28.4). To facilitate communication, two elements are necessary. First, visual notification devices are required for alerting individuals to incoming phone calls or knocks at the door (9.3.1). Second, permanent telephones should have volume controls (4.31.5) and should be near enough to an electrical outlet to allow usage of a text telephone (9.3.1). As an alternative to these measures, portable visual alarms and communication devices may be offered upon request (9.3.2). Owning these portable items is a good idea for hotels, since they allow patrons who are deaf to occupy rooms other than wheelchair-accessible rooms, leaving these open for patrons with mobility disabilities. Hotels might also consider purchasing TV decoders and TDDs to be available for loan to patrons with hearing losses.

3. Under the ADAAG regulations "Transportation Facilities" (10) is reserved. However, a designer involved in hotel design should alert the management that under Title III (Public Accommodations) they are responsible for making all facilities and programs accessible, including shuttle-bus services. Considering this aspect of hotel service demonstrates a sensitivity to the needs of people with disabilities that is likely to increase patronage among this group.

MEDICAL OFFICE

Design considerations for this office should begin with sensitivity to the needs of the patients. Children who may already be nervous or fearful when they arrive can be made more so by adult-size furnishings and decor. Figure S6–3 illustrates alterations in Dr. Adams's office that take this into account. In the reception area a standard height reception desk countertop can hide those behind it from the childrens' view. To make patients feel that they have access to the staff, one portion of the counter should be lowered to anywhere from 28 inches to 34 inches AFF (4.32.4). This also makes the counter accessible for parents or children in wheelchairs. A play area should be added to the reception room to allay fears and boredom. This might include small chairs or stools, a table with chairs for coloring or other activities, and a toy bin. Small-scale seating here and in consultation rooms can add to the children's comfort. Steps to reach exam tables help patients to maintain their independence, while

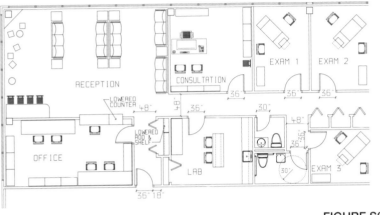

FIGURE S6-3.

keeping tables at a comfortable height for the physician.

Although the main emphasis of the alterations is to suit the children who will visit the office, this does not preclude the necessity of ensuring an accessible office for adult or child visitors with disabilities, as well as an accessible path of travel to the office. To this end the closet nearest the door should be enclosed on the hall side, reduced in depth, and opened only in the lab to leave adequate clear space in front of the door (4.13.6). Also, a portion of the closet rod should be lowered for use by children or wheelchair users (4.25.3). Restroom facilities should be brought into compliance for visitors in wheelchairs (4.22). In order to do this it is necessary to relocate the door to exam room number 3 and extend the bathroom to provide adequate maneuvering clearance (4.22.3). The door to the accessible bathroom should be 36 inches (4.13.5). Appropriate signage is one of the many considerations that must be included, for instance, to indicate the location of the accessible bathroom facility (4.30).

Also, low handrails for children are a useful addition to ramps or stairs in a pediatric facility (A4.8.5). This scenario is a good reminder that universal design is for everyone, not just people with disabilities.

HEALTH CLUB

When a health club is provided in a multiuse building, it is considered a public accommodation and, as such, must be made available to everyone regardless of physical ability. A health facility in a private club is exempt from Title III.

Figure S6–4 illustrates the following solutions. The doors to both the aerobics room and the exercise room are of adequate width (4.13.5), and there are no physical barriers in the aerobics room. However, the exercise room does not leave access aisles between pieces of equipment. A configuration that allows at least 32 inches between machines will enable wheelchair users

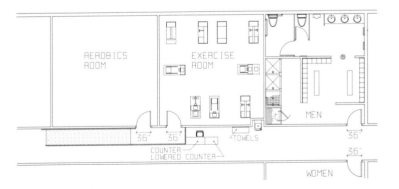

FIGURE S6–4.

or others with mobility aids to gain access to the equipment (4.2.1, 4.2.4.1). This access is necessary for equipment designed for either upper or lower body workouts, since some people who use wheelchairs have residual leg strength that must be maintained. For people with visual disabilities equipment that requires digital programming is a problem, and there should be staff assistance as a means of providing access for patrons who wish to use such equipment.

The staircase leading to the exercise rooms must be ramped (4.8) and supplied with a handrail on each side (4.8.5). The counter for obtaining towels or service is too high, and either a portion should be lowered to a maximum height of 34 inches AFF (4.32.4) or the counter should be replaced with a desk. The drinking fountain is inaccessible and should be brought into compliance (4.15).

The locker room has adequate space for maneuvering, and the bathroom has accessible facilities. However, the sauna does not have an accessible doorway, and it is architecturally infeasible to retrofit given the width of the space. Although the shower stalls are of acceptable size and have no inhibiting curbs, one of them must have the required seat and grab bars (4.21.3, 4.21.4). Likewise, the controls and shower heads must conform to the guidelines (4.21.5, 4.21.6). Note that a visual alarm was added to the locker room for safety purposes (4.28.3), and proper signage should be installed to indicate accessibility (4.30).

MUSEUMS

The fact that specific groups have scheduled tours should in no way influence the exhibit design, simply because these groups represent the wide variability found in the general public. A universally designed exhibit would enable everyone to participate and would not require any adaptations for "special" groups. The exhibit designers must be sensitive to all possible disabilities from the beginning of the project.

A major consideration for the exhibit is the layout. A clear path of travel is necessary for people in wheelchairs, and also for good traffic flow through the exhibit (4.2, 4.3, 4.4). Some seating should be provided to allow patrons to rest. This is especially important for people who tire easily due to some physical condition (such as heart disease or pregnancy), but is also ideal for children, elderly people, and anyone who would simply like to sit and enjoy a piece of art. Lighting should be carefully planned so that there are no glares on glass or on descriptive captions. This is essential for the enjoyment of all patrons, but particularly for those with visual disabilities who need good lighting conditions to see. Taped audio tours giving detailed descriptions of the artworks are valuable aids for visitors who are blind, and if practicable, tactile replicas of major pieces can enhance their understanding of the art. Similarly, printed versions of the audio tours should be provided for people with a hearing loss. These audio and print tours can be educational for other patrons as well.

RESTAURANT ALTERATIONS

The overall preliminary plan works well, but some alterations are needed as shown in Figure S6–5. The seating and planters in the lobby area should be repositioned to allow more clear floor space (4.2), and the entrance partition should be shortened.

and decor are provided in both areas, and the accessible space in the main dining room is not restricted to people with disabilities (5.4). The table configuration provides sufficient access aisles (5.3, 4.32) and accessible seating, which is located throughout the main dining area so that choice of seating is not limited (5.1).

The adjustments discussed thus far have all been related to space requirements for wheelchairs. Other disability groups must be considered, however. Using marble floors for the path of travel and low pile carpet under the tables will be convenient for wheelchair users, but also will provide good directional cueing for people with vision problems. Because restaurants are generally noisy, sound absorption is a factor to consider in choosing wall and floor coverings, particularly to benefit people with hearing losses. As mentioned earlier, the lighting must be carefully planned, especially with respect to Mr. Ortega's friends who require both an accessible table *and* good lighting. One way to maintain ambient lighting but still provide enough light for reading menus is to offer auxiliary lighting upon request to accommodate people who may need it. Although ADAAG does not require Braille menus, waiters should be sensitive to the needs of people who are blind and offer to read the menu to them.

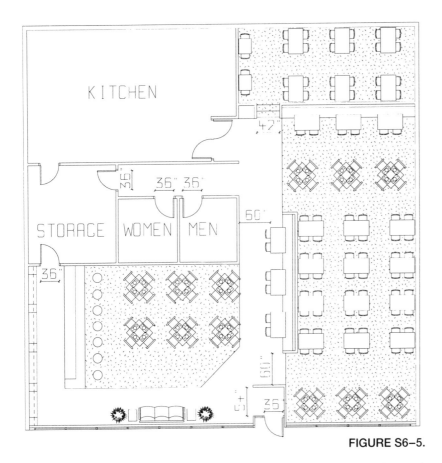

FIGURE S6–5.

CLASSROOM ACCOMMODATIONS

Classrooms are treated as assembly areas, as are conference rooms, movie theaters, concert halls, sports arenas, and the like. In the existing classroom the only accessible seating is on the top tier, but ADAAG mandates integrated accessible seating

Fewer bar tables should be used and these should be positioned to allow for access. Although the bar is at standard height, a portion of it does not have to be lowered since service is available at tables in that area (5.2). Similarly, the two-level dining area does not pose a problem as long as the same service, menu, and a sensitive design would provide a reasonable number of choices (4.33.3). To achieve this the stairs will need to be ramped (see Figure S6–6). Because the tiers are 66 inches deep, they are adequate for landings (4.8.4) and will also leave enough space for wheelchair users to make the turn into the first seat on the tier (4.2.3). The legs of the fixed tables may limit maneuvering space, however, so they have been removed in favor of cantilevered desks with adequate knee clearance (4.2.4, 4.32.3). The ADA guidelines require that accessible spaces be dispersed throughout an assembly area only in assembly areas with seating capacity of more than 300, but a sensitive design should include choices no matter how large the assembly area (4.33.3). The dais must be ramped as well to accommodate lecturers who use wheelchairs (4.8) in the event that the classroom is used for standard teaching or conferences rather than long-distance broadcasting. In terms of depth the dais is already accessible.

To help people with hearing losses, assistive listening devices should be installed in individual fixed seats not more than 50 feet from, and in full view of, the front of the classroom (4.1.3, 4.33.6). Wiring for this should be installed when the room is wired for telebroadcasting. Signage indicating the availability of these devices should be posted (4.30.7). For students who are deaf, closed captioning may be used on video monitors and sign language interpreters also may be made available. Because some future participants may be blind or visually impaired, it is important to consider lighting throughout the classroom, especially with respect to glares on the dais area. The large TV viewing screen is legible enough to accommodate everyone in the classroom. If smaller TV monitors were chosen instead of a large screen, several would need to be strategically placed to be sure of adequate viewing thoughout the classroom.

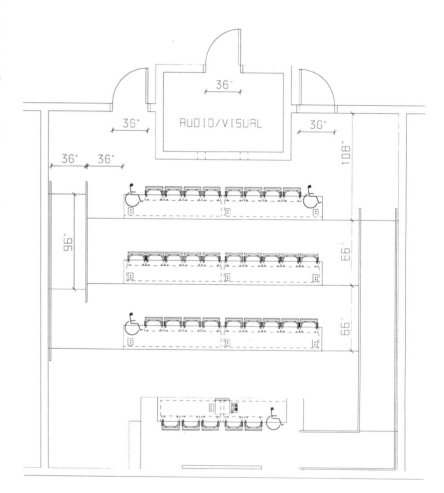

FIGURE S6–6.

OFFICE ENVIRONMENT

Because of her limited reach capabilities, the configuration of Ms. Allen's work station should provide her easy access to all her equipment and work surfaces. Figure S6–7 illustrates some possible changes. Height is an important factor to consider. The work surface must be at a proper height to allow her to pull her motorized wheelchair into a position to access her computer terminal and fold-away keyboard (4.32.4). Personal file drawers, overhead shelving, and storage cabinets should be properly placed within her reach, as should light switches, electrical outlets, and similar items (4.2.5, 4.2.6). The wardrobe can be re-

placed by coat hooks at an appropriate height, which makes space available for a guest chair for conducting interviews. Because she has limited dexterity, the drawers and doors available for Ms. Allen's use must have properly designed pulls and the force required to operate them should not be too severe (4.25.4).

The interior path of travel from Ms. Allen's work station to all common-use facilities must be in compliance (4.3). This might include the restroom, drinking fountain, elevators, conference room, library, copy room, and lounge. In addition, it is recommended that emergency evacuation procedures be rehearsed within the organization in order to assist any employees with disabilities to exit the building safely.

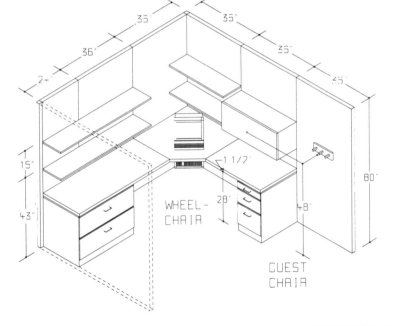

WHEEL-
CHAIR

GUEST
CHAIR

FIGURE S6–7.

Index

2.6.95 COUTS 26.96 54397